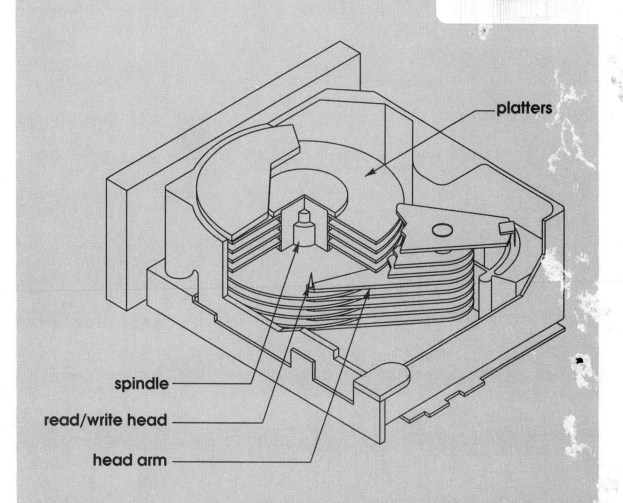

platters

spindle

read/write head

head arm

Understanding

Hard Disk

Management

on the

Macintosh

Understanding Hard Disk Management on the Macintosh®

J. RUSSELL ROBERTS

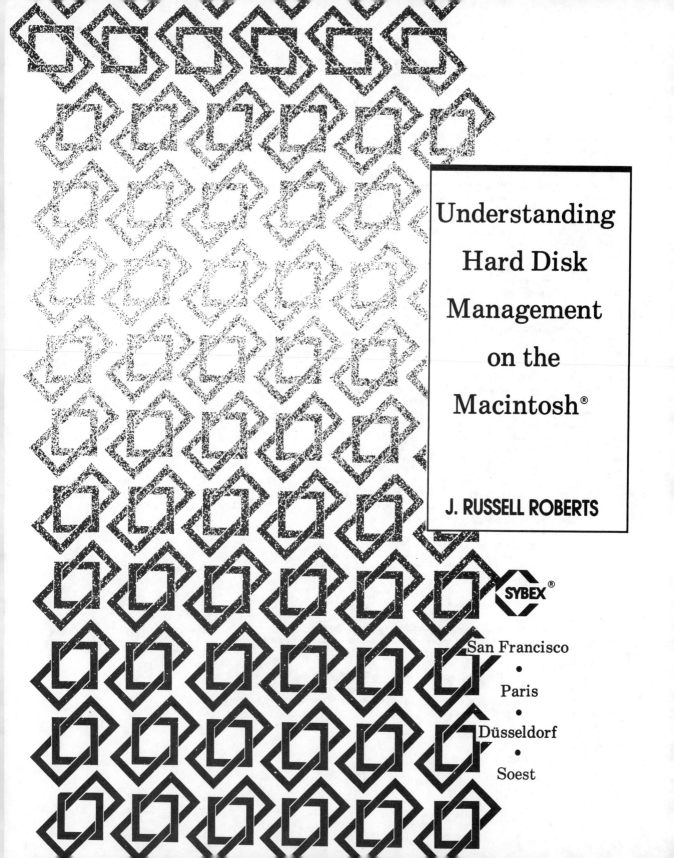

SYBEX®

San Francisco
•
Paris
•
Düsseldorf
•
Soest

Cover design by Thomas Ingalls + Associates
Cover photography by Michael Lamotte
Series Design by Julie Bilski
Technical drawings by Jeff Giese

To
Elizabeth Nicole
Kadetsky

Acknowledgments

This book is, in every sense, a collaboration. Without the support, expertise, and accommodation provided by a host of others, it couldn't have come into being. To these people, I owe a debt of gratitude.

At SYBEX: My thanks go to editor Vince Leone, who gracefully bore my many delays and coaxed the book to completion. I'd also like to thank Dianne King, who proposed the topic and helped shape the project; copy editor Peter Weverka; technical editor Dan Tauber; technical support supervisor David J. Clark; word processors Chris Mockel and Bob Myren; proofreader Kristen Iverson; typesetter Olivia Shinomoto; and indexer Paula Alston.

In Santa Cruz: Bob Chapler and the rest of Chapler & Company for providing workspace and sympathy, and Brad Widelock for his daily doses of encouragement.

At Apple Computer: Much of the information in these pages was gleaned from members of the Cupertino crew—Sandy Tompkins, Leona Guthrie, Carol Crews, Rich Biasi, Linda Williams, and others.

Contents at a Glance

Table of Contents

FOUR
ORGANIZING AND NAVIGATING YOUR HARD DISK   83

FIVE
PROTECTING YOUR DATA   113

Introduction

You get a lot when you purchase and use a Macintosh-compatible hard disk. You get more productivity, overall convenience, and the ability to do things not possible with floppy disks alone. Just having data centralized and quickly accessible makes your hard disk an unbeatable investment.

But hard disks come with an entirely new set of issues, options, and problems. Without an effective organizing plan, data may get lost in the clutter of files and folders. Hard disk centralization is a double-edged sword—an unreadable floppy is bad enough, but the prospect of a hard disk malfunction strikes fear in the heart of many users. What's more, the hard disk marketplace has its own jargon: SCSI, interleave ratios, built-in termination, and so forth.

THE GOALS OF THIS BOOK

Understanding Hard Disk Management on the Macintosh is designed as a guide to the technological and practical aspects of your hard disk. I start with the basics of data storage by explaining the concepts behind it and a few things about Macintosh technology. Then I move on to the subject of using hard disks in your day-to-day work, explaining what tools and strategies are available for keeping your data organized and optimized. Next I tackle the issue of hard disk security—how to make sure your data won't be lost, corrupted or accessed without authorization. And since even the most savvy hard disk user isn't exempt from Murphy's Law, I cover troubleshooting techniques for the most common hard disk problems. Finally, I discuss maximizing and expanding your hard disk system.

The aim of this book is not just to increase your knowledge about hard disks. Reading this book will ultimately increase your confidence. Armed with the right information, you should be as comfortable with your hard disk as you are with your Macintosh.

WHAT THIS BOOK IS NOT ABOUT

This book is a user-oriented guide. You may use it as a powerful diagnostic resource, but it's not a repair or installation manual—you won't find instructions for disassembling a hard disk or installing an internal drive in a computer. Neither is this book a guide to storage device standards for the Macintosh; if you're a programmer seeking in-depth information about SCSI or other Macintosh data pathways, you'll have to look elsewhere.

WHAT YOU NEED TO KNOW ABOUT THIS BOOK

This book assumes you're already familiar with the basics of Macintosh operations: clicking, dragging, menu selection and the like. If you're not familiar with these techniques, check your user manual. Aside from the basics, I have taken little for granted.

Because Macintosh terminology in common usage is often unclear, redundant, or downright misleading, I have defined even the most basic Macintosh terms in order to make sure that you acquire a clear understanding of the more advanced topics.

HOW TO USE THIS BOOK

Of course, you'll benefit most if you read this book from beginning to end. Still, books like this are often bought by users who have a specific task in mind. If you haven't purchased a hard disk yet but are considering one, read Part One, "Macintosh Hard Disk Essentials." Part One, besides covering basic hard disk technology and terminology, explains some of the features and flaws to look for when shopping for or evaluating a hard disk. If months or years of regular use has made your hard disk a morass of confusion and crowding, you'll need to analyze your needs and get organized. Part Two, "Managing Your Hard Disk," explains the principles behind data management and presents several strategies and scenarios for structuring your work. If you bought this book because your hard disk isn't working, you'll want to read all of Part Three, "When Something Goes Wrong," which explains how to diagnose and treat hard disk problems, with emphasis on how to recover lost data. Part Four, "Maximizing Hard Disk Performance," explains various ways to expand your system. New technologies, including networking, are described. You'll find *Understanding Hard Disk Management on the Macintosh* useful as long as you own your hard disk.

ICONS USED IN THIS BOOK

Three visual icons are used in this book. The Note icon

indicates a note that augments the material in the text. The Tip icon

represents a practical hint or special technique. When you see the Warning icon

pay particular attention—it alerts you to a possible problem or offers a way to avoid a problem.

P A R T   O N E

MACINTOSH

HARD DISK

ESSENTIALS

This section is a guide to hard disk technology—how it works, and how to get it started working for you. Chapter 1 explains some of the technical principles behind hard disks, and Chapter 2 lays the groundwork for getting your hard disk system up and running.

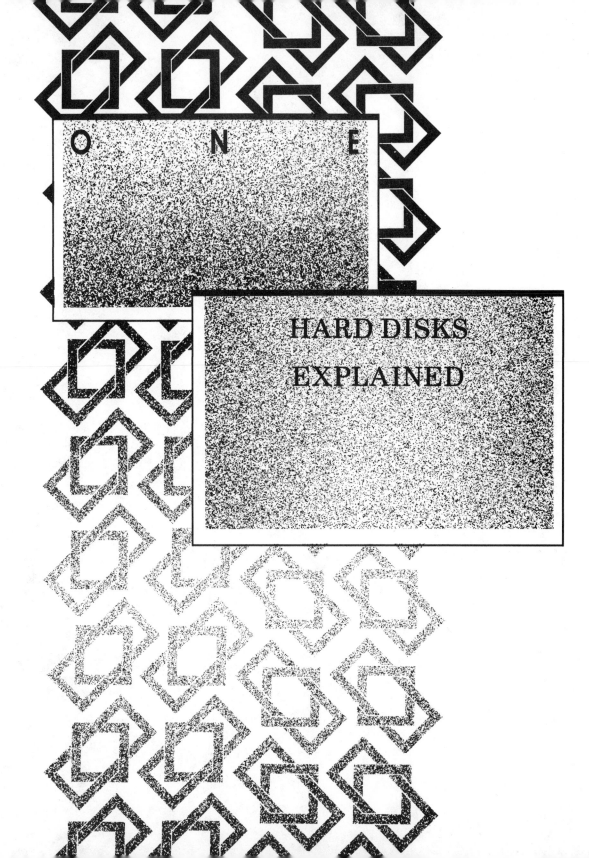

O N E

HARD DISKS
EXPLAINED

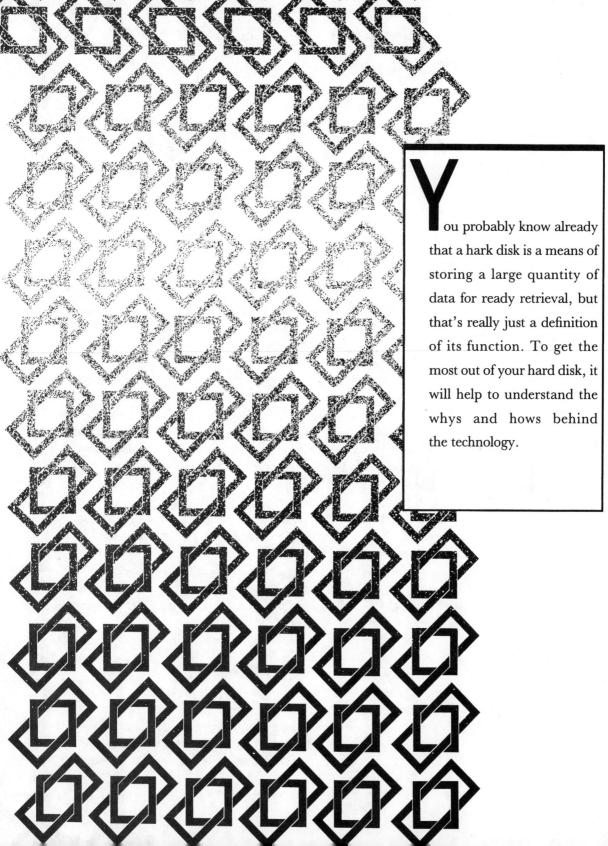

You probably know already that a hark disk is a means of storing a large quantity of data for ready retrieval, but that's really just a definition of its function. To get the most out of your hard disk, it will help to understand the whys and hows behind the technology.

This chapter introduces you to that technology, to storage devices, and to the Macintosh in general. In it, I'll survey the history of data storage and explore the inner workings of hard disks. Then I'll trace the evolution and the changing, challenge-filled role of hard disks for the Macintosh computer. Finally, I'll explain the SCSI peripheral standard and look at some of the factors affecting hard disk performance on the Macintosh.

A BRIEF LOOK AT STORAGE TECHNOLOGY

The hard disk is just one of a family of machines collectively known as *storage devices*. A computer, no matter how powerful, only processes data. To obtain that data in the first place, and to preserve it afterwards, the computer relies on storage.

In the early years of computing, information was stored on paper that the computer read much like a blind person reads braille. For years, thick stacks of keypunch cards or reels of ticker-tape-like paper had to be fed to the computer to run even the simplest program.

This was a cumbersome process, so *magnetic medium devices,* the computer equivalent of tape recorders, displaced the paper storage method. Magnetic medium devices manipulate *tape*—a thin sandwich of plastic and metalic particles. A magnetic recording head arranges the particles in a distinctive pattern and then a similar head reads them; but instead of translating the patterns into sound waves, the computer interprets them as bits and bytes.

Reels of stored information had a distinct advantage over their paper predecessors: they could store information to a higher density, they could be erased, and they could be reused at will. Many large computers still use this technology today.

Still, reels are limited by their linear nature—to retrieve data, the computer must spool and unspool the tape, which takes time and causes wear and tear. That's why the next generation of magnetic media was devised: the *floppy disk*. Floppies operate on the same principle as magnetic tape, only the plastic-metalic sandwich is in platter form and encased in a protective covering. Just as a compact disk player can skip from one track to another in seconds, a computer's floppy disk drive can readily access data anywhere on the disk.

Yet once again, with innovation came limitation. Whereas data tapes could be quite lengthy, floppies were limited to a uniform size. That's why a second approach was being developed concurrently with the floppy disk: the *hard disk*. Instead of plastic, hard disks are made of rigid platters of metal or glass. They can store data with a very high degree of density. But because of this density, the slightest imperfection on the surface, up to and including a mote of dust, can cause data loss. Hard disk technology was promising, but for a while it seemed destined to exist only in isolated environments, far from the dust and dirt of the everyday world.

To make hard disk use more practical, a number of tactics were tried. Most of them involved encasing the disks in a dust-free medium and hermetically transporting them to the *read/write heads*, the recorders and retrievers of data from the hard disk. This kept the platters more or less clean, but the delicate read/write heads were still exposed, if only for the time it took to change disk packs. It was at best an expensive, high-maintenance solution to the problem of keeping the hard disk clean.

In the early 1970s, scientists and engineers at IBM began developing what proved to be the most successful strategy. They combined and contained the hard disks and read/write heads in a single, sealed unit cooled by highly filtered air. Users wouldn't be able to slip disks in and out at will, but dust and other contaminants wouldn't slip in, either. This type of storage unit is often still referred to by its IBM code name, the *Winchester drive*. Most hard disks used by personal computers today are variations and permutations of the Winchester drive.

Impressive as they may be, hard disks aren't the apogee of storage technology. The compact disk (CD), write once, read many (WORM) optical drives, magneto-optical drives and the digital audio tape (DAT) drive represent yet another generation of storage technology.

Perhaps the most popular method for moving sealed disks to the read/write heads involved floating the disks on a bed of air. The popular and reliable Bernoulli Box backup units still use this method.

AN INTRODUCTION TO MEMORY

Your hard disk is a means of storing information, but it's not what most people mean when they refer to computer "memory." Memory is the "place" information is held so that it can be accessed and manipulated by the computer's *central processing unit* (CPU). This place is actually two places, commonly known as the *RAM* and the *ROM*.

All information in RAM is erased when the power is turned off or interrupted. Prevent information loss by regularly saving to disk.

You cannot erase the information in ROM—that's what ''read-only'' means.

When you launch a program, that program is loaded, or read, into RAM or *Random Access Memory*. When you open a file, that goes into the RAM too. Since the RAM can get filled to capacity quickly, the computer regularly purges and rearranges the information stored in it, getting rid of the data it no longer needs.

Yes, but how does it know what it doesn't need? That's one of the tasks of the information stored in ROM, or *read-only Memory*. It's the manager of the microprocessor world, a set of rules, instructions and other information that is permanently inscribed—it doesn't disappear when you turn the computer off, or trip over the plug. This data is known as *firmware*, whereas the data that gets loaded into RAM from storage devices is known as *software*.

The smallest unit of memory is the *bit*. Bits are either ''off'' (0) or ''on'' (1). A *byte* is a unit consisting of eight bits.

You'll often see the letter *K* (or *Kb*) after a number. That stands for *kilobyte*, and although kilo usually means a thousand (as in kilometers), a kilobyte is actually 1,024 bytes, or 8,192 bits. The extra bits are there because computers use a base 2, or *binary*, number system (because the bit is the basic unit of data), and 2^{10} equals 1,024.

A *megabyte* is 1,024 kilobytes; it's usually abbreviated as *meg*, and sometimes *M*. Personal computers are beginning to deal in *gigabytes*, a unit of measure equal to 1,073,741,824 bytes. At present, a single CD-ROM disk has a raw storage capacity of nearly a gigabyte, and gigabyte-size hard disks are commercially available for the Mac II.

INSIDE YOUR HARD DISK

If you're lucky, you'll never need to see the inner workings of your hard disk. All units are sealed to ward off dust and other impurities, and they should be opened only for major repairs and only by qualified technicians in an especially clean environment. That sort of advice is given about a lot of electronic equipment, but in the case of hard disks it should be taken to heart: most hard disks operate to precise tolerances and even a highly informed nonprofessional can easily do more harm than good. Simply touching or breathing on an exposed hard disk can obliterate data.

Unless it has a storage capacity of 20 megabytes or less, your hard disk is probably a collection of disks, usually called *platters*. Platters, stacked one on top of another like records on a multiplay turntable, rotate on a central spindle.

When you power up the hard disk, an electric motor turns the spindle and the platters start spinning very rapidly. A Macintosh drive is supposed to keep its platters spinning at 3500 revolutions per minute, more than one hundred times faster than a long-playing record. Because it usually takes a few seconds for the platters to attain that speed, I recommend that you turn on your external hard disk a moment or two before you start up your computer, although disks installed inside the Macintosh have circuitry that essentially does the same thing for you.

Why do the platters spin so fast? Because the faster they spin, the less time the computer has to wait for the right block of data to come around on a platter. Remember, a hard disk is a mechanical device serving a solid-state electronic one; on the microprocessing level, a tenth of a second is a long, long time.

READ/WRITE HEADS

The read/write heads of your hard disk are something like a cross between a tape head and a phonograph stylus. They are small, light, and suspended on a metal arm; but they don't actually touch the surface of the platter. Instead, floating very close to the platter, they swing back and forth to cover the entire surface area.

How close? The gap between them is usually measured in thousandths of an inch, a distance smaller than a hair's breadth. The residue left behind by a fingerprint or by cigarette smoke can fill the gap and cause the read/write heads to touch the platter surface. When this happens, a condition known as *head crash* often occurs; the damage can range from momentary data loss to permanent impairment.

Head crashes are also caused by moving or dropping the drive while it's in operation. Most units have a shock absorption system to minimize this danger, but extremes of motion—say, knocking the hard disk off your desk—are likely to cause damage.

THE CONTROLLER

The *controller* manipulates the read/write heads and passes data to the computer or disk. If you've ever wondered why Macintosh hard disks are much more expensive than their PC counterparts, the controller is a large part of the answer: on the IBM and compatible PCs, the hard disk controller board can be plugged directly into the computer's data pathway with an add-on card. The Macintosh II has a similar add-on architecture, but earlier Mac designs required newer, more elaborate—and hence more expensive—controller circuitry.

INITIALIZATION

Initialization, also called *formatting*, is the process by which a hard disk is organized and mapped to make data storage and retrieval proceed as quickly as possible. An initialized disk is divided into concentric rings called *tracks*, which are divided into segments called *sectors* (see Figure 1.1). The amount and size of the tracks and sectors on an initialized hard disk vary according to the unit's capabilities and the manufacturer's standards. Commercially available hard disks come from the factory already initialized, but you may reformat them if you want to.

Besides the neat division of platter space, initialization involves identifying areas that are unusable or unreliable, and "walling off" these areas from future use. Unusable or unreliable platter space is created by dust motes, manufacturing impurities, and jolts that cause the read/write heads to touch the platter surface. The presence of these unusable areas should not be seen as a sign of a defective product, since they are an inevitable consequence of using your computer.

Information about the locations and usability of the sectors is stored in a file called the *file allocation table* (FAT). The FAT is usually stored on the outermost tracks of the hard disk. Whenever the Mac needs to read or write data to the disk, it reads the FAT first. Although the FAT keeps track of all sector locations, a list and description of each sector's contents is stored in a single *directory*.

Together, the FAT and the directory are what make the hard disk work. If either is damaged or missing, the Mac is unlikely to recognize the drive or make any sense of its contents; as far as the computer is concerned, your disk is blank. In fact, putting a hard disk file in the trash doesn't actually delete the file, it just purges its listing in the directory. When you reinitialize a previously formatted disk, all you're really doing is creating a new FAT and directory.

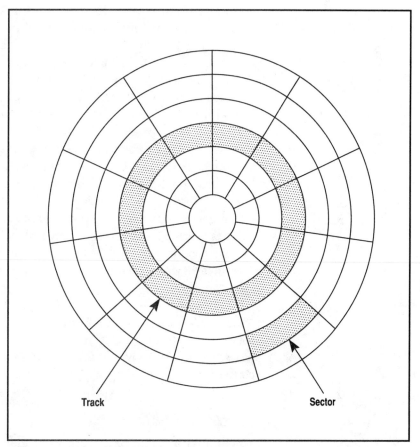

Figure 1.1: Hard disk tracks and sectors

MACINTOSHES AND HARD DISKS

The Macintosh that debuted in 1984 was a far different machine from the Mac Pluses, SEs and IIs of today. The user interface icons, windows, and pull-down menus set new standards for ease of use, but the hardware had severe limitations, some of it intentionally built in by the machine's designers.

The Macintosh was designed to be the "Model T" of personal computers—a single, utilitarian unit without any options. The idea was to keep third-party developers from tinkering with the Macintosh and turning it into a confusion of modifications and permutations. To do this, the Mac was built as a "closed box" computer—it lacked *expansion slots,* which allow users to augment computers by adding circuitry. When it came to storage devices, users were supposed to be satisfied with adding a single external floppy disk drive.

Users weren't satisfied. Personal computer technology was advancing rapidly; soon 400K or 800K of floppy storage seemed far from adequate, especially compared with IBM PCs and compatible computers and their 20 and 40 megabyte hard disks. Soon the Mac's beige box, intended to be sacrosanct, was being regularly cracked open by third-party "upgraders." A number of companies started offering *internal hard disks* for the Macintosh by 1985.

These early drives, though comparable to other Winchester drives in construction and quality, had the disadvantage of having to survive in a hostile environment. The interior of the Macintosh was already crammed with hardware, and even well-engineered internal hard disks, makeshift solutions at best, succumbed all too often to the Mac's lack of circulation and inadequate power supply. The accessory market soon shifted its impetus to *external hard disks*, which didn't have to be mounted within the central shell and didn't depend on the computer's power supply. Yet these, too, had their drawbacks.

SERIAL HARD DISKS

A *port* is a cable-and-connector pathway that conveys data from an attached device to the CPU. A *serial* port can only transmit one bit at a time.

The first wave of Macintoshes, which had 128K and 512K of RAM, were built with the expectation that adding another floppy disk drive would be the most advanced enhancement necessary. So only one external port, a serial port, was provided. That's why the first generation of external hard disks, in effect, had to masquerade as floppy disks (which are serial devices), albeit very large ones. As far as the computer's operating system was concerned, the first serial hard disks were more or less the same as floppies.

These serial disks could store more information than floppies, but the Mac couldn't access that information any faster. Data flow remained bottlenecked at the serial port, which could process at the rate of only 62.5K per second. In spite of their popularity, external hard disks had many performance limitations, and in general they contributed to the misconception that the Macintosh is not a "serious" computer.

SCSI HARD DISKS

Fortunately, by 1986 Apple faced up to reality, acknowledging that hard disks are a necessary part of personal computing. With the introduction of the Macintosh Plus, they added an *SCSI* (Small Computer System Interface) port, a new feature designed primarily for hard disks and related peripherals. The computer could access data from up to seven different devices at once through this port at speeds several times greater than could be achieved through the serial port. Almost immediately, the Mac hard disk industry blossomed in earnest. And with the increased power of mass storage, the Mac began to make headway in the business marketplace.

What is SCSI?

SCSI (pronounced "scuzzy") isn't a computer unit or piece of software, but rather a set of rules for ensuring compatibility between devices. SCSI is a complete set of mechanical, electrical, and functional standards developed by the American National Standards Institute (ANSI), an organization that develops and promotes industry standards in order to eliminate product incompatibility. SCSI devices and accessories often display a special symbol (Figure 1.2).

Figure 1.2: The international SCSI Symbol

A device built to SCSI standards can communicate with other SCSI devices via circuitry known as a *SCSI bus*. Hard disks aren't the only machines built to SCSI specifications; the Macintosh itself is a SCSI device, and other peripherals such as high-speed printers and backup drives are also available in SCSI versions.

Under SCSI rules, each device is either an *initiator* or a *target*: the initiator requests the target to perform an operation such as the reading or writing of a certain block of data. At present the Macintosh always acts as the initiator on the SCSI bus, but "intelligent peripherals" that initiate commands of their own are in the wings.

Multiple SCSI devices—up to eight, counting the Mac—can be linked to the SCSI bus at once. But only one of those devices can be a Macintosh.

SCSI Ports for Older Macs

If your Macintosh was manufactured before the introduction of the Macintosh Plus, that doesn't mean you can't use SCSI. Many hard disk manufacturers offer accessory SCSI ports that take only a few minutes and require no special tools or technical knowledge to install, either by the user or by a qualified dealer.

Before you buy a SCSI port, however, make sure it's compatible with your hard disk. Usually, the best port for the task is offered by the manufacturer of your hard disk (others might not work at all). The typical port is installed through the battery compartment in the rear of the Mac.

If you have a 512Ke Mac (the *e* stands for enhanced), a port is all you need; your computer's ROM has routines that facilitate SCSI. Your machine won't be as fast as a Mac Plus, but having a hard disk will make a big difference in your computing.

But if you have one of the original 128Ks or an unenhanced 512K, an Apple-authorized memory upgrade is highly recommended before the purchase of a SCSI disk or port. You'll need the enhanced RAM and ROM in order for the speed of SCSI to make a noticable difference.

> Pre-SCSI Macs can be upgraded with add-on SCSI ports.

EXTERNAL HARD DISKS

Today, every Macintosh in production can use SCSI devices. Serial hard disks are no longer manufactured, and SCSI hard disks are available with capacities from 20 megabytes to 200 megabytes and beyond. Because the majority of Macs in use today are still the "closed box" type (the Mac Plus and its predecessors), the most popular hard disks are *external disks*. These are attached through external cabling, and have separate power supplies, cooling systems, and control circuitry. We'll discuss their set-up, installation, and formatting in Chapter 2.

It's important to note that even though the same external hard disk can be used with a Macintosh Plus, an SE, and a II, it's configured for optimum performance with only one member of the Mac line at a time. This topic, along with information on how to determine configuration and how to reconfigure for your computer, is explored in Chapter 8.

INTERNAL HARD DISKS

In 1987, the Mac was fully opened for business. The Macintosh SE (for System Expansion) retained the distinctive size and shape of its predecessors and added a single expansion slot and room for an internal hard disk. The Macintosh II, introduced at the same time, was designed with an unabashedly open architecture: there was room under the hood for no less than six expansion slots and two hard disks.

These models ushered in a new generation of internal hard disks—engineers no longer had to make design compromises in order to shoehorn the units into the computer's casing. The new internal drives are several times more reliable than their predecessors, and significantly easier to install. The user can install the Mac II with tools no more specialized than a screwdriver.

Internal drives for the SE fall into two categories: those designed to fit directly above the floppy drive (in the front), and those designed to take advantage of the accessory access port (in the back). Internal disks designed to fit in front require professional installation but free the access port for other add-ons, such as enhancement cards. Internal disks designed to fit in back can usually be installed by the user, and free up space for a second floppy drive.

Internal drives are an excellent choice when desk space is hard to come by, or when sound needs to be kept to a minimum (internal disks are cooled by the computer's fan). The disadvantage is that internal disks can't be transported easily from one computer to another; many users with both an office and a home system prefer external hard disks that they can shuttle back and forth.

HARD DISK
PERFORMANCE ON THE MAC

Most SCSI Mac external hard disks can work with any member of the Macintosh family—the same would go for internal hard disks, except for the fact that design differences between the SE and Mac II require different configurations. But just because they'll work, that doesn't mean they'll work exactly the same when teamed with any model of Macintosh. The degree of performance depends on many factors, but especially on the limitations imposed by the computer and the hard disk controller. Primary among these performance factors are *transfer speed* and *access time*.

TRANSFER SPEED

Transfer speed, measured in kilobytes per second (Kps), is the rate at which information is conveyed from the disk to and from the CPU. Transfer speed varies with the traffic coordination capacity of the CPU. Like the miles-per-gallon rate of a car, the official transfer speed of a hard disk is put at the optimum level. However, optimum transfer speed is usually attained only in short bursts—continual transfer at optimum speed would quickly overwhelm the CPU. Transfer speeds for the Macintosh line are summarized below.

- The Macintosh Plus SCSI port accommodates 312Kps, a considerable increase over serial port hard disks, which average 62.5Kps, and floppy disk drives, which average 56Kps.

- The Macintosh SE's port is more than twice as fast as the Mac Plus'. It operates at approximately 656Kps.

- The Macintosh II can port at a lusty 1250Kps, or 1.25 megabytes per second (Mps), nearly a twofold increase in transfer speed over the SE.

Interestingly, even the Mac II's capacity doesn't begin to tax the capacity of the SCSI standard itself, which allows a maximum transfer rate of 5Mps. This capability guarantees that SCSI will be a part of Macintoshes to come.

Interleave Ratios

In order to accommodate the transfer speeds of the different Mac models and also retain compatibility with all of them, hard disk manufacturers adopted *interleaving*. When interleaving has been implemented, the read/write heads deliberately skip sectors. In other words, information stored on the disk is broken up so that *logically* continuous sectors are not *physically* continuous. Changing the number of physical sectors between logical sectors changes the number of platter revolutions required to completely read or write 1 track, thereby changing the disk's transfer speed to accommodate the transfer rates of different computers.

The fastest hard disks match the transfer speed of the Mac II, which means that the *interleave ratio* is 1:1—the heads can read or write a complete track in 1 platter revolution. For the Mac SE, the standard ratio is 2:1, which means it takes 2 revolutions to read or write all the sectors on 1 track. For the Mac Plus, the ratio is 3:1 (see Figure 1.3).

Some drive manufacturers offer products that allow a 1:1 interleave on all three models. Given the limitations of the SCSI port, such options might seem to be more the product of marketing than engineering. Unless your Mac has undergone a CPU enhancement that includes new SCSI capability, you're unlikely to benefit from an interleave ratio faster than the standard for your model. This means that a hard disk with a 1:1 ration is unlikely to operate faster on a Mac Plus than one with a 3:1 ratio.

ACCESS TIMES

A common benchmark of hard disk performance is *access time,* the time it takes the read/write heads of a hard disk to locate a given track. Since tracks vary in distance from one another, access time is usually given as an average. Current averages range from 65 milliseconds for older hard disks to 20 milliseconds or less for the newest, most expensive hard disks.

Access time is measured in milliseconds and the time difference between the slowest and fastest hard disks is imperceptible except when several hundred sectors have to be located and read (a regular occurrence when launching an application). In this case, a delay of milliseconds is multiplied to the point that it becomes noticeable.

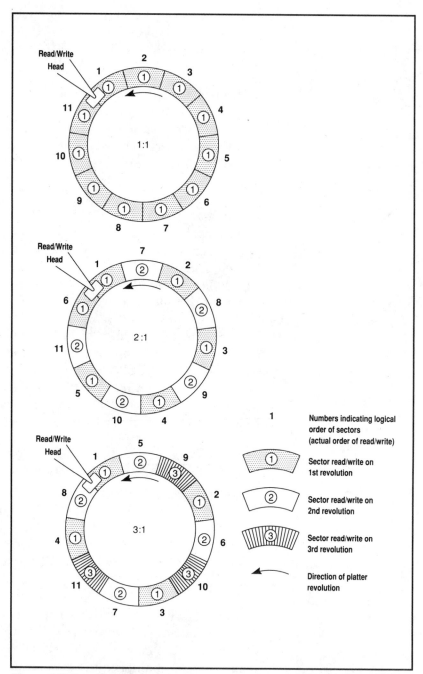

Figure 1.3: Interleave ratios change the order in which physical sectors are read and written to; the top ratio is 1:1, the middle 2:1, and the bottom 3:1.

However, the increased performance of a faster drive can often be cancelled out by the limitations of the SCSI bus and the CPU. A hard disk that runs swiftly on the Mac II will seem to run slowly on the SE, and no faster than a standard disk on the Mac Plus if the drive's transfer speed is faster than the computer's.

CODING METHODS

Another factor affecting performance is the method by which information is read, or *coded,* into the sectors. Most information is coded in a conventional bit-by-bit fashion (the same format used by floppies), but some of the more expensive drives now employ *run-length limited* (RLL) coding.

RLL coding squeezes more data into each sector—sometimes over 50 percent more, although a lot depends on the controller and the nature of the data being stored. Because it places data close together, RLL coding can shorten access time and make a drive perform faster. However, it is primarily viewed as a means of increasing storage capacity, not of enhancing performance. RLL coding requires a special controller, so it's not a viable upgrade option for most regularly coded hard disks.

COATING, PLATING, AND SPUTTERING

Like floppies, the magnetic media on most hard disks are made of iron oxide particles suspended in a neutral, binding coating. But floppies endure only a fraction of the wear and tear of hard disk platters, so their oxide surfaces are overlayered with a thin sheet of plastic. Hard disks require a more durable coating.

There are two prevailing approaches to hard disk coating: *plating* and *sputtering*. Plating uses an electrical and chemical process like alloying to bind the oxides to the platter's metalic surface. This is the cheapest—and most popular—coating technique. Sputtering creates oxide adhesion by an electrical-vacuum process, which is more expensive but achieves a higher density of oxides.

What are the advantages from the perspective of a user? Sputtered hard disks can pack more megabytes onto a platter, but that's an important factor only in high-capacity drives of 100 megabytes or more, where space is at a premium. Plated drives cost less, but the plating process is done to various degrees of quality; poor plating has been known to flake off and render the drive unusable.

Manufacturing techniques shouldn't be a major factor in evaluating hard disks—the real criteria should be convenience and quality. The number of platters isn't as important as storage capacity, and the coating method doesn't matter as much as the reputation of the manufacturer.

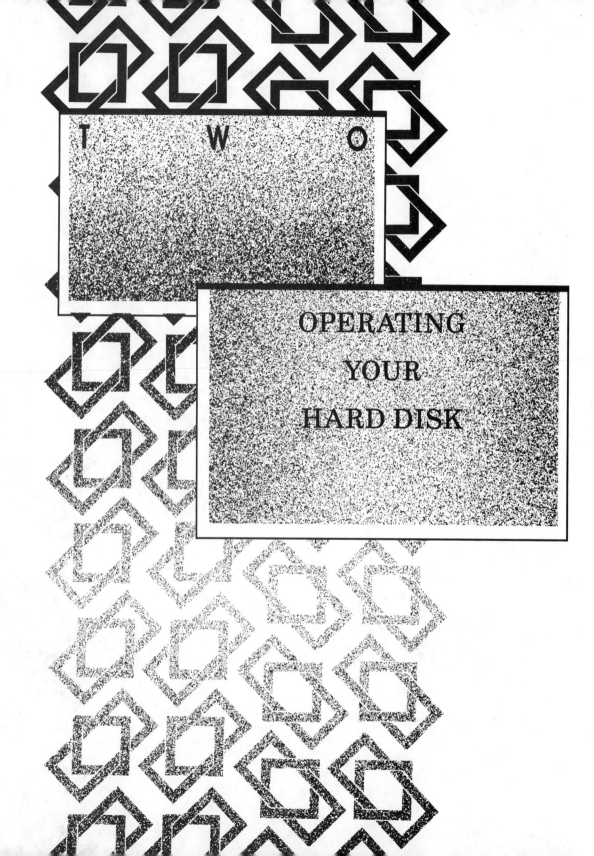

T W O

OPERATING
YOUR
HARD DISK

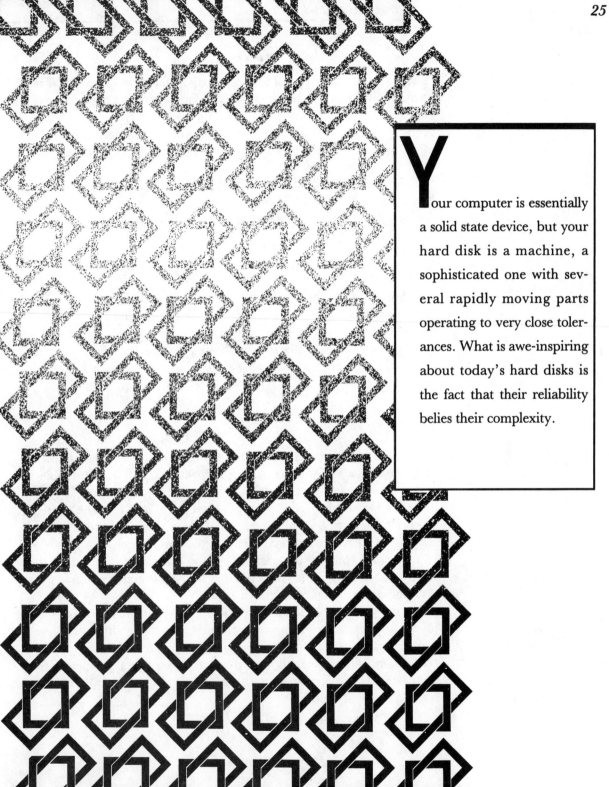

Your computer is essentially a solid state device, but your hard disk is a machine, a sophisticated one with several rapidly moving parts operating to very close tolerances. What is awe-inspiring about today's hard disks is the fact that their reliability belies their complexity.

This chapter is designed to help you get started with a hard disk system. I'll cover the details of setup, installation and connectivity. I'll cover how to fit your hard disk into your workplace, and what precautions you should take for trouble-free operation. Then I'll move on to the software side, demonstrating how to prepare your hard disk for its role at the core of your computing.

Even if you already have your hard disk up and running, you can benefit from reading this chapter. In it I introduce several of the concepts you might need for troubleshooting a hard disk related problem.

HANDLING YOUR HARD DISK

A hard disk is not a box of nitroglycerine, but it's not a brick either. When handling your hard disk, strive for a balance between confidence and caution. Don't get it wet. Don't subject it to extremes of temperature (below freezing or above 100 degrees). Don't place it under a heavy weight. And try to keep it from being sharply jostled or violently shaken.

UNPACKING

When unpacking your hard disk, try not to mangle the container or the foam padding. Once you've unpacked the disk and double-checked for stray paraphernalia or documents, set the packaging aside for safekeeping. You may never need it, but if a time comes when you have to transport your hard disk through the mail or by package express (perhaps to return it to the manufacturer for repair), you'll be glad you kept the packaging. You could ship your hard disk in any reasonably padded package, but nothing is better suited to the task than the original container.

Before you move on to the hardware, take a moment to peruse and fill out any warranty or registration cards that come with your hard disk. Surprisingly, the majority of new equipment purchasers fail to return consumer information of this sort, even when it's clearly to their benefit. It's a good idea to take care of this now, rather than waiting to get around to it.

TRANSPORTING

A hard disk is most vulnerable when it's operating. Before you move your disk, give it ample time to shut down. Don't just turn off the computer it's attached to; if your hard disk has its own power supply, make sure to turn that off as well. Before moving it, wait a minute for the platters to stop spinning and the read/write heads to return to an at-ease position.

Once turned off and disconnected, the hard disk is a relatively hardy breed. You can put it in your briefcase, place it in the backseat of your car or even send it through the mail (but be sure to package it well and make a backup of all data first).

HEAD PARKING

Moving the read/write heads to a stable location is known as "parking the heads." This is an important procedure, because an unparked head, hovering a fraction of an inch above the platter surface, can be jolted into contact with the platter surface. When this happens, data loss or the much-dreaded head crash may result.

Most of the hard disks on the market today offer automatic head parking, in which the parking procedure is automatically triggered by the off switch. Others park their heads by means of software. To complicate matters even more, the definition of parking itself varies from company to company. For some, head parking means retracting the head entirely, for others it means moving the head to a "safe" area of the platter (usually an area currently void of data).

Make sure you know whether your hard disk is parked automatically or with a software program. If you've bought it used or lost the documentation, ask the manufacturer or someone who owns the same kind of hard disk you have. If yours parks automatically, determine if "automatically" means when the power is discontinued, or only when the off switch is hit. If your hard disk parks when the power is discontinued, you can turn it off by flicking a floor switch, rather than by reaching around the back of the unit.

If your hard disk parks by means of software, you won't necessarily have to run the parking program every time you shut down. Consider how susceptible to hard knocks your hard disk is. If your computer is in an out-of-the-way place, you don't need to park the read/write heads each time you finish working. Make sure you have the correct and current software, and that it is installed on a backup floppy as well as on the hard disk itself. Park the heads whenever you're moving your hard disk more than a few feet.

SETTING UP

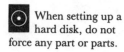

When setting up a hard disk, do not force any part or parts.

Most of the following refers specifically to hard disks of the external, self-contained variety, but the information will be useful to owners of internal hard disks as well. If the documentation that came with your hard disk is complicated, inadequate, or entirely absent, the following should help you on the way to proper installation. For installation instructions, however, you'll have to rely on the manual or the manufacturer. The best way to ensure the correct setup of your external hard disk is to read the instructions. There are too many variations on the installation process for us to cover all of them; and since each variation involves direct contact with the computer itself, you need to be sure of every step you take. Meanwhile, no matter how correct an action might seem, don't force any part or parts. Computer peripherals are designed to stand up to heavy use, not heavy abuse.

WHERE TO PUT IT?

Most external hard disks are *horizontally oriented,* designed so that the platters spin parallel to the desktop. The majority of these fit easily under the Mac Plus or Mac SE. In fact, most people prefer that location. It has the advantage of raising the Mac screen a few inches, which many people find easier on the eyes. If you do put your hard disk under your computer, make sure your unit is designed for that position, that it has ample vents for circulation and that the vents aren't blocked by the bottom of the Mac.

To see if this arrangement works for you, place the still-unconnected hard disk under your computer. Now fire up the Mac and operate with floppies for a while. If your taste or your workspace doesn't accommodate the added height, simply place the hard disk elsewhere.

Just where that ''elsewhere'' is might be dictated by the length of your SCSI cable—it might not be long enough. If you'd like to clear your desktop or put your hard disk in a place where you won't hear it (most have fans), look into the purchase of a longer SCSI cable. They can be up to seven meters long. Consider placing your hard disk in a corner, a cabinet, or even a closet. Make sure the location meets the following criteria.

Ventilation Resist the temptation to use your hard disk as a bookend or paperweight; a single sheet of paper placed flat against a vent can impair cooling. There should be at least three inches of open space on both sides of your hard disk, unless your unit has a special air intake and filtration scheme. Check your documentation to see what kind of filtration system you have.

Most hard disks are designed to be placed on a flat, hard surface. Instead of placing it on a soft surface like pile carpeting, first lay down a piece of wood or firm cardboard large enough to cover the unit's entire bottom. This will allow air to flow underneath.

Cleanliness A hard disk draws air through a series of high-mesh filters. These are more than adequate for filtering out the dust and dirt found in office and household environments, but not for extremes of grease, moisture and dirt, which can overwhelm them. It is probably okay to store your hard disk under your desk, but not under the kitchen sink.

Accessibility You want your hard disk to be where you can get to it with ease, both to check on its operation and to flip its power switch. Depending on your power supply setup, you might need to flip the power switch every time you start a computing session. We'll cover power switch strategies in a bit.

Safety Keep your hard disk out of harm's way. This goes not only for the hard disk, but also for your computer system's cords, cables and connectors. Keep them away from pets, children, vacuum cleaners and the like.

You can store or transport a hard disk—when it's properly disconnected—in just about any position, but you should operate it in the position for which it was designed. If you place a horizontally oriented hard disk on its side, chances are it will still work but not for as long as it would have otherwise. Changing a hard disk's orientation puts a torque and gravitational strain on the internal bearings and other mechanisms, which can lead to failures.

Keeping your hard disk level doesn't mean you have to get out a carpenter's level; any reasonably flat surface will do nicely.

PLUGGING IN

If you want to put your hard disk under or near your Mac, it's probably easiest to plug both of them into the nearest socket. This way you can turn them on and off by reaching around the back of the units. However, if the hard disk is placed in such a way that the on/off switch isn't easy to reach, you might consider a *power strip* setup.

Use a power strip only if your hard disk parks its heads automatically when the power is shut off.

A power strip is a sophisticated extension cord with multiple outlets, an on/off switch and, in some cases, a circuit breaker. With your hard disk's cord and your computer's cord plugged into the strip, you can leave the unit's on/off switch in permanent "on" mode. This way, you can simply power up and power down by flicking the switch on the power strip. However, to use a strip your hard disk must head park automatically when the current is shut off. Most hard disks do park the read/write heads automatically; but if yours doesn't, using a power strip makes it susceptible to head crashes.

For many, the best solution is to plug the computer, hard disk, printer, modem, and all other accessories into one power strip. With this arrangement you don't have to spend time searching for on/off switches. No matter how you configure your setup, make sure the computer and the hard disk don't power up simultaneously: the hard disk needs a few moments to get up to speed before it can be recognized by the Mac. In fact, Apple recommends starting a hard disk at least ten seconds before switching on the Mac. If both are plugged into the same power strip, you can keep the hard disk switched on, but you have to activate the Mac with the power switch in the rear or with the keyboard.

USE SURGE SUPPRESSORS FOR SAFETY

Every computer user should have a *surge suppressor* to filter off excess voltage. Surge suppressors increase the reliability of your hard disk and add years to the life of your computer and its peripherals.

AC current supplied through the wall sockets of most buildings doesn't flow at a consistent voltage. The standard flow rate in the U.S. is supposed to be 120 volts, but in reality the rate often varies plus or minus 10 to 15 volts, depending how old the circuitry is and the demands placed upon it. When, for example, lightning strikes a power pole, a large electricity user goes off-line, or a large household appliance goes on, a sudden strain is placed on the system, causing a momentary voltage imbalance that sends surges through local outlets. These have little effect on lights and appliances, but they can cause data loss or even permanent damage in microprocessors and magnetic media.

Some hard disks come with built-in surge protection. Most add-on surge suppressors are simple plug-in devices that range from $15 to $100.

Surge suppressors won't protect you from brownouts, blackouts or other abrupt power outages. That's why it's a good idea to save your data regularly. If you want a guaranteed, reliable source of electricity, consider buying an *uninterruptible power supply* (UPS). These units work like temporary batteries, switching on so quickly and smoothly that the Mac doesn't register the power loss. Most UPS units provide power for less than a minute, enough time to save your work and shut down, and others operate for an hour or more. A UPS unit costs more than a surge suppressor but it makes your Mac oblivious to brief power outages.

Some surge suppressors shut off the power if the voltage drops below a certain point. This protects hardware but not unsaved data.

SETTING UP A DAISYCHAIN

Most external hard disks come with one SCSI cable and two SCSI ports. That's because each SCSI device, including a hard disk, can serve as a link on the SCSI bus, passing on information to and from the SCSI device on either side. A number of SCSI devices linked together this way is called a *daisychain*. Up to seven devices can be daisy-chained at once. A SCSI port's capacity to transmit information is greater than the CPU's capacity to process and transmit it, so

The length of all the cables in one daisychain should not be more than 20 feet.

even a fully loaded daisychain can perform as fast as a single SCSI device. Regardless of how many devices are connected to a daisychain, the total length of the cables used should be no more than 20 feet. If SCSI signals travel more than that distance, the slowed response time can confuse the Macintosh.

On most hard disks, it doesn't matter which port is connected to the computer and which is connected to another SCSI device. But even if you're only hooking up a single hard disk, you're establishing a SCSI bus that must have a clearly defined end. This definition is achieved with a terminator, which is discussed below.

Do not attach anything to the Macintosh SCSI port unless you are sure that it is a SCSI device. The 25-pin connectors on SCSI devices are manufactured to a common design format called DB-25, and this format is shared by products that use another device standard known as RS-232. (Certain other products employ the DB-25 format as well.) The connectors on these products will fit, but their input can burn out the SCSI circuitry.

If you're using the cables and connectors provided with a SCSI device, there's no need to worry—if the other end mates properly with the device's port, it's SCSI. But if you're in doubt, look for the SCSI symbol (see Figure 1.2). Some don't display it, but most do. Apple connectors place it on the top surface of the coupling assembly, while some manufacturers imprint it underneath the assembly, or on the cable itself.

Termination

Daisy-chaining isn't just a fringe benefit of SCSI, it's what the standard was designed for—to overcome the limitations created by data port bottlenecks. For the SCSI bus to support multiple devices, it must be capped with a termination resistor, or *terminator*. The terminator tells the SCSI bus when to stop searching for connected devices. Internal hard disks are automatically terminated, but most external drives aren't.

Your Mac is constantly sending and receiving signals up and down the SCSI bus, signals that contain commands, status messages, target addresses and, of course, data. Some signals are directed at a specific SCSI device, but others of general significance are intended to

Both ports on most hard disks have 50-pin connectors. Because the cables supplied with these disks usually have a 25-pin connector at one end (to match the port on the Mac), you'll probably need to get a cable with two 50-pin connectors if you want to link two hard disks.

Don't connect non-SCSI devices to the SCSI port—this could damage the Mac.

be read by all the devices in the daisychain (even if only one device is connected). Unless there is a terminator at the end of the daisychain, general-significance signals travel up the SCSI bus and then "bounce back," colliding with other signals and disrupting the entire bus. But a terminator safely dissipates the signals.

Most terminators are external, in the form of a short female/male adapter. If you intend to attach only one SCSI device to your Mac, attach it in one of the following ways:

- connect the SCSI cable directly to one device port and place the terminator on the other

- place the terminator between the SCSI cable and the device port

Of the two, placing the terminator between the SCSI cable and the device port is more convenient for users who occasionally daisy-chain another SCSI device. Connecting the SCSI cable to one port and placing the terminator on the other becomes necessary when multiple devices are on the bus—that's when you need to make sure that termination is active only on the last device in the chain. A terminator placed in the middle of the chain effectively cuts off other devices from the bus.

Unfortunately, some external hard disks have internal terminators that can't be deactivated, or terminators that are not removable. Most of these were manufactured in the early days of Macintosh SCSI by companies who assumed that most users would need only one hard disk at a time. If your terminator is one of these, get in touch with the manufacturer; most can at least recommend a means of removing or circumventing the termination. If the manufacturer's no longer around, try taking it to a qualified service technician and hope for the best.

Of course, a permanently terminated hard disk isn't obsolete. It will work fine when directly connected to the Macintosh, or when placed at the very end of a daisychain.

Setting SCSI Addresses

Daisy-chaining is a means of ordering devices along the SCSI bus, but there's another order to the setup: each device has an *address* that

When buying an external hard disk with an internal terminator, make sure that you know how to turn the terminator off and on.

serves both as an identifier and as a means of prioritizing data traffic. The address order bears no relation to the physical order, and you can change it without reconnecting any cables.

The SCSI bus has a total of eight addresses—0 to 7—and no two devices can have the same address. The address 7 is reserved for the Macintosh itself, since the computer is also a SCSI device. Internal hard disks for the SE and Mac II are always set at 0. You can set your hard disk to any of the six addresses in between.

Different drives come with different means of setting addresses. Some come with a preset address that can only be changed with software after the drive is up and running. Others require the setting of switches, and still others have a simple dial or knob on the rear of the unit for changing addresses. And, of course, there are some units that can't be reset at all—a drawback only when you need to daisy-chain two units with the same permanent address.

When looking for a startup disk, the Mac first looks at the floppy drives and then looks at the SCSI bus.

If you have a choice, it's a good idea to set your main external hard disk to the address 6. Six is the next address, after the floppy drive and internal hard disk (address 0), that the Macintosh looks for when you start up the system. When two or more devices are trying to feed the SCSI bus at the same time, the one with the highest address gets priority. Be sure that no devices share the same SCSI address.

You must shut down and restart your computer before attempting to access a re-addressed device. Otherwise the Mac will send data to the wrong addresses. Also, never change addresses in the middle of a work session.

Reset addresses only when the computer is turned off. Or if your system uses software to change addresses, be sure to change them only under the conditions specified by the software. In any case, before you attempt to access a re-addressed device, shut down and then restart the system all over again. And never change addresses in the middle of a work session. The Macintosh reads SCSI addresses only once, during the startup sequence. If you change addresses in the interim, the computer will remain oblivious; it will blithely send commands and data to wrong or nonexistent devices.

BREAKING IN YOUR HARD DISK

Your first impulse with a brand new hard disk may be to go easy on it, perhaps by only loading a few applications and files and only adding to them sparingly. Whereas a gentle breaking in period may be appropriate for a new automobile, for hard disks you should take the opposite tack.

It's best to uncover any defects in your hard disk in the early phase of use before the warranty expires. Here's a three-step strategy for ferreting out defects while there's still time to do something about them.

Keep the unit running. If your hard disk has a separate power supply, it can operate (but not read or write data) while the computer is turned off. So long as the noise from the fan doesn't present a problem, keep it running for a week or so. If the platter bearings, the exhaust fan, or the drive motor are defective, intense use may bring these problems to light while your unit is still under warranty.

Copy as much data as possible. Bad sectors and controller problems are usually discovered while reading and writing. As soon as you're finished setting up, transfer the applications and files you expect to use regularly to your hard disk. And if it's not too much trouble, load up the drive too. You needn't struggle to fill up every megabyte—taking up a significant block of hard disk space is surprisingly fast and easy.

Instead of laboriously feeding in floppy disks, create a folder. Next, into this folder, insert a duplicate of everything currently on the drive. Then open the folder, create another folder within it, and place all the duplicates inside that one. Now select the folder containing the duplicates, and duplicate it. Repeat the process as long as possible; you'll encounter the out of room message (Figure 2.1) soon enough, but that just means there isn't enough space to hold the large folder you're copying. Continue copying, but select smaller folders to duplicate. Be sure to discard these folders and their contents before getting down to work, however: multiple copies of files and applications could cause the system to crash in confusion. If this copying process causes any complications (such as system malfunction or incomplete copying), the hard disk may be defective. Refer to the troubleshooting techniques in Chapter 6 or consult the drive's manufacturer or merchandiser.

Make the hard disk drive the startup device. You'll want to do this anyway, since nowadays even a modestly equipped System

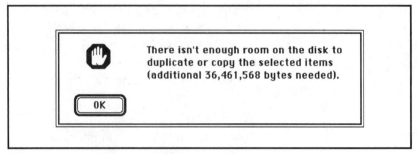

Figure 2.1: This dialog box indicates that there isn't enough free space on the disk to fit the item you are trying to copy.

Folder can take up more than 800K (the capacity of a double-sided floppy). Your Macintosh probably reads and writes the contents of the System Folder more than any other software, so its presence on your hard disk ensures a workout. System installation and startup designation is discussed below.

GETTING THE SYSTEM RUNNING

Now that your hard disk is properly situated, installed and connected, it's time to see if the computer recognizes the drive. First, start up the computer. If your drive comes preformatted with a resident System Folder, all you need to do is make sure everything is turned on. The computer should boot automatically (make sure no disks are in your floppy drives). If, starting up, all you see is the Macintosh's request for a disk icon, this means your hard disk doesn't have a valid System Folder. Keep the hard disk running, but boot up from a floppy. When the desktop appears, note that the hard disk icon looks different from the floppy disk icon. Hard disk icons differ from manufacturer to manufacturer, although most icons resemble the unit they represent.

On the other hand, if you've had to boot from a floppy and a Hard Disk icon doesn't show up on the desktop, shut down the Mac. Check the power cord and SCSI cable to make sure they're securely connected. It's important to do this with the computer switched off. Often the Macintosh doesn't recognize SCSI connections made after starting up. If you make SCSI connections with the computer on, the

Macintosh might send data to the wrong addresses, which can cause system crashes. If securing the power cord and SCSI cable doesn't do the trick, see Appendix A.

If you have a serial hard disk, watch out for instances when the hard disk icon is replaced by a floppy disk icon. This means the Mac has confused the drive with a floppy. Although they are rare, subsequent performance problems can occur. When the Mac displays an incorrect hard disk icon, immediately save all data, shut down and restart.

⊙ If the Mac displays an incorrect hard disk icon, save your data, shut down, and restart.

INSTALLING THE SYSTEM FOLDER

In Chapter One, we discussed the role of ROM in running the Macintosh. But the ROM provides only a part of the Mac's operating system: the rest must be loaded into RAM at the beginning of each session. This software usually makes up the bulk of the System Folder contents—it's the first software you should install on your hard disk.

Apple has released several versions of the System since 1984. (Apple is currently upgrading it every six months.) Unfortunately, though, it isn't safe to assume that the latest version is the best one to use. The best System Folders are often a mix-and-match collection of system components, custom-configured to match the needs of the user and the limitations of the machine. We'll take up the subject of system software in detail in Chapter 4.

You may choose eventually to upgrade the System Folder resident on your hard disk, but for the moment the best version to install is probably one you've been successfully using with your floppies. One way to determine if your System Folder will meet your short-term needs is to examine the System Folder icon. Does it have an image of a miniature Macintosh in the middle (Figure 2.2)? This symbol is called a "blessed" folder: it means the system files within are sufficient to operate the computer. If you had rebooted on another system and removed vital files from this folder, the "blessing" would be absent. The miniature Macintosh image has been a feature of all Finder files since Version 6.0: it's a sign that the software is recent enough to handle your hard disk effectively.

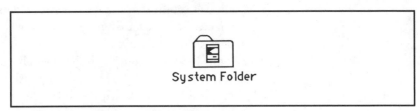

Figure 2.2: The "blessed" System Folder

You can also press
⌘-I on the keyboard to choose Get Info from the File menu. Be sure to select the File or Folder item first.

Another way to determine if your System Folder meets your short-term needs is to read the Get Info entries. If your active System Folder does not display the "blessed" folder symbol, use the Get Info command to determine its version number. Open the folder and find the file named System. Click on it once to select it (Figure 2.3), then choose Get Info from the File menu. An information box similar to the one in Figure 2.4 should be displayed. Get Info boxes exist for every visible file on the Macintosh and they are storehouses of useful information.

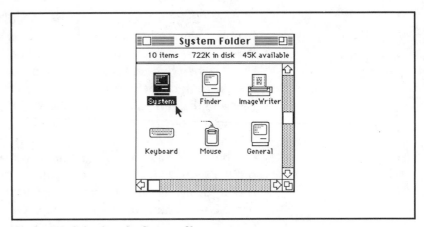

Figure 2.3: Selecting the System file

Do not use System
Version 3.1 or
earlier.

Note the version number. If you have Version 3.1 or earlier, *do not use it.* Such Systems are remnants of the *Macintosh File System (MFS),* a file management approach long since abandoned by Apple. The *Hierarchical File System (HFS)* has supplanted the MFS version. Unlike its predecessor, the Hierarchical File System is capable of handling

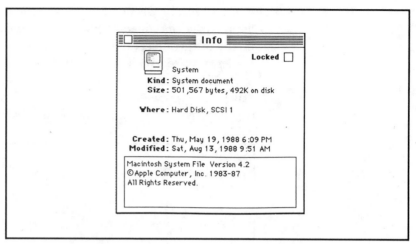

Figure 2.4: The Get Info box

the multiple nested folders generated by a hard disk system. If your system is an MFS version, replace it with an HFS version, which you can obtain at an Apple dealer or through a Macintosh user group. Now that you've checked the System file, make sure that the Finder file with the same icon is present (see Figure 2.3).

Once the System Folder has passed the test, copy it as you would any other file by selecting its icon and dragging it over the hard disk icon. The System Folder won't disappear from the floppy, but a duplicate will be created on the hard disk. Double-click on the hard disk icon to confirm its contents, then shut down.

To eject a floppy after startup, press ⌘-Option-1 or drag the floppy icon into the trash.

Now, while continuing to hold the mouse button down, start the Mac back up, once again making sure that the hard disk is turned on first. If the floppy disk wasn't automatically ejected when you shut down a moment ago, it should eject itself now. If it doesn't, wait until startup is completed, select the floppy and choose Eject from the File menu. Now shut down and restart again, and your Mac should be up and running from the hard disk alone. If it isn't, see Chapter 6.

THE STARTUP SEQUENCE

When starting up from a hard disk, make sure the floppy drives are empty.

When the Mac is switched on, it displays the Disk Requested icon (Figure 2.5) and looks for a startup disk. First it searches the "native" internal floppy drive that it's sold with (not the optional internals for the SE or Mac II). Next it looks in the second internal floppy drive and the external floppy drive. If the Mac finds a floppy in any of these locations, and the floppy does not contain a System Folder, it rejects the floppy. But if the Mac finds a System Folder in one of those locations it will begin to boot up. Make sure the floppy drives are empty—or at least not occupied by disks containing System Folders—when you want to start up from a hard disk.

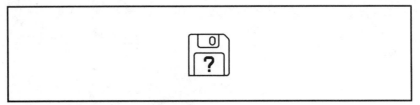

Figure 2.5: The Disk Requested icon

After searching the floppy drives, the Mac starts searching the SCSI devices, from SCSI 6 on down in descending address order. Again, the search stops as soon as a System Folder is found. At this point, booting up begins. If you have only one SCSI device in the daisychain, and it is set at a SCSI address other than 7 (the address of the Mac itself), this device becomes the default startup device. If, however, two or more units are in the daisychain, you'll have to establish a hierarchy—you'll have to give the startup unit of your choice a higher address. (SCSI address priorities need bear no resemblance to the physical order of devices in the daisychain.)

> If you use System Version 4.2 or later, you can use the Startup Device Program to change SCSI priorities without resetting addresses. Access this program through the Control Panel.

Users working with System Version 4.2 or later have another option: the program called Startup Device. This program lets you change SCSI priorities without resetting addresses. Access it through the Control Panel desk accessory. First open the Control Panel, then click on the Startup Device, then click again on an icon corresponding to the drive you want, as in Figure 2.6.

Why all this effort to ensure that the Mac boots from the same System Folder every time? Speed and consistency, for the most part. You can operate your hard disk with a floppy-based startup file, but the time wasted reading and writing from the floppy will slow your work considerably. And even if there is a System Folder on another hard disk in the daisychain, it may lack a number of the elements (most notably fonts)

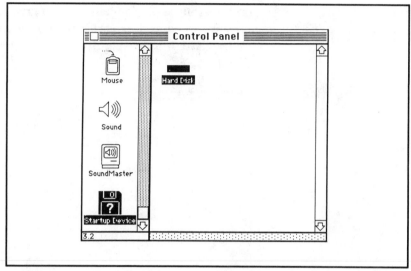

Figure 2.6: Designating the startup device with the Control Panel

that were used to create your files, elements needed to accurately reproduce those files when reopened. Remember, not every system configuration works on every Macintosh. To keep chances and unpleasant surprises to a minimum, it's best to boot your system from the same System Folder each time you operate.

CUSTOM STARTUP SCREENS

As the bootup process begins, the screen display changes the "Happy Mac" to the startup screen. Usually the screen shows a stylized version of the Mac and the Welcome to Macintosh message. This screen is automatically written into the *boot blocks* of each startup disk. Boot blocks are the sectors on the hard disk platter that tell the Mac how to find and interpret the data on the rest of the disk. The screen image however, can be modified or overridden by a customized image. This is a very helpful feature when working with a hard disk. With a customized startup screen, you can tell at a glance whether your Mac accidentally booted from the wrong System Folder.

The easiest way to create a custom startup screen is with Super Paint, a paint/drawing program from Silicon Beach Software. Super Paint operates much like MacPaint or other graphics programs, but it can also convert bit-mapped images into the Mac's startup screen format; just choose Save or Save As... from the File menu, then enable this option (Figure 2.7).

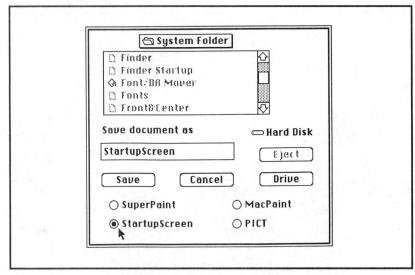

Figure 2.7: Creating a custom startup screen with Super Paint

Note that *StartupScreen* is one word and that each *S* is capitalized. Once saved, you'll need to give that precise name to the file, and then place it in your System Folder. (One of the boot block commands directs the Mac to search for a document by the name StartupScreen only.) The Super Paint application does not have to be resident on the disk for the customized startup screen to be displayed.

Custom screens can also be created with utility programs such as ScreenMaker, and ready-made screens are also available. Both can be obtained commercially through electronic bulletin boards or user groups.

PART TWO

MANAGING YOUR HARD DISK

In this section, we'll explore the elements of effective hard disk usage from the basics of the data structure to performance-enhancing software options. Chapter 3 explains how to make the transfer from floppies to the hard disk and defines and discusses applications, documents, and related resources. Chapter 4 details numerous approaches to organizing files on your hard disk. Chapter 5 assesses the task of keeping your hard disk safe, not only from accidental loss but also from virus corruption and unauthorized access.

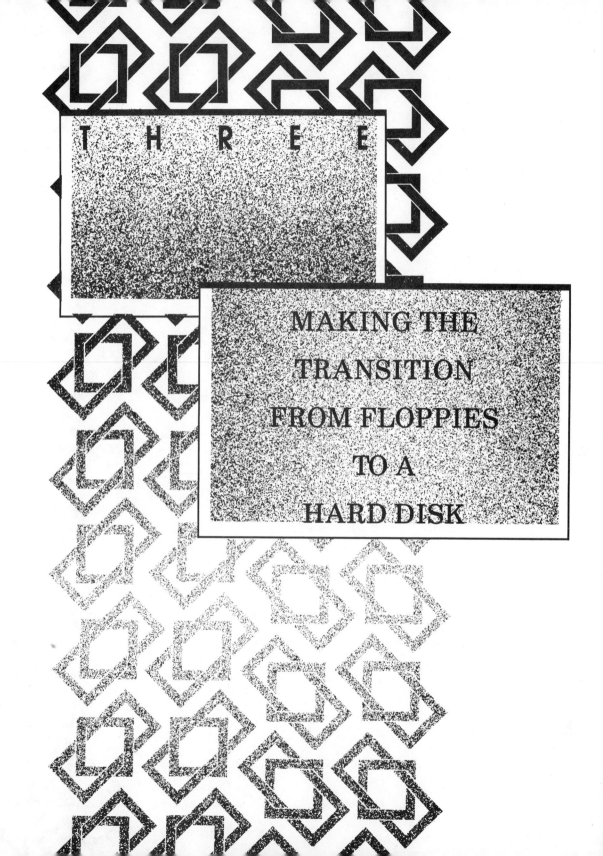

THREE

MAKING THE TRANSITION FROM FLOPPIES TO A HARD DISK

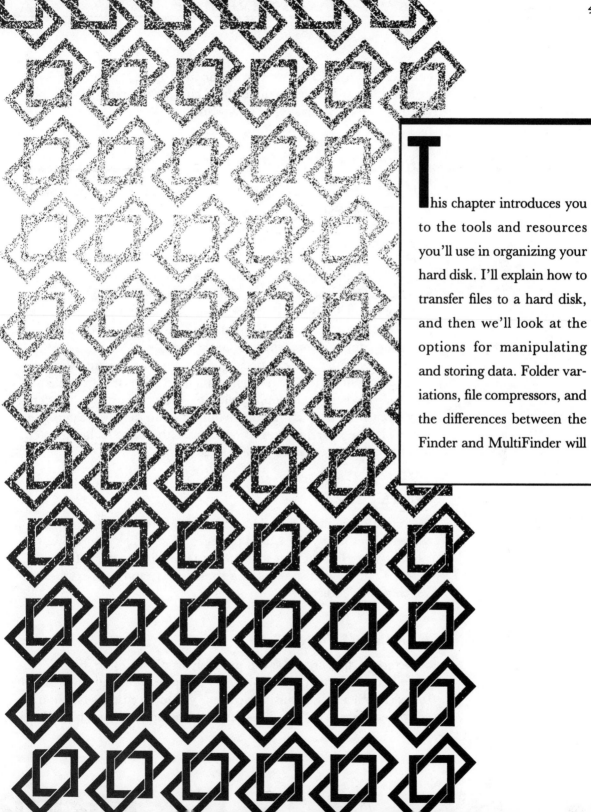

This chapter introduces you to the tools and resources you'll use in organizing your hard disk. I'll explain how to transfer files to a hard disk, and then we'll look at the options for manipulating and storing data. Folder variations, file compressors, and the differences between the Finder and MultiFinder will be covered. I'll conclude with an explanation of the Macintosh's data structure that will help you understand how the computer works and why hard disk organization is important.

ORGANIZING YOUR FILES

If you've already installed a working System Folder on your hard disk, the next step is to transfer your applications and documents from your collection of floppies to your hard disk, so you can do most of your work there.

If you're new to hard disks, all those megabytes of storage space can seem awfully tempting. You might feel an understandable impulse to fill up your hard disk with every piece of software on hand. But a bit of advice is in order: don't copy software to your hard disk just because you have one. Copy the software because you need it. And only copy software when you need it.

Of course, only you can decide which applications and files you need at your fingertips, and when you'll need them. It helps to take a cold, hard look at your floppy collection before you begin transferring in earnest. Start by dividing your files into the three categories below. I'll be referring to these categories throughout this chapter and the next as we discuss storage strategies.

WORK FILES

Work files are the applications and documents you use regularly—the ones that justify the Mac's presence in your life. You might be surprised how little of your software actually falls into this category—perhaps only a word processor, a spreadsheet, and a few games to which you're addicted.

REFERENCE FILES

Reference files are those you probably won't use often, but which you should have on hand anyway. For instance, you may never need to take another look at the invoices you've sent to customers, but if a customer refers to last April's order while making this month's order, it's a lot easier to go to the hard disk for the order than to search through floppies.

Reference files are also the type that benefit from centralization. If you had a spreadsheet to project the profitability of several investments given a number of different scenarios, you would want all the investment files on the same hard disk as the spreadsheet, rather than scattered across several floppies. You can do serious number-crunching without a hard disk, but the flexibility and ease of making speculative analyses is severely impaired.

ARCHIVAL FILES

Archival files comprise the remainder of your software, the files that might come in handy someday, although there's no telling when "someday" might be. This category might include little-used applications, documents ready for storage, exotic fonts, and other electronic bric-a-brac.

MANAGING APPLICATIONS

Of all file types, applications are probably the easiest to manage. They require no special installation, can be stationed anywhere on a hard disk, and can be renamed with impunity. Yet there are a few general principles to keep in mind when loading applications on your hard disk.

- Watch for duplicate versions, as two copies of the same application on one hard disk—even if they're different versions—can cause system hangs, crashes, and lost data. If you have multiple versions of the same application, copy and transfer only the latest one. However, having multiple versions of an application on separate hard disks should present no problem, as long as there is only one copy on each.

- Keep track of resource files and drivers. Many applications create and require dependent documents—dictionaries, user preference settings, device drivers, and so on. Be sure to transfer every dependent document necessary to produce your normal working environment within an application to your hard disk. Unlike applications, dependent documents may need to have a certain title and be in a certain folder in order to work. Consult your software manual if it has a section on hard disk installation. Once again, try to avoid having multiple versions of a dependent document on the same SCSI volume.

- Be prepared for your hard disk to introduce certain changes to your files. When a document is transferred to a volume with another System, the new System file may introduce changes to the document's appearance. Elements such as spacing, columnization and alignment may be affected. If you created your document with a font that isn't present in your hard disk's System Folder, the application may automatically convert all text into another font, which will cause changes in formatting. The accurate placement of page elements is probably crucial in your documents, so make sure all the necessary fonts are installed in your hard disk before you transfer files there. And open a few documents under the new System to see what changes, if any, occur. If you don't want to save any changes made during the transfer, you can still retain the original document by choosing not to save the changes upon closing. The Save Changes? dialog box governs System- as well as user-initiated modifications.

Changes created by a new System file vary in degree from the obvious to the invisible. In some cases, when you close a transferred document, you may be asked if you want to save changes even if you've made no changes and no changes are apparent. In these situations I recommend that you give the document close scrutiny to make sure it is acceptable, then save the changes. If you don't, the Save Changes? dialog box will continue to appear every time you close your document.

LOADING NON-COPY-PROTECTED FILES

With a few rare exceptions, any application or file that you can copy from floppy disk to floppy disk can easily be loaded onto a hard disk as well. You use essentially the same procedure:

1. Click once on the floppy icon to select it, then drag it over the hard disk icon.

2. An interim dialog box appears, then a subsequent dialog box lists the number of files to be transferred, and this number decreases during the transfer. You can cancel the transfer at any time by clicking the Cancel button in the dialog box, but this will only stop the copying in midstream. Any files already copied to the target volume will remain there.

Copying icon by icon can be tedious as well as disorganizing, since it may separate an application from its documents. In practice, you'll probably prefer to transfer larger groups, either folders or entire floppy disks.

Moving all of a floppy's files into a folder and then copying the folder to the hard disk is probably the most convenient means of transferral. If that's the method you choose, be sure to open the new folder and see if it contains a System Folder. If it does, drag the System Folder into the trash (and don't forget to select Empty Trash afterwards). Many floppies are startup disks, so it's important to police your hard disk for System duplication. Of course, transfer any resource files, INITs, DAs, and the like before deleting the System Folder.

Transferring a floppy without putting all its files into one folder requires an interim step. Here's how to transfer a floppy to the hard disk:

1. Drag the floppy disk icon onto the hard disk icon. This brings up a dialog box like the one in Figure 3.1. If for some reason your Mac does not present this dialog box, that indicates the Mac may have confused your hard disk for a floppy—which could mean that it will erase the hard disk! Stop the operation immediately by turning off the power or pulling the plug on the computer.

2. Select the OK button in the dialog box and a copy of the floppy disk will appear as a folder on the uppermost, or *root level* of the hard disk.

Resource files, INITs, and DAs are explained in the "File Types" section later in this chapter.

If you are trying to copy a floppy to a hard disk and the dialog box in Figure 3.1 does not appear, stop the operation immediately.

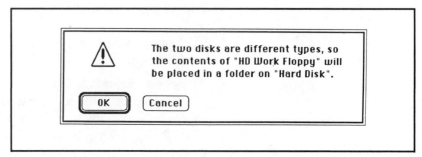

Figure 3.1: A dialog box for copying a floppy to a hard disk

3. Drag the floppy disk icon to one of two places: the hard disk icon, or the open root level window of the hard disk (the window that opens when you double-click on the hard disk). If you try to copy the icon to a preexisting folder on the hard disk you will probably be unsuccessful—Systems 4.0 and later won't let you do this. No matter how you copied the floppy, you should probably then delete any system folders from the copy on the hard disk.

No matter how you've made the transfer, it's a good idea not to start transferring other floppies until you've done the following:

- Don't just cause the drive to eject the disk. Make sure a dimmed version of the floppy icon is present on the desktop before you eject it. There's a quick though scary shortcut for ejecting a floppy icon: drag it into the Trash. The disk will not be erased, just ejected.

- Examine the copied files to see if the application and document icons you just transferred have been changed into default icons. Default icons are displayed in Figure 3.2, but you should note that some of the more modest applications don't display custom icons to begin with. If you find that *any* icon has been *changed* to a default icon, or that a file name has been changed, you should immediately delete not only the changed file, but all files that were transferred along with it— that is, with the same copy command. Do not attempt to launch or open an altered file and investigate why your file icons were changed; by so doing you would damage your System Folder.

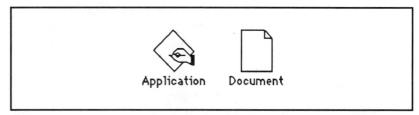

Figure 3.2: Default icons for applications (left) and documents (right)

- Launch an application or two and look for glitches, incompatibilities, or System-file-related changes. Now's the time to find about them. Open a few documents and see if you can spot any changes there as well. If an application's menus do not reflect user settings or other custom information, double-check to see if all the resource files are in order and in their proper place.

If a test launch fails, this may indicate that the application is copy-protected. Some copy-protected applications cannot be transferred at all, others are transferred in garbled form, and still others demonstrate their copy protection only when the user attempts to launch the copy. These types of software require a separate approach to hard disk transfer.

LOADING COPY-PROTECTED FILES

In the Macintosh world, the issue of copy protection has more or less been decided in favor of the user. In fact, you can thank your hard disk for the fact that nowadays hardly any Mac software is released with copy protection. Users grumbled when they couldn't make backups of their floppies, but when they found that copy protection kept them from consolidating their work on hard disks, the grumbling became a roar.

Although copy protection is on its way out, many users still find themselves with an application or two that has some sort of protection scheme. In general, copy protection falls into three categories:

- Key disk software can be copied freely but will only run when the original or "key" disk is placed in a floppy drive. The most nefarious of these programs demand the key disk not just at startup, but at random times during use. Software of this type can probably be copied to your hard disk, but since you'll have to use the floppy anyway it's hardly worth the bother.

- Uncopyable software either can't be copied, or else the copied "duplicate" version will not work (or at least not work very well). This category comprises the bulk of copy-protected software. Much of it can be successfully transferred to a hard disk with a protection-overriding utility such as Copy II, which is discussed below.

- Semicopyable software can be transferred to either a floppy or hard disk, but only a limited number of copies can be transferred, and of those only a few are copyable. With semicopyable software, you can opt to expend one of the allowed transfers on your hard disk, or you can use Copy II (discussed shortly) or another utility to make a nonregistering copy.

For the most part, each of these copy protection categories applies to applications, not to the documents created with them.

Before you attempt to overcome a copy protection scheme in order to load an application onto your hard disk, look instead into getting an upgrade that isn't copy-protected. In most cases, if you're a registered user and the software company whose application you wish to copy is still in business, you can pay a small fee and upgrade to a protection-free version. Only game manufacturers may take exception, since most of them have no plans to abandon copy protection in the near future.

Using Copy II

Copy II Hard Disk is the application you'll want to copy to your hard disk. When it comes to overcoming copy protection, the Copy II family of applications is practically the only choice. It has almost no competition in the Macintosh market, and no other program is nearly as comprehensive and effective when it comes to floppy-to-hard disk transfers. It's updated quite often to incorporate new copy protection schemes, so make sure your copy is a current one before getting down to work.

Once you've loaded Copy II on your hard disk, you can transfer a copy-protected floppy onto the disk by following this procedure:

1. Insert a copy-protected floppy into your native internal drive. On a two-internal drive Mac II, it's the one on the right; on an SE it's the one on the bottom.

2. Click on the Copy II icon. You'll see a dialog box similar to the one in Figure 3.3. Under the Information menu is an item called ''Copyable Programs,'' which features a list of copy-protected software known to transfer smoothly with Copy II. If the application you're dealing with isn't on the list, it's still worthwhile to give copying a try.

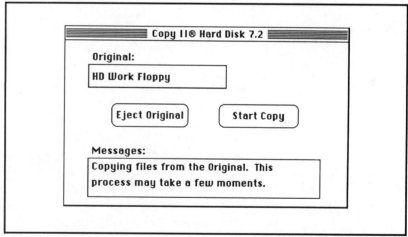

Figure 3.3: The Copy II Hard Disk dialog box for transferring copy-protected programs

3. Click the Start Copy button. Copy II may ask you to insert other, related disks in the copying process, but don't worry about erasing any floppies.

4. A dialog box appears asking you to specify where the copy-protected floppy should be loaded on the hard disk (Figure 3.4). Scroll down the list of files and folders and click on the one to which you want the copies transferred. Transferring may take anywhere from a few seconds to several minutes, depending on the volume of data and the sophistication of copy protection. A Copy Complete! message will notify you when the transfer is done.

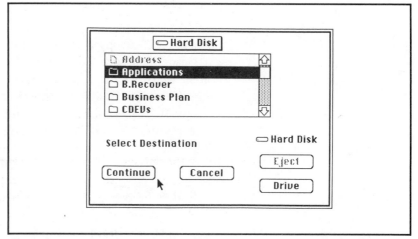

Figure 3.4: The Copy II Hard Disk dialog box for designating the target destination

Unlike floppy to hard disk transfers performed by the Finder, Copy II will not automatically create a new folder for the files you've transferred to the hard disk. Get around this by creating and naming a new, blank folder before launching Copy II. Also, Copy II is programmed not to transfer all files commonly found in the System Folder (System, Finder, Clipboard, etc.). These files are never copy protected, however, so you can copy them directly.

It's important to note that Copy II's Copy Complete! message does not mean "Copy Successful!" All too often, when a transfer appears to have been flawless, the application bombs or crashes upon

After you've transferred an application to the hard disk, don't launch it until you've saved the other open files and applications on the disk. A head crash or bomb could ensue.

launching. Again, watch out for changed icons or file names, and test each application after you transfer it. Take care not to launch an unproven application while any other file or application is open on your hard disk.

If Copy II Hard Disk can't transfer a copy-protected application, you probably can't use the application successfully on your hard disk, but that doesn't mean you can't store documents created by the copy-protected application on your hard disk. Also, the floppy-to-floppy version of Copy II, available on the same disk as Copy II Hard Disk, will most likely allow you to at least transfer your copy-protected files from floppy to floppy for preservation purposes.

Copy Protection and the Law

The microcomputer software industry has made many million-aires (and a billionaire or two) since taking off in the seventies. It's easy to understand why software companies seek to protect their copyrights to the full extent of the law. Unfortunately, most national and international laws regarding copyrights were written for the printed media, not for the interactive, changeable electronic media. Statutes will eventually catch up with the Information Age, but for the present the legal issues implied in software ownership are some-what fuzzy for the average consumer: what industry figures call "software piracy" is often an act of innocence or ignorance.

Only a lawyer can understand all the implications of software copyright law. From a user's standpoint, you should know a few principles (unless otherwise stated by the manufacturer) that apply to most of the software commercially available for the Macintosh.

- You have a right to preserve and transfer all files and applications. Even if your software is copy-protected, it's okay to duplicate it for purposes of convenience, safety, or just to protect your investment. That includes backups and hard disk transfers.

- You may duplicate freely, but you cannot use your duplicates in a situation that would legitimately require you to purchase another copy of your software. In other words, you can make a backup program for your office computer, and the co-worker who shares your office computer can use the backup program at work. Your co-worker, however, can't use the backup program at work while you're using the same program on your home computer. It helps to think of software copyrights like a book. You can loan it, borrow it, and carry it back and forth between locations, so long as no two people are reading it at the same time. If two people are reading it simultaneously, one would have had to make a copy, which is illegal. Software designed for multiple users and software sold under a "group user" or "site" license are exceptions to this rule.

- Your documents are your property. Copyright laws apply to applications and other programs, not to the documents created with them. If you use a graphics program to create artwork, you can copyright that artwork in your name and sell it or give it away as you see fit. You cannot, however, distribute copies of the application you used to make the artwork, even if your intent is solely for the application to be used as a means of viewing the artwork.

There is one important exception to all of the above rules: *shareware*. Shareware was developed as a means of distributing software without the hassles of marketing and retailing. If a program has been designated as shareware, you're encouraged to give away copies to anyone who might need one. Each new user is asked to send a fee to the developer and voluntarily become a registered user. Usually, the "About…" portion of the Apple menu tells you if a program has been designated as shareware. I will discuss several shareware applications in this book.

No matter what the distribution method of your software, there are compelling reasons for being a registered, legal user, reasons beyond compliance with the law. Legitimate users get more than software—they get documentation, technical support, and free or inexpensive upgrades when the product is improved. Given the growing ability and complexity of Macintosh applications, it's getting harder and harder not to be a registered user.

SPLICED APPLICATIONS

There's a third type of application, one that isn't exactly copy-protected but can't be easily transferred from floppy to hard disk. Usually it is called a spliced or merge application, and it exists in two states: unassembled and assembled.

Spliced applications are packaged and sold with the software spread across several floppy disks; at least one of the disks also includes an "installation" program, which reassembles the segments of the application on a hard disk or other storage device. Spliced applications may be used because the application itself is too large for a single floppy, or because effective installation (with the supporting resource files in all the right places) involves more than simply dragging icons. PageMaker, for example, now requires four floppies to contain all features and attendant files.

Try to copy multi-disk applications to the hard disk by launching the application's installation program from the floppy.

If you have a spliced application in unassembled form, try to install it on your hard disk by launching the installation program from the floppy and then following the prompts. Avoid making a floppy-to-folder copy of each of the disks. You'll save time and space by using the installation program from the floppy, and you might save yourself a system crash. (If you use the floppy-to-folder method, you will have to launch the installation program from the hard disk, which may be difficult because of assumptions it makes about floppies and drives.)

If you have already assembled a spliced application on another storage device, you can transfer it by simply daisy-chaining your hard disk to the device and copying over all files. It's the floppies that present the biggest problem when transferring spliced applications: a failure of any floppy in the set to transfer can render the whole program unusable. Moreover, floppy-by-floppy copies made onto other floppies don't always produce a working duplicate set. In these instances, the user is in the unique position of using a hard disk as a backup for a floppy! If you are forced to do this, be sure to back up your hard disk regularly.

MULTIFINDER: NEW WINDOWS ON YOUR WORK

Merely by copying the bulk of your work data to your hard disk, you've already significantly increased the efficiency and productivity of your computer. You've eliminated the time you used to spend juggling floppies and feeding them to the machine. Most of your applications will run noticeably faster.

MultiFinder can only be used with the Macintosh Plus model and up.

But there's a quantum leap in the wings: *MultiFinder*, a feature of all Apple system software since Version 5.0. MultiFinder is not a multitasking application in the literal sense, but it does allow you to launch and work on several applications at once. Because of its size, MultiFinder isn't feasible for floppies, but it runs well on any SCSI device.

Unfortunately, MultiFinder isn't for everyone. It requires at least 1 megabyte of RAM and its effectiveness depends upon the characteristics of the applications you use most often. Yet if you can get your hands on a copy of System 5.0 or later, why not install it? At the very least you can take advantage of its many advanced features, and you can disable MultiFinder if necessary. MultiFinder can only be used with Mac Pluses on up; new Apple software no longer supports earlier models.

INTRODUCING MULTIFINDER

Like the Finder, MultiFinder is an application that opens, manages, and manipulates Macintosh files in accordance with your commands. When you launch an application with the Finder, the application is simply read into the RAM; since only one application can run at a time, the Finder's only concern is that there's adequate memory, and any unused RAM remains unused.

In contrast, MultiFinder not only reads the application into RAM, it confines the application to a designated region. This frees the rest of the RAM for other applications, as many as memory allows. MultiFinder keeps the applications carefully segregated, expanding or contracting the designated regions as necessary. The Finder is always the first of the applications launched, so normal operations (the desktop, etc.) are always just a mouse-click away.

I've already mentioned that MultiFinder doesn't give you true multitasking. That's because only one application can actually be operating, or *active*, at a time; the others are frozen until the one is finished operating. But you can activate an application simply by clicking on its window, so you can use MultiFinder to perform several meaningful tasks at once.

If you're equipped with System 5.0 or later, you can activate MultiFinder by selecting Set Startup... from the Special menu. Notice that the dialog box (Figure 3.5) contains several options; after you select MultiFinder, you can choose what files, if any, you'd like to open automatically when you start up your Macintosh.

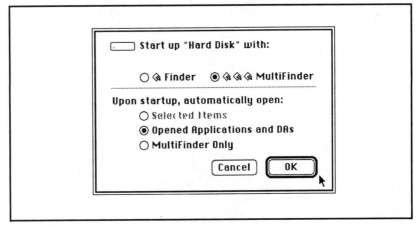

Figure 3.5: A dialog box for enabling MultiFinder and other startup options

If you want to see the familiar desktop setup whenever you start up your Macintosh, click on the MultiFinder Only option—MultiFinder will be active, but the only application automatically launched when you open your Macintosh will be the Finder. If you'd like to open with a different application or file, just click to select the desired icon before you open the dialog box. You'll find the name of the application or file where the phrase Selected Items is in Figure 3.5; that's the button you'll want to select.

If you'd like to go directly to a commonly used work environment, say, a word processor, select the Opened Applications and DAs option. But you'll have to shut down and restart the Macintosh under MultiFinder first—you'll need it in order to keep the application open when you switch back to the Finder.

There's only one obvious indication when a Macintosh is running MultiFinder: in the upper-right hand corner of the screen, a miniature version of the icon belonging to the currently active application is displayed. This is a helpful identifier, but it's also a button; click on it and it will change to the icon of another loaded application (if another is loaded), making that window the active one. If you have three or more applications loaded (including the Finder), click here to activate each one consecutively, in alphabetical order.

The limitation imposed by alphabetical order can make icon clicking inefficient. Why activate HyperCard when you're trying to shift from Backgammon to MacWrite? The easiest way to shift active applications is to simply click on the desired window, but sometimes that window is obscured by others. That's why a third method exists: under the Apple menu, below the DAs, notice the list of loaded applications. The active one has a checkmark next to it; you can activate another application by selecting that one.

Once you've experimented with MultiFinder and feel comfortable with its features, you'll want to give it a try in your day-to-day work. On the other hand, if you don't have to shift rapidly from one application to another, you may not need it. Also, if you work with several large applications, you may not have enough RAM to load two or more applications at once with MultiFinder. An off-the-shelf Mac Plus, for instance, can't run HyperCard under MultiFinder, and some programs written before the advent of MultiFinder can't be loaded on any Macintosh running MultiFinder (they make assumptions about RAM that render them unmanageable). We'll describe a number of hard disk organization scenarios—both with and without MultiFinder—in the next chapter.

OPTIONS FOR STORING DOCUMENTS

You create, save, and store documents because you want to preserve your work, and you can choose from a number of formats for saving your documents. You preserve disk space if you choose wisely. The first step to selecting a file format is an analysis of your requirements: do you only want to store the information contained in the file, or do you need to store it in a specific form?

NORMAL MODE

Unless you've selected other options, most applications automatically save your work in normal mode. If you store a document this way, it will look more or less the same when you reopen it (although using a different System can wreak changes). Normal mode is the most memory-intensive format—it saves a file in a way closest to the way you created it. Normal mode is the best choice for work data, for documents in an unfinished state, or for documents you want to open, consult, and perhaps borrow from quickly.

You can always save a new document in normal mode and save it later in another format. If you try to save a document in a different mode with Save As..., the original document is usually not changed; instead, a copy of the document is saved under the new format, often with a slightly modified name. You'll have to return to the Finder, throw away the old document and give the new document the correct name.

TEXT-ONLY MODE

Many applications that deal mostly with words, such as page layout programs and word processors, offer the option of saving only the text in a document. In these files, all formatting information—fonts, headers/footers, pagination—is discarded.

Along with the advantages they offer for saving space, text-only files are useful for transferring documents larger than the Clipboard can handle from one application to another. Some text-only files can also be transferred to other operating systems, such as MS-DOS or CP/M.

The resource fork is described later in this chapter under the heading "Introducing the Fork."

The text-only format can be useful, but take care to use it only when you're sure that the words alone, and not the formats, are worth saving. Otherwise, you may save disk space but lose a lot of time in laborious reformatting. And just how much space can be saved is a function of how full the resource fork is: an elaborate 5K document may be half the size in text-only mode, whereas a 500K one with few format variations may stand to lose only a few kilobytes.

OTHER MODES

Depending on the parent application, document files can also be saved in a variety of other modes. Experiments and experience will help you make the most of these options, but bear in mind that because an application can save a document in one format, that doesn't mean it can read the resulting file. Below is a discussion of other modes for saving files.

- Word processors often let you select a format that changes the parent application. Microsoft Word documents, for example, can be saved as MacWrite documents. Another common option is the *Interchange format,* which can pass text and formatting data among incompatible applications. If you want to open a WriteNow file in Microsoft Word, you'll need to convert it to an Interchange file first.

- Graphics applications can often import, export, and convert documents in a number of formats. For example, ImageStudio can use both Encapsulated PostScript (EPS) format or Tagged Image File Format (TIFF) to save files in MacPaint. Choosing either of these is more an act of modification than preservation, since the resulting document will be radically different from the original, and suitable for different uses. Unless you need to use multiple applications on the same graphic file, you're probably better off saving in normal mode.

- Spreadsheets are applications that can generate multiple document types: text files, charts, graphs and the spreadsheets themselves. When saving such files, you may be faced with the option of linking or unlinking. Linked documents draw their raw data from the spreadsheet; they can change to reflect changes in the spreadsheet. If you don't want a linked document to be changed by the spreadsheet, either unlink it or save it in the format of another application.

COMPRESSING FILES

Document format options can be used to save disk space, but if you're seeking real compactness you'll want to turn to a *file compressing utility*. These can squeeze most files down to a bare minimum, but they do have drawbacks.

Most file compressors available today weren't created to save space on a hard disk—they were created to save money on phone bills. Electronic bulletin boards offer files for transferring, or *downloading*, with a modem, but even with high-speed modems the downloading of a single application can take an hour or more. Compressing programs like StuffIt, PackIt, and MacArc were invented to cut downloading time drastically. The file is "passed through" compression before it's placed on the bulletin board. Once downloaded, the file must be decompressed (usually with another copy of the same utility) before it can be used.

Compressors reduce the size of a file significantly, but you must spend time compressing and decompressing the files. A 1 megabyte file, for example, can be squeezed to less than half that size, but reconstituting it may take five to ten minutes. For that reason, compression is a useful tool only for archival data, where saving space is more important than accessibility.

Of the current file compression utilities, the shareware program StuffIt is the fastest and most efficient. It offers three choices of compression methods: RLE (automatically used if the file is under 25K), LZW and Huffman. The respective advantages of these depends upon the characteristics of the file itself, but you can instruct the application to simply select the one most appropriate for the task. StuffIt has the added advantage of being able to open and convert files already compressed with PackIt.

StuffIt saves files in an archive, which is much like a folder except that you can only open it from within the application. This is convenient when an application and its related files need to be bundled in a single package; but it can lead to confusion when unrelated files are in the same archive. Name archives on a logical basis. For example, keep business correspondence in an archive titled "Business Correspondence.sit." (All StuffIt files are automatically given the .sit extension.) You can add new files to an archive at any time, but you can't transfer a compressed file from one archive to another. You'll have to decompress it first.

One quirk of StuffIt is especially worth noting. It doesn't recognize folders at all, which means that only individual files can be selected for inclusion in an archive. It also means that if you select a folder for compression, StuffIt will ignore your choice and compress instead the file on that directory level with the highest alphabetical order.

COMPACTING THE DESKTOP FILE

One of the largest files on your hard disk may be an invisible one. It's called the Desktop file, and although you can't see it without a special utility program (such as ResEdit), it usually resides on the root level of each volume. It's essentially a list of all the information the Macintosh needs in order to accurately represent the contents of every file on the volume: the icons, the type ID of files, instructions on where to find the application needed to launch a document, and so on. It's read whenever you open a folder or double-click on an icon.

The more files and folders you have on your hard disk, the bigger the Desktop file—and since much of the information isn't automatically purged when changes are made, it can grow even bigger with time. In fact, the bigger it is, the longer it takes the Macintosh to read it, and it can become so big that normal operations start to slow down. This shows up most often on hard disks of 80 megabytes or more (the more files to keep track of, the bigger the Desktop file), but it's not uncommon on drives of lesser capacity.

You cannot compact the Desktop file under MultiFinder.

Fortunately, you can compact the Desktop file: just open up the System Folder, simultaneously hold down the Option and Command keys and double-click on the Finder icon. Doing so will not affect operations in any way, but the display formats of some folders may be changed—some custom icons may be replaced with default versions.

AN OVERVIEW OF THE MACINTOSH DATA STRUCTURE

Thus far, I've discussed aspects of Macintosh technology that are easily apparent to the user. Now it's time to delve further, to look under the hood and explore the internal structure of the Mac's approach to information management and processing. Although I won't get too technical, I will touch upon concepts and elements that may prove essential when it comes to retrieving or repairing lost and damaged files.

Even if you never need to perform first aid on your data, you'll find this section a useful insight into the Mac's inner workings. It'll also help clarify Mac terminology.

Figure 3.6 shows three discrete levels of data, the volume level, the file level, and the fork level. *Volume* refers to any element of storage medium that has a single identity and root directory, such as a floppy disk, a hard disk, or another storage device such as CD-ROM or WORM drive. These devices can usually contain only one volume apiece, but with the Mac volume recognition doesn't depend on the kind of hardware you're using. A single storage device can be broken up into multiple volumes; on hard disks this is known as *partitioning*. With partitioning, the computer treats the disk like several small but separate disks, each with its own desktop icon and directory. The other two data levels, forks and files, are discussed later in this chapter.

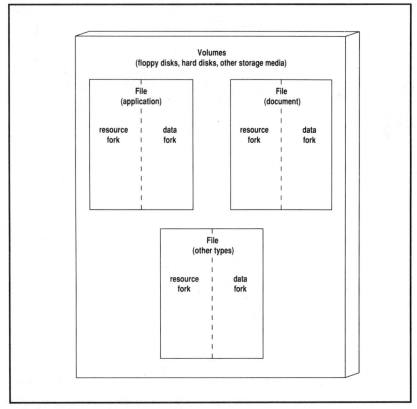

Figure 3.6: The three levels of Macintosh data

When a volume is on-line and accessible to the computer, it is called a *mounted* volume. Inserting a floppy or booting up a SCSI device are means of mounting a volume. You can tell that a volume has been mounted when its icon appears on the desktop.

FILE TYPES

If volumes are the libraries of the Macintosh world, then the *file* level would be the books on the shelves. Yet Mac files can be more than mere storehouses of information. Below I will discuss several different types of files. Together they cover the entire spectrum of the Mac's operations and capability.

Applications   These are programs that allow you to perform a task or tasks. Word processing, number-crunching, and desktop publishing are all performed by applications. Most allow the work you do to be saved and stored in files, but not all; the Finder, for example, is an application that's constantly running whenever you use your Mac. The Finder is the software that displays and updates the desktop and related icons; it translates your clicking and dragging into meaningful commands for the System file to read. (The system file is not an application—it is the software portion of the operating system.) When you click on an icon like the ones in Figure 3.7 and launch an application, you're actually using one application, the Finder, to load another one.

Documents   These are the products of the applications. They are files that contain the work you've done. Documents also have their own distinctive icons (Figure 3.8), which you can open by double-clicking. In Mac jargon, documents are opened, but applications are launched.

Before a document can be opened, an application capable of reading it must also be present on a mounted volume. In fact, to open a document usually means to simultaneously launch the application with which it was created. It used to be that a document could only be read and edited by the parent application, but now many applications can *convert* or *import* files created by other applications. Mac software is becoming more feature-laden. Chances are that most word

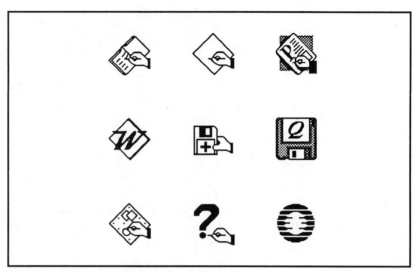

Figure 3.7: Some examples of application icons

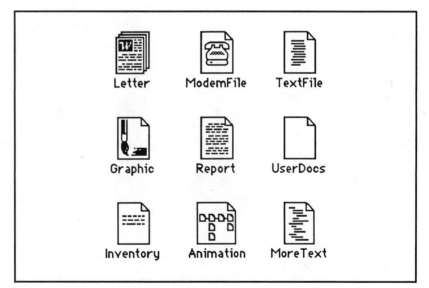

Figure 3.8: Document icons

processing or desktop publishing applications will be capable of importing any text or graphic document, and spreadsheets will be capable of importing any numerical document.

Resource Files   These store user preferences and customization information. Usually neither created nor readable by the user, these files are usually referenced, updated, and filed away automatically. In fact, some applications automatically create resource files.

For example, the word processing application Microsoft Word uses a number of resource files to perform different tasks (see Figure 3.9). The Hyphenation file stores the hyphenation breaks of commonly used words; the Main Dictionary file has a similar list of correct spellings; the Temp file provides temporary storage for handling long or complex documents; the Glossary file holds frequently used text for easy access; and the Settings file contains the user's default choices for menus and formatting. You can't open and peruse these files, but you make Microsoft Word open, read, and modify them every time you use that application.

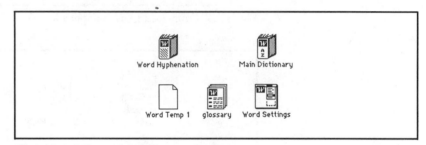

Figure 3.9: Microsoft Word resource files

Keep track of where resource files are stored and which application created them. Copy all resource files to your new hard disk or system.

Resource files are usually placed in one of two locations: the home folder of the application or the active System Folder. I recommend that you keep track of which applications create Resource files (and where the files are stored). Whenever you need to work on a different disk or system, copy them along with the applications.

Desk Accessories   Also called DAs, these are small, easily accessed programs. You don't even have to quit application to access a DA because they are incorporated into the System file. They all have the same icon, a suitcase (see Figure 3.10). Once you've installed one, you launch it via menu selection (under the "Apple" symbol). To install and remove a DA, you use an application known as Font/DA Mover, which comes bundled with all System software disks from Apple.

Figure 3.10: The Desk Accessory icon

DAs were originally intended to be simple, accessible tools—extensions of the Mac's computer-as-desk metaphor. Some of the most common ones—the Alarm Clock, the Calculator, the Calendar—are still simple and small, but others offer features and capabilities that rival applications. Word processors, spelling checkers, graphics programs and spreadsheets are all available in DA form. Not only have programmers transcended the limitations of DA size (they generally cannot occupy more than 32K), they've managed to circumvent Apple's limitation of fifteen DAs per System file. Now up to five hundred DAs can be available thanks to utility programs like Suitcase.

Despite the growing versatility of DAs, their days may be numbered: under the MultiFinder, a Mac with enough RAM can run multiple applications at once. MultiFinder could make DAs obsolete.

Fonts Files   These contain instructions about managing type. Specifically, they tell the Mac how to display and modify particular type styles. There are two kinds of fonts.

- *display fonts* govern the bit-mapped display of a typeface both on the screen and on a dot-matrix printer

- *downloadable fonts* are used with laser printers to translate the choppy bit-mapped font into smooth characters. Downloadable fonts for the Macintosh are written in a language called Post-Script.

The Display Font icon is similar to a Desk Accessories icon (Figure 3.11). Like DAs, display fonts are incorporated into the System file by means of the Mover application. A properly installed font is usually available in every application that uses fonts, although some applications (like Microsoft Word) require special installation steps. The number of fonts that can be installed in a System file is limited to 256, but software programs such as Suitcase can make thousands of fonts available at once. In practice, however, all but the most extensive desktop publishing systems use only a few dozen fonts.

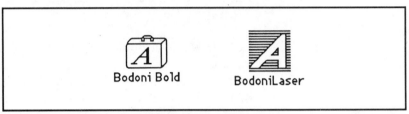

Figure 3.11: An icon for a display font (left) and for a downloadable font (right)

When you download a font, be sure not to rename it accidentally. If you get the names mixed up, your printer might print a display font when you intend to use a downloadable font.

Downloadable fonts (Figure 3.11) are not part of the System file. In order to work with a LaserWriter or another PostScript printer, downloadable fonts need to be in the System Folder. When you place them in the System Folder—place them in that folder only, not in a subfolder—take care that you don't accidentally rename them. If, while processing printing for a Postscript device, the System cannot find the downloadable font, it will rely on the display font instead and create a bit-mapped version of that font.

Because of their ability to produce characters nearly as good as those from a typesetter, downloadable fonts are expensive, whereas most display fonts cost little, are shareware, or are free. For example, the leading PostScript font manufacturer, Adobe, sells its downloadable fonts but makes the display versions available for free to user groups and electronic bulletin boards. You don't need downloadable fonts unless you have a Postscript device—and even most of those have a number of downloaded fonts in ROM. So even with a PostScript device you don't need many external files to make quality reproductions.

Drivers   These are programs that allow the Macintosh to control a device. A *device*, in Mac parlance, means a piece of equipment or part of the computer that transfers data in and out of the machine. Devices include floppy drives, hard disks, keyboards and printers. The video screen on the Macintosh II is also considered a device, although it is not considered a device on the Mac Plus and the SE (due to their direct use of QuickDraw routines).

Most drivers are built into the ROM; others are incorporated into the System file along with fonts and DAs. In the case of printer drivers, you must place the icon in the System Folder and then select it from the Chooser desk accessory to make the drive available. Figure 3.12 shows some driver icons.

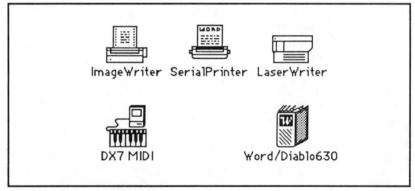

Figure 3.12: Examples of printer-driver icons

Drivers can work as nested programs; that is, one driver may be built upon another driver. In Figure 3.12, the SerialPrinter file is an application-specific driver written to manage a generic serial printer, and the Diablo630 file is a driver for a specific serial printer. When you select the SerialPrinter file in Chooser, the Diablo630 is presented to you as a selectable option. The Diablo driver would be useless without the serial driver file. This is why it's necessary to keep track of which combinations of drivers your hardware requires, and to store, install, and transfer them as a unit.

INITs Files These install and activate themselves automatically. After you place one in the System Folder, it will often remind you that it's installed by adding some sort of notice to your startup screen, either a graphic symbol or textual statement (Figure 3.13).

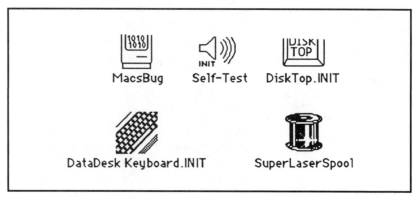

Figure 3.13: A few INIT icons

The INIT (short for initial) is a useful file format for utility programs that you'll want to have in the background at all times. Because their features are automatically put into action, you'll never forget to "turn them on." A laser spooler, a network communications system, and a debugger are examples of INIT files.

Some INITs pop up as another menu in the Finder, some are accessed by way of the Apple menu, and some are virtually invisible to the user. If you have a file that doesn't look like a document yet can't be opened by double-clicking, chances are it's an INIT. A word of caution is appropriate for INIT experimentation, however: because it modifies your system's startup sequence, a buggy, bad or incompatible INIT installed on your hard disk could make it unable to boot. When in doubt, try out the INIT on a floppy-based System Folder first. Just make sure the floppy is placed in the floppy drive before you power up the Mac. To deactivate an INIT, just remove it from the System Folder—it won't be loaded the next time you start up.

CDEVs   These are accessed only through the Control Panel selection under the Apple menu. A subcategory of INITs, CDEVs are also loaded automatically when you place them in the top level of the System Folder. CDEV is short for Control Device. Figure 3.14 shows some of the more common CDEVs.

The Control Panel was originally just another Desk Accessory. As options increased, however, Apple realized that different users needed to control different aspects of their systems. The DA was

INITs modify your system's startup sequence, so a buggy or incompatible INIT on your hard disk could prevent it from booting. If you think you're having trouble with an INIT, try it out on a floppy-based system folder.

INITs are automatically loaded in alphabetical order. If for some reason you want them to be loaded another way, simply add a new first letter to their name. For example, change LaserSpool to "ALaserSpool" or "ZLaserSpool."

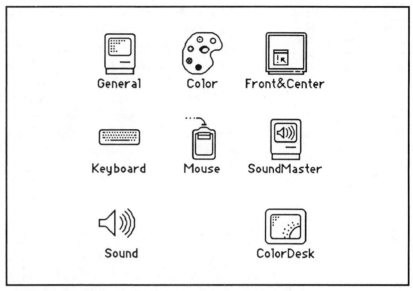

Figure 3.14: CDEV icons

rewritten to encompass CDEVs, which now appear in a window on the left side of the Control Panel box (Figure 3.15). Clicking on an icon in this window will cause the options controlled by that CDEV to be displayed in the main window of the box.

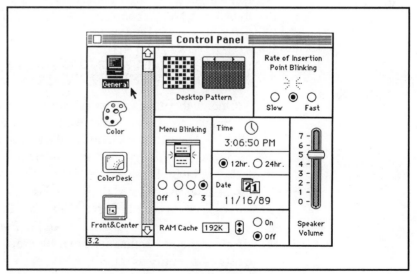

Figure 3.15: The Control Panel, with scrolling CDEV field

The Control Panel recognizes CDEV files by name only. Don't rename CDEVs when you install or remove them.

The Mac Plus and the Mac SE don't need the Monitors CDEV. This CDEV manages color and shade settings for the Mac II.

CDEVs are becoming a popular format for utilities effecting operations (such as Front&Center, which moves dialog boxes wherever the mouse pointer happens to be). They're installed and removed in the same fashion as INITs, but take care not to rename them—if you do they won't be recognized by the Control Panel. Apple bundles a lot of CDEVs with System software, but there's no need to load ones that don't pertain to your setup. The Mac Plus and SE, for example, don't need the Monitors CDEV, which manages color and shade settings for the Macintosh II.

CHOOSING THE RIGHT FILE TYPE

Some of the tasks that used to be achieved only by means of an application can now be done by DAs and INITs as well. When choosing software, which file format is better? If you have a Mac with multiple megabytes of RAM, you can probably work under Multi-Finder, in which case the limitations of a DA or INIT will prevent those file formats from becoming a consideration.

On the other hand, if your RAM resources are more modest (or if you work with memory-hungry applications such as HyperCard), MultiFinder may not be the file format that solves all your hard disk problems. Convenience may be an important factor—even with MultiFinder, an application must be located and launched in order to be available. In contrast, DAs and CDEV-type INITs are always just a menu selection away.

INTRODUCING THE FORK

One of the most important concepts to grasp is that of *forked data*. Essentially, forking is the process of storing a file in two files; as another glance at Figure 3.6 will indicate, the fork is the final level of information organization. Though they are fundamental to Macintosh technology, forks are invisible to the casual user. But an understanding of them is essential when you need to retrieve lost or garbled data.

To put it in a nutshell: every file—applications, documents, etc.— is in fact two files, a *resource fork* and a *data fork*, both stored under a single filename. Either fork can be empty, but an empty fork still exists as an entity as far as the Mac is concerned. Both forks collaborate to launch a file.

The Resource Fork

Stored in the resource fork (sometimes called the "resource file") are all the *resources* required by the file. What are resources? Generally speaking, resources are the building blocks of Macintosh programming—the elements that build a file. Icons, menus, dialog boxes, and other discrete portions of fonts, programming code are all resources. Resources are broken down into *resource types*, which are stored in the fork and arranged by function in logical groupings. Resource types are identified by distinctive four-letter codes; each resource in the type is in turn identified by a *resource ID* number.

Why is all this code broken up into so many discrete units? There are two primary reasons. The first has to do with memory management: because the data is so fragmented, it can be loaded into RAM more efficiently than it could if it were still in large chunks of code. The Macintosh has highly sophisticated firmware in ROM known as the Memory Manager, which uses this flexibility to great advantage.

But the second, perhaps more significant reason why resource codes are so fragmented has to do with the user interface. The resource approach gives Macintosh software a standardized look and feel—it's a rare application that deviates from the familiar arrangement of pull-down menus, dialog boxes, and scrolling windows.

With many operating systems, the programmer has to build the "world" of the program practically from scratch. When a pull-down menu is called for, the programmer has to design the menu right down to the typeface and write a code that draws it on the screen. If the program is later translated into, say, Italian, the programmer has to draw the code all over again. What happens if the Italian versions of the commands are too long to fit in the original menu box? The menu code itself has to be rewritten, which means that codes would have to be modified throughout the software.

Fortunately, this isn't true for the Macintosh programmer. All he or she has to do to create a new pull-down menu is redefine the MENU resource (the four-letter code for that resource type) with its own ID number. The definition would not only describe the menu and every item on it, it would also specify what other resources are to be accessed when a particular menu item is selected. With the resource codes redefined and stored in the resource fork, the Macintosh takes over from there, displaying the menu and initiating the commands.

Since all this can be done without writing a single line of code, even a nonprogrammer can make menu modifications. Want to market an Italian version of your Mac? Just type in replacements to the English words in the resource definition fields. If the menu must be wider to accommodate Italian words, you can modify the menu too.

The ROM routines that create and manage these resources are collectively called the User Interface Toolbox, or more commonly the *Toolbox*. A Mac programmer could bypass the Toolbox and build an application entirely from scratch, but the application would be slow running, incompatible with other applications, and difficult for users to master.

You can use applications such as ResEdit to explore and modify a file's resource fork. I'll explain the whys and hows of doing so in Chapter 7.

The Data Fork

More mundane but just as important as the resource fork is the *data fork*. As the name implies, the data fork is the storehouse where the data that's manipulated by the program is kept. This data is broken down and saved as numeric code.

The process works like this: let's say you launch a word processing application by double-clicking on its icon. If it was designed to industry standards, the application should open with a document screen labeled "Untitled." But "Untitled" isn't a document just yet; it's the more-or-less empty data fork of the application.

If you type the word *Macintosh*, then save the document, the application works with the Toolbox to create a new file (which you're requested to name). This new file is still controlled by the application, but now it has its own data and resource forks. The data fork contains only the letters *M, a, c, i, n, t, o, s* and *h*, while the resource fork contains a recipe of sorts, a list of all the resources you used while typing that word—the font, font size, letter spacing, position in the document, and so on. The resource fork also contains information about which application created it, which is why opening a word processing document simultaneously launches the word processor.

The separation between data and resources is the main reason why formatting changes are so easy to make on the Macintosh, even with huge blocks of text. Instead of loading the text into RAM in order to alter its appearance, the Mac simply changes the rules by which the text is displayed. An application's data fork is useful because the application can use its own data fork, rather than RAM, as a storage area while you are working on a document. This fork is copied to the document data when you answer yes to the Save changes? dialog box.

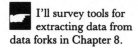 I'll survey tools for extracting data from data forks in Chapter 8.

One fringe benefit of the fork structure pertains to data retrieval. When the resources in a file's resource fork have become garbled, the file is usually unreadable by the system. But an ''unopenable'' document still has an intact data fork, and the information it contains can often be salvaged.

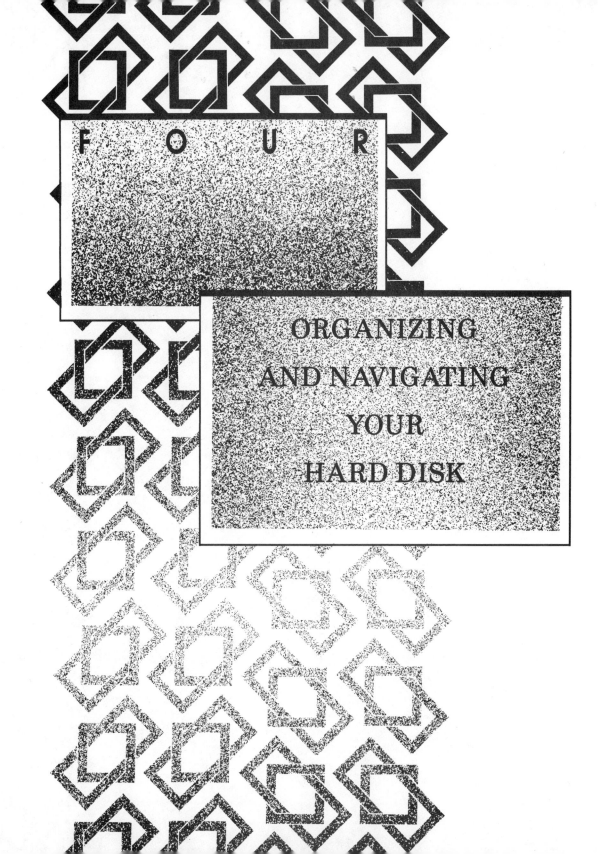

F O U R

ORGANIZING
AND NAVIGATING
YOUR
HARD DISK

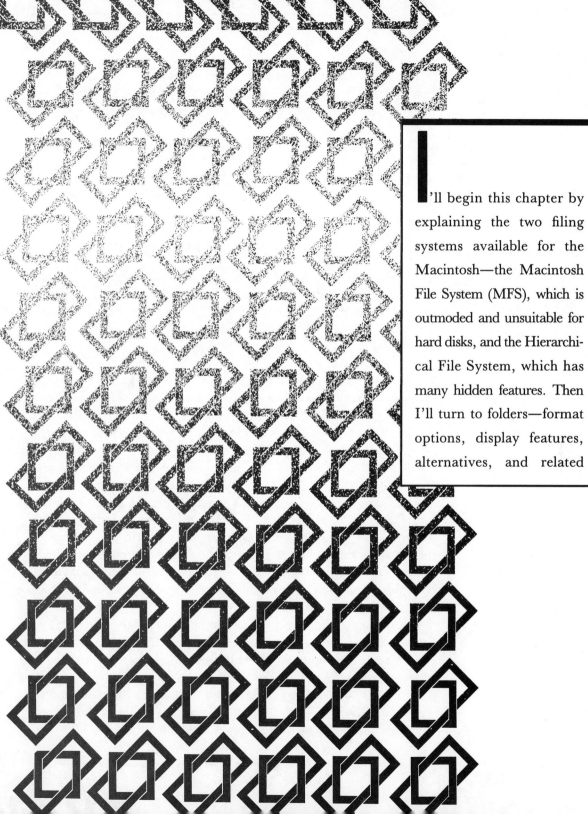

I'll begin this chapter by explaining the two filing systems available for the Macintosh—the Macintosh File System (MFS), which is outmoded and unsuitable for hard disks, and the Hierarchical File System, which has many hidden features. Then I'll turn to folders—format options, display features, alternatives, and related information and advice. I'll also review alternative data locations, such as on the desktop and on partitioned volumes. Finally, I'll display these elements in action, with real-life scenarios for three organizational plans.

Next, I'll cover how to navigate through your hard disk's directory, and how to locate a file quickly, easily, and with a minimum of confusion. And, since files can get lost on even the most thoroughly organized hard disk, I'll show you how to do high-speed searches.

THE HIERARCHICAL FILING SYSTEM

⊙ Use only HFS on a hard disk system. Some instructions in this book do not apply to MFS.

In Chapter 2, I mentioned that the Macintosh has had two distinctly different means of file organization: the Macintosh File System (MFS), and the Hierarchical File System (HFS). HFS was designed to replace MFS, and it's the one you want operating on your hard disk.

Here's why: MFS was created with the expectation that all Macintoshes would work with only one or two floppy disk drives and that the floppy disks would hold a relatively small amount of information. Therefore, MFS does not truly allow you to *nest* files and folders within other folders. All files and folders placed in other folders don't actually exist on other organizational levels—they're still on the same root level. Although MFS folders are a convenient way to designate a group of files, the organization is cosmetic only. To see the difference between representation and reality, try to open a file from within an application, as in Figure 4.1. The desktop in the figure may seem uncluttered (top), but in the application you still need to scroll through every file (bottom) because the folders are nowhere in evidence. With the advent of double-sided floppies, serial port hard disks, and finally SCSI buses, MFS soon became unmanageable. HFS replaced it in 1986.

HFS creates folders in true nested subdirectories. Under HFS, because files are stored in a useful folder structure (Figure 4.2), you can navigate through volumes within an application far more rapidly. HFS has its drawbacks, however. A misplaced file can be difficult to find. And the proliferation of folder levels can lead to "overorganization," with files tucked away so far down the hierarchy that simply locating one becomes a tedious process.

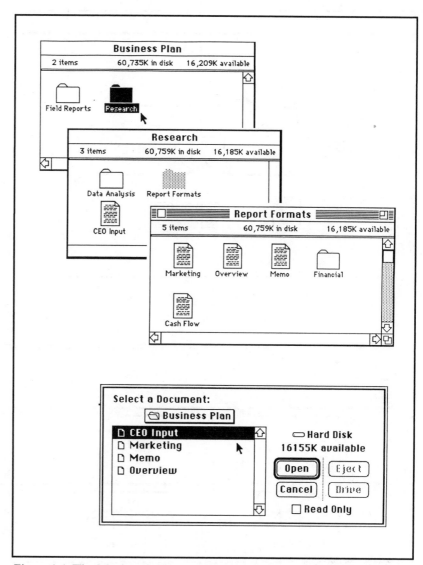

Figure 4.1: The Macintosh File creates an illusion of nested folders (top), but all files are actually on the same directory level (bottom).

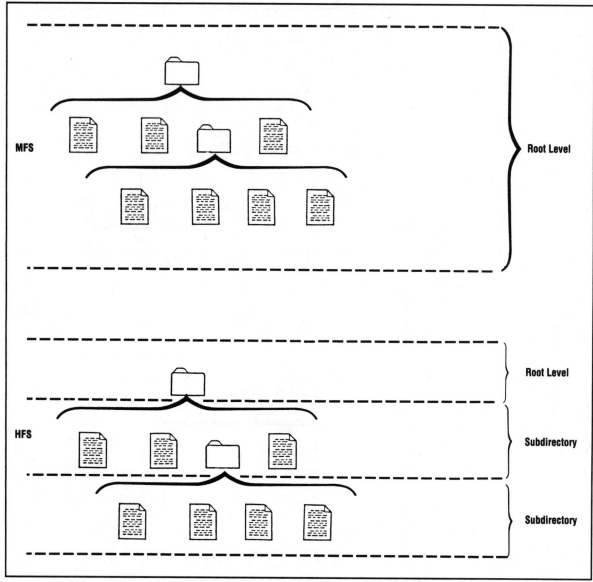

Figure 4.2: Where MFS (top) stores all files on a single level, HFS (bottom) creates a complete, pyramid-structured hierarchy of folder subdirectories.

THE DIFFERENCES BETWEEN HFS AND MFS

Unlike other System features, which are apparent only when a volume is made the startup volume, the file system is active whenever a volume is mounted. Which is why you'll want HFS not only on your hard disk, but on any reasonably full floppies you use regularly.

There are a number of ways to determine which file system is present:

- Check the Finder file by selecting About the finder... from the apple menu; if you're running Finder Version 5.0 or earlier, it features MFS.

- All your disks may not contain a Finder file, so try seeing if folders disappear when the Open... command is selected from within an application, as in Figure 4.1. If they disappear, MFS is present.

- In every folder window there are two closely spaced lines right under the space where the column headings are displayed (Figure 4.3). On an HFS system, the space between

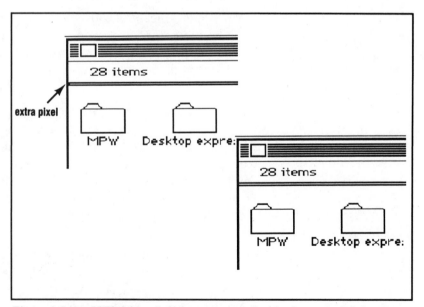

Figure 4.3: An HFS folder (left) has an extra pixel in the upper left-hand corner; an MFS folder (right) does not.

these lines is filled (by one pixel) at the far left. Under MFS, the space is entirely clear. This method for determining the file system is especially handy when working with multiple, unfamiliar floppies.

If you want to convert an MFS floppy to HFS, make a backup of the disk (and make sure the copy is a functional one). Then select the disk and choose Erase Disk from the Special menu in the Finder. If you take these steps and you are running the Macintosh on an HFS startup System file, the disk will be reformatted for HFS. Copy all files back to the disk, and dispose of the backup duplicates you made earlier.

HFS is more efficient and convenient than MFS, but that doesn't mean there are compatibility problems between the two standards. You can keep using MFS disks with your Macintosh should you so choose. In fact, some early versions of popular applications, such as Excel and MacDraw, won't work correctly with Finder Version 5.1 or later, which excludes the HFS option anyway.

WORKING WITH FOLDERS

More than a means of conveniently grouping files, folders are one of the best tools for structuring your Macintosh work environment. The first step in using folders is to understand their features. Let's take a look at the most important ones.

Folders remember their place on your screen.   Double-click on a folder to open it. Click on the title bar area to move it anywhere on the screen. Then close it and click it open again; until you reposition a folder window, it will continue to open in the location you specify. This feature lets you work with multiple folders without getting lost in the clutter of overlapping windows, an advantage that's especially handy when running under MultiFinder.

Folders remember their size on the screen.   Double-click on a folder to open it, then move the size box to make the folder window as long or thin, large or small as you like. Now close it and open it again. Until you change its size, the folder window will open to its *set size,* the size it was the last time you opened it. (You can, of course, change the set size at any time.)

Folders can expand to full screen size. Click on the zoom box in the upper right-hand corner and expand the folder window to *full size*, a width of 9 inches and a height roughly equivalent to the depth of your monitor's screen. For all single-unit Macintoshes, full size is effectively the equivalent of full screen size, although the Mac II and some large add-on monitors allow even more room for resizing.

Most document windows within applications can be toggled between set size and full size via a similar zoom box, although in such cases the full size mode usually takes up the entire screen on the Mac II as well.

Folders remember their View format. There are seven different ways for a folder to display its contents. When created, a folder automatically displays by Icon, but this can be changed by selecting another format from the View menu while the folder is open and active—that is, when it's in the foreground.

VIEW FORMATS

View formats are probably one of the most underutilized features of the Macintosh—even experienced users often prefer only one format, which they apply uniformly to all folders. But each format has its own distinct advantages, and used in combination they can greatly add to the clarity of hard disk organization. Following is a discussion of the seven View formats offered by Macintosh.

View by Icon

Choosing View by Icon (Figure 4.4) shows all the folders and files and their full-size icons. This view is useful because you can identify applications and documents at a glance, and because the large-scale icons are easy to select, drag, and double-click with the mouse.

However, the format takes up a lot of screen space; it's best to use it for folders with relatively few files. And since you can arrange the file icons in any which way, the folder often becomes sloppy and cluttered. To tidy up such a folder, select Clean up Window from the Special menu, and use the mouse to arrange the icons in alphabetical order or in any fashion that suits your work. Watch out for icons that

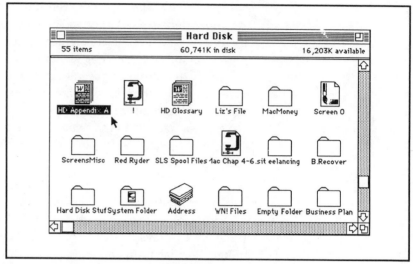

Figure 4.4: The View by Icon folder format

get lost by being placed too far below the main grouping. You can scroll around to find an icon, but often it's easier to simply change the folder format to View by Name.

View by Small Icon

Viewing by Small Icon is similar to viewing by Icon, with the notable difference that the icons are one-quarter the size, and the names are listed to the right rather than underneath. The advantage of small icons is that they fit more densely into a window, and the disadvantage is that, being miniature versions, they are often difficult to distinguish from one another (Figure 4.5). Small Icon size may not be a problem if you're familiar with the identities of your applications (and their documents), but if you are familiar with them, why not use another, even more compact folder format?

View by Name

Under the View by Name format, all files and folders are listed in alphabetical order in a single column. The icons are smaller, in fact so small that many are unidentifiable. That's why the Macintosh substitutes standard default icons for all folder and file icons: all

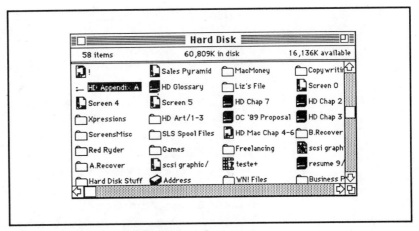

Figure 4.5: The View by Small Icon format

applications share the same icon, as do all documents (Figure 4.6). You can drop one folder into another, but you can't change the order of files and folders without changing a name or two. (When you change names, the reordering won't take place until you close and reopen the window.) The format's alphabetical order places numbers, spaces, and symbols before letters.

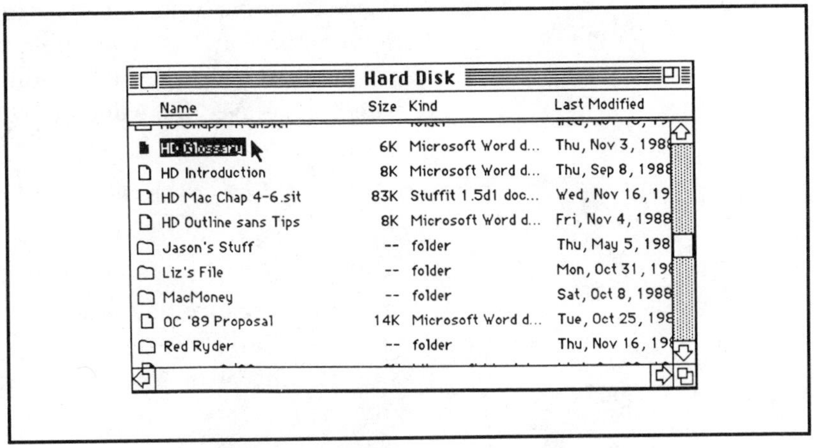

Figure 4.6: The View by Name format

Icon standardization can lead to confusion. To let you know which document you're launching, the View by Name window has a Kind column, which lists the parent application of each document. Entries in the Kind column are limited to 18 character spaces; if this space is insufficient for the information, the entry is truncated and ends with an ellipsis (...). When this happens, select the file and choose Get Info from the File menu to see a complete Kind entry. View by Kind has two other, self-explanatory data categories: Size and Last Modified. Notice that the Name column heading is underlined in Figure 4.6. When you choose View by size, View by kind, or View by date, the Size, Kind or Last Modified column headings are underlined instead.

Not only does the View by Name format display more information than the View by Icon and View by Small Icon formats, its innate orderliness and compactness make for a very neat desktop. Yet there are a few cautions that you need to take:

- Select a file or folder not just by clicking on its icon, but by clicking anywhere across the row—on any of the column entries (Name, Size, Kind, Last Modified) or on any space in between the columns.

- Be careful about clicking the mouse. You might accidentally select and start dragging a file or folder, then dump it inadvertently into another folder.

- When dragging from one folder to another, don't let go of the mouse until you're sure no subfolder is highlighted in the target folder. Otherwise, if a subfolder is highlighted, that's where the moved file will end up.

View by Date, by Size, by Kind, and by Color

The View by Date, by Size, by Kind and by Color formats are variations of View by Name. The data columns, the default icons and the automatic organization are the same, but the organizational criteria varies. As with View by Name, you can determine what the format is by looking at the column headings: the underlined one serves as the main criterion (Figure 4.7).

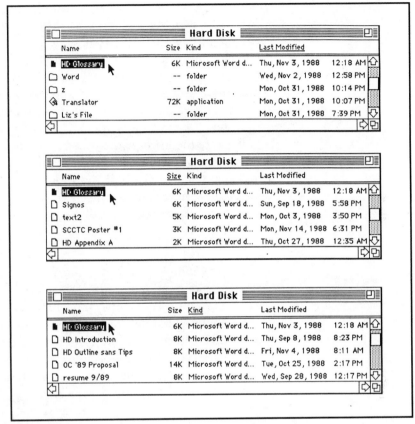

Figure 4.7: View by Date, by Size, and by Kind formats

View by Date This format arranges the folders by order of the date you last modified them. (The date a folder was created is recorded in each file or folder's Get Info... box.) The Last Modified date is drawn from the calendar settings in the Control Panel.

View by Size This format arranges the files from the largest to the smallest according to the number of kilobytes they use. This view is especially useful with applications. Since most applications are larger than documents, they'll be readily accessible at the top of the list. Folders, on the other hand, bring up the rear since their size is minimal no matter how large their contents. If two or more files are the same size, they will be listed alphabetically.

View by Kind   This format lists the folder contents in order of their type, with applications first, documents second, and folders last. But the order of that order can vary depending on the order in which files are placed in the folder. If the first file in the folder is a document, then documents become the first subcategory in the folder. On the other hand, if the first file is an application, then applications will be the first listed. Folders are always listed last. Within the subcategories, the files and folders are in alphabetical order.

Because the file type order can be customized, View by Kind is a versatile organizational tool. To customize a file, just empty the folder and put the files back in the order you desired. Or you can simply create a new folder, transfer the contents from the old one, and give it the same name as the old, emptied folder once you've discarded it.

To color-code an icon, click on the icon and then select a color from the Finder's color menu.

View by Color   This format is only an option for Macintoshes that employ color monitors; it won't show up in the View menu unless the Monitors Control device (CDEV) in the Control Panel is set for 16 or more colors. Although current color-capable Macintoshes can display 256 colors at once, the system only reserves eight colors for file and folder designation—orange, red, pink, light blue, dark blue, green, brown, and black. Files are listed in the window in the same order as on this color list, with orange first and black last. Files and folders of the same color are arranged in alphabetical order. To color-code, click on an icon, then select a color from the Color menu in the Finder. Until you change their color, all files and folders will be displayed in black.

There are three types of monitors available for the Mac II: color, black and white, and grayscale (which displays shades of gray as well as black and white).

If your Macintosh can use View by Color, you'll find it one of the most useful of folder formats: you can group applications, documents and folders together in any combination, based on any criteria. For example, you could put your current project files at the top of the list by coloring them orange. But this format requires continual updating—you need to color-code everything as it's created. And the subtleties of color organization will be lost if you need to transfer your work to a noncolor Macintosh. Interestingly enough, View by Color works on a Macintosh II with a black-and-white monitor that isn't grayscale, although all eight colors are displayed in solid black and only the computer can tell them apart.

STORING ON THE DESKTOP

Folders aren't the only place where files (or other folders) can be placed. Another valid, especially useful location is the desktop of the Macintosh itself—the home base screen, with the trash icon in the lower right-hand corner and your hard disk's icon in the upper right-hand one (Figure 4.8). Although you may at first feel a bit uneasy about parking important data near the trash can, you'll soon find storing on the desktop a useful feature.

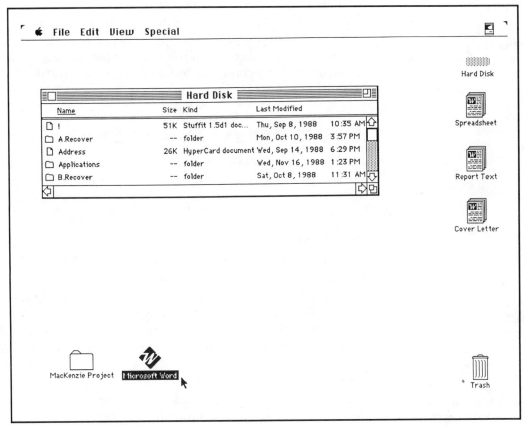

Figure 4.8: Files and folders stored on the desktop

To place a file or folder on the desktop, just drag it from its folder to a vacant spot. You'll notice that no matter what the view format of its previous home, the icon is automatically displayed in full size. You can arrange any number of icons on the desktop in any way you wish, and then shut down with confidence. Upon rebooting, the icons will be right where you left them. (If they aren't, it's probably because your hard disk isn't the startup volume at the moment.) The Finder handles desktop icons just like any others, except when making duplicates, in which case the new icon will appear in the right-hand column (underneath any volume icons), rather than adjacent to the original.

As far as the HFS system is concerned, the desktop is simply a part of the startup volume's root level. You can't use a file box to place a document on the desktop, however.

Use the desktop as a location for the applications you use most often, or as a means of giving top priority to projects that demand special attention. Of course, if you really want to make an application or document as prominent as possible, use MultiFinder's Set Startup... feature to launch it automatically upon booting up.

Keeping too many files at the root level will ultimately slow you down.

CLEANING UP AND CLOSING UP

With icons in a folder, or multiple folder windows on the screen, it often seems like the rule is "the more, the messier." Following is a discussion of some shortcuts to keep things more tidy and less tiresome.

Organizing Icons

Icons or small icons are *placement-sensitive;* unlike the other folder formats, which are automatically organized, they can be arranged in any order on the screen. And when your file folders get disorderly, try the following methods for cleaning them up.

If the Clean Up Window command reads Clean Up Selection instead of Clean Up Window, that's because an icon inside the folder is currently selected. Deselect it by clicking elsewhere and try again.

Select the Clean Up Window command from the Special menu in the Finder. This command will move all icons from their current position to the nearest coordinate of an invisible grid. If an icon is not visible in the current window size, it will be moved into any spare space that may exist in the window. This command is useful for minor organization, and you may want to select it from time to time just as a helpful habit.

To maximize folder organization, hold down the Option key while selecting the Clean Up command from the Special menu; you'll note that instead of Clean Up Window, it now reads simply Clean Up.

This command will align all icons, but instead of simply moving them to the nearest grid coordinate, the entire window's contents will be redrawn in a new, close formation. Icons will be reshuffled so that the whole constitutes a rectangular block. The Clean Up command is especially useful for thoroughly disorganized folders, and should be used whenever a format change is made from icons to small icons and vice versa.

Keep in mind, however, that both the Clean Up command and the Clean Up Window command organize the display in the window of the folder, not the folder itself. That means that icon reorganization is based on the size and shape of the folder window. For example, if the folder window is long and skinny, the icons may be placed in single file. If you're unsatisfied with the results of the clean up commands, resize the folder window and try again.

Closing Folders

Locating a certain file often entails plunging far into the depths of the hierarchy, which can mean opening a half-dozen or more folders on the way there. Fortunately, there are alternatives to the tedious method of closing up by clicking on each folder's close box:

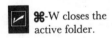
⌘-W closes the active folder.

- To close folders one at a time, hit ⌘-W. This command closes the currently active folder, and if that folder is nested inside another open folder, the next folder automatically becomes the active one. Thus you can repeat this command until all nested folders are closed. If you make a mistake and want to go back a step, press ⌘-O to reopen the previous folder.

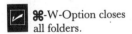
⌘-W-Option closes all folders.

- To close all the folders at once, hold down the Option key while closing any one of them (either by clicking in the Close box or pressing ⌘-W) This closes all folders, including the root level window for the hard disk itself. This is the quickest method, and the only way to go when the multiple windows cluttering up your screen are from non-nested folders.

CHANGING FOLDERS
WHILE APPLICATIONS ARE OPEN

Take a look at the two dialog boxes in Figure 4.9. Both are actually versions of the standard file dialog box, a feature that most applications take advantage of, often with minor modifications. The first time you save a document, and every time you choose the Save As... option, you'll probably see some version of the box on the top. But every time you open a preexisting document from within an application, chances are you'll see a variation of the one on the bottom. (If you select Delete from the File menu you will also see a similar dialog box.) I use the generic term *file dialog box* to refer to any of these boxes.

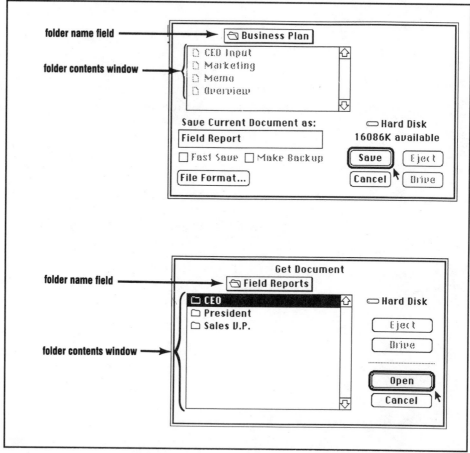

Figure 4.9: Variations of the file dialog box for saving a document (top) and importing one (bottom)

Next to the Finder, file dialog boxes are the prime portals through which you'll navigate on your hard disk. These HFS boxes have features that may not be obvious to the casual user. Let's take a look at a few.

USING THE PATH MENU

The path menu displays the current folder at the top of the list and the root folder at the bottom, but in this book *up* will always refer to the direction of the root (highest) level.

When you save a file, where does it get stored? Unless you specify otherwise, it will be stored in the same folder as the application you're using. The complete sequence of nested folders that starts with the root and ends with the folder in which a file is stored is called the file's *path* (or *pathname*). The path is displayed whenever you click on the folder name field directly above the folder contents field in the Save As... dialog box (Figure 4.10). This path display is more than a box; it's a menu, and you can leap up the hierarchy any number of levels simply by selecting the folder you want.

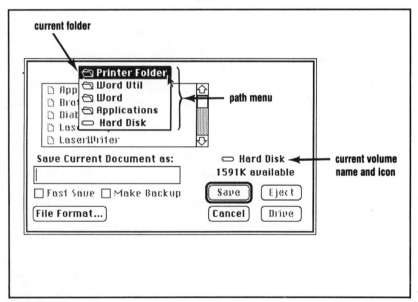

Figure 4.10: The Save As... dialog box after clicking on the folder name field

To navigate down the hierarchy, double-click on any folder in the folder contents window and, if necessary, scroll the contents window to locate the desired folder. Being able to go up and down the hierarchy means you can save—or seek—a file anywhere on any volume currently mounted on your system without having to quit your current application.

By the way, there's a shortcut to climbing back up the hierarchy: click on the name or icon of the current volume. This will automatically move you one level up the hierarchy.

In a Save or Save As... dialog box, only the folders can be opened, but in an Open dialog box both folders and files are accessible. Don't panic, however, if a folder containing valuable data appears to be empty—an Open dialog box can present a misleading picture. Files that the application cannot recognize are sometimes not just dimmed, they're not listed at all. And the files that can be selected do not necessarily belong to the application you're in at the moment. While in Microsoft Word, for instance, it looks as if you can select all MacWrite documents in the Open dialog box, but trying to open a MacWrite document actually triggers a conversion process—a copy of the document will be converted to Word's format and then opened, and the original will not be altered.

Path navigation should be done before the Save or Save As... button is selected; once the path is set, all subsequent versions of the file will be saved to that locale. Creating a file from within its intended folder is the most efficient way to go, but there are limitations: once you've saved a file, you can't use the standard file dialog boxes to relocate it, nor can you create a new folder, or rename a file or folder. For those tasks, you'll need to use the Finder.

USING THE FOLDER CONTENTS WINDOW

Since folders can hold a large number of files and other folders, the folder contents window in a file dialog box can become very long. You can scroll up and down the field until you find the file or folder you're looking for, but there are a few mouse-free shortcuts that make the task easier.

The contents of an open folder field are always listed in alphabetical order, with the first file or folder automatically selected whenever you open the dialog box. Skip down the list by typing in a character or two from the keyboard: the first file beginning with those characters will be selected. In other words, typing *h* will select the first file starting with *h* or *H* (the function ignores upper- and lower-case). If you want to be even more specific, type the first two characters of the file or folder name. But do it quickly: typing *j* and *o* in rapid succession should select a file named Job File, but if you pause between characters the Mac may interpret the second key press as a separate selection and move on to select a file with a name that begins with *o*.

The Mac tries to match alphabetical commands as closely as possible, but there is a margin for error. If you type *z* and no file or folder beginning with that name exists, it will select the one that comes nearest, one that begins with *y*, or *w* or *v*. Numbers, spaces and other nonalphabetical characters come before letters in the folder field, so any one of those keystrokes will send the user to the top of the list.

SEARCHING AN ENTIRE VOLUME

Even the most thoroughly organized hard disk can sometimes bury files in a labyrinth of path and nested folders. If you have at least a vague notion of the whereabouts of a file, you can try prospecting for it with the Finder. But if you don't know the general location, the type of the file, or even its name, you'll discover that the Finder is little more than a time-consuming last resort. A number of *mass volume search* programs have been developed to search the entire contents of a storage volume at very high speeds, using a varying range of criteria. Let's examine two of these, the most popular one and the one with the most features.

WORKING WITH FIND FILE

Find File will not distinguish between capital and lowercase letters.

Find File is a mass volume search DA from Apple Computer, currently included as part of the System Disk software package. It searches for file and folder names only, and it can't differentiate between a whole name and a string of characters within a name. It's capabilities border on the minimal, but it has the advantage of being free. To use Find File:

1. Select it from under the Apple menu. A window will appear (Figure 4.11).

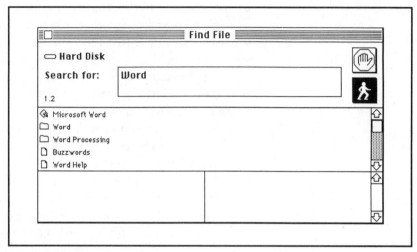

Figure 4.11: The Find File window

2. To initiate a search, type a name or set of characters into the Search for field. In the example, *Word* was typed in. If you want to search another hard disk or a floppy, click on the Hard Disk icon until the volume you want appears.

3. Either click on the symbol to the right that looks like a pedestrian "Walk" sign or hit the Return key.

4. The program searches from the root level down, and as the search commences it displays the names of all the files and folders it finds that match what you typed in the Search for field. When the search is over, the Macintosh beeps (unless you've turned the volume down), and the Stop symbol is selected automatically.

Fortunately, you don't have to wait until the entire volume has been searched before you can monitor Find File's progress. Each time a match is made, the result is added to the scrolling field in the center of the window. In the example in Figure 4.11, all files containing *Word* now appear in the scrolling field. Note that the program doesn't distinguish between names and strings within names. You can inspect any of these files in midsession by clicking on the Stop symbol. This won't end the search, it will just freeze it. Click on Walk again to make the search resume.

To examine the file information for a matching file, you don't have to stop a search even temporarily—just click on the file name in the scrolling field. This will fill the two bottom rectangles of the Find File window. On the left you'll find the pertinent information usually found in the Get Info box (the file type, the dates created and last modified, and the size). On the right you'll see the path you use to locate the file itself.

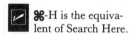
⌘-M is the equivalent of Move to Desktop.

You can use this path as a map to the file or folder, but if you want to permanently rescue it from its present obscurity, select the Move to Desktop command from the Find File menu. This will automatically transfer the file from its current location to the desktop, the area in which the trash icon and volume icons are displayed.

⌘-H is the equivalent of Search Here.

The Search Here... command under the Find File menu allows you to start a search at any level, in any folder. When the Search Here... command opens its dialog box, select the folder in which the search will begin. That folder and any nested within it will be searched. You can also use this command when one of the criteria matches appears in the scrolling field. In this case, when you click on the Search Here command, it will inform you of the other contents of the matches' home folder.

Find File can also do its work in the background: taking care not to hit the close box (which would cancel the search), click on another open window. The DA will continue to do its work and beep you when it is ready.

Working With GOfer

GOfer is a fast, versatile, easy-to-use mass volume search utility. Not only can it search file names, it can search the text of the files themselves for text strings, key words, or any combination thereof. It can also locate text with a very specific set of command parameters. For instance, you could use GOfer to identify all the word processing files that mention the names Chrysler and Chevrolet, or even to identify files that include either Chrysler or Chevrolet but only when mentioned in proximity to the name Buick.

Once installed, the GOfer DA can be accessed from within any application. The GOfer window (Figure 4.12) shares many features with Find File window. Notice, however, the three buttons at the top. These bring up dialog boxes that allow you to customize the searches you want to make.

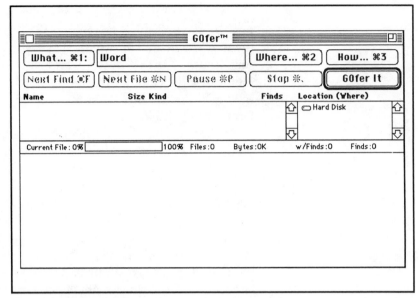

Figure 4.12: The GOfer window

- What... sets up the object of the search. It tells GOfer what to look for, in what context, and how close a match to make. With GOfer, you can seek an exact match, you can ignore upper- or lower-case letters, and you can even have GOfer list matches that it considers close to the ones you're looking for.

- Where... saves time by specifying exactly where to look. You can direct GOfer to search in a combination of folders, and you can narrow the target to include or exclude all files created by any application or file type. If you want, you can even limit the search to only text forks or data forks.

- How... lets you spell out how you want the search results displayed, and when you want the program to notify you by beeping.

Once you've defined what you want to look for, GOfer works extremely rapidly. It only takes about one minute to search one megabyte, and it's rarely necessary to search an entire hard disk thanks to the Where... command. Unfortunately, GOfer has a glaring weakness: it can't search for file and folder names alone. So even when you're sure of a file name, you'll have to wait while GOfer reads for matches in the text of the files as well. Fortunately, this weakness of not being able to search for file and folder names by themselves happens to be Find File's greatest strength. Find File searches file and folder names only, so if you install both Find File and GOfer the full spectrum of your volume search needs will be covered.

GOfer offers a major fringe benefit: it can display the contents of every file's text fork, and this text can be cut and pasted from one application to another. Since cutting and pasting can be done without leaving one application or launching another, GOfer can be a useful text-only alternative to the Clipboard.

CLEANING HOUSE WITH SEARCH UTILITIES

Search utilities are useful not only for locating misplaced files, but for weeding out the redundant, the obsolete and the superfluous. Keeping only one version of a file has three benefits: it saves space, it eliminates user confusion, and it guards against possible confusion on the part of the Mac. (Duplicates can cause data loss and system crashes.) Here's a brief rundown of the software most likely to profilerate on a hard disk:

- Duplicate system files are a likely cause of operational glitches. Such duplicates commonly come into being when a startup disk is copied whole onto a hard disk. Use Find File or another search utility to remove duplicate files named System, Finder, Clipboard, ImageWriter, LaserWriter, or any related duplicate file.

- Desk accessories and fonts can often be found in multiple versions, since the act of installing them in the System file itself creates a copy. Once properly installed, the individual icon of the desk accessory or font does not need to be present anywhere on the hard disk (with the exception of downloadable fonts, which need to be placed in the System Folder). Look also for multiple versions of the Font/DA Mover application.

- Temporary files are often created by applications (such as Microsoft Word) for a multitude of reasons, most notably to free up RAM by storing portions of an active document to disk. Once you've saved your document, these temporary files are usually drained of their contents but not deleted from the Finder. You can often find these discarded files in the System Folder. Although most take up hardly any storage space, they can lead to clutter and confusion. Temporary files usually have the default document icon (the page with a bent-over corner and no lines), and a title that indicates the application of their origin, such as "Word Temp 1" in the case of a Microsoft Word file.

Before you permanently delete any file, make sure that you can do without it, and that the one retained is the desired, up-to-date version. Two or more documents can share the same name, and the most used copy of an application may not be the one with the most features. When in doubt, open the documents, look them over, and check the Get Info boxes of the applications for version numbers.

PARTITIONING YOUR HARD DISK

A hard disk can be partitioned—formatted so that it functions not as one volume, but as two or more. The Mac handles partitioned volumes as separate entities, each with its own directory, icon, and SCSI address, and each capable of being mounted and unmounted at will. What are the benefits of giving your hard disk a split identity? Although they're not for everyone, partitions can be useful organizational tools.

When two or more people share a single Macintosh system, assigning each a partition may make matters easier for all concerned. With partitions, compromises and confusion can be eliminated: each user arranges his or her files according to individual needs and preferences, and any organizational changes made to one partitioned volume will not affect the others.

Partitions can also be helpful when information has to be quickly accessible and segregated too. For example, a scientist working simultaneously on several experiments may have generated similar sets of statistical files for each one. If the scientist assigns these files to separate folders on the same volume, the scientist could accidentally file information in the wrong folder, which could prove disastrous. It would be safer and faster for the scientist to store each file on its own partitioned volume. If only one volume is mounted at any one time, the prospect of a misfile is minimal.

System Folders can be configured and augmented in numerous ways—by changing fonts, DAs, INITs—but a single set of customizations may not be useful for every kind of work. Each partitioned volume can have its own System Folder, and each can be used as the startup volume when its features are needed. For example, a volume for page layout projects could be installed with ample fonts and a LaserWriter driver. One dedicated to spreadsheets, on the other hand, may need fewer options.

The uses of partitioning go beyond file and folder organization. Used in conjunction with password protection (discussed in Chapter 5), a partition can create a *software safe,* a storehouse that keeps important files off-limits and leaves the rest accessible. If you're fortunate enough to have a hard disk with more than twice the capacity you need, you could use one partition as backup storage for the other. But since they would both be vulnerable to the same hardware problems, you would still need a conventional backup.)

Some partitioning utilities, such as Symantec Utilities for the Macintosh (SUM), are commercially available as part of a general utility package. Others are installed as standard equipment on some hard disks models. Before you use partitions, consider the drawbacks:

- Partitioning erases the drive's current contents.

- Extra formatting files take up space, and a hard disk partitioned into several volumes will store less than a single volume on the same unit.

- Once created, the size of partitions can't be modified by anything short of reformatting. Different sets of files grow at different rates, and it's frustrating when one volume is filled to capacity while another has room to spare.

CREATING PARTITIONS WITH SUM

To partition a hard disk with SUM, you need to install two files into the system. The first is HD Partition INIT, and it needs to be dragged into the System Folder. It will be loaded every time the Macintosh is started. During startup it will display its icon on the screen to remind you of its presence. The second file is HD Partition DA (see Figure 4.13), and it has to be installed into the System file with the Font/DA Mover. HD Partition DA allows partitions to be created, mounted for use, unmounted, and deleted.

To create a new partition with HD Partition DA, select the Create button and specify the partition name and size in kilobytes in the appropriate text boxes (see Figure 4.14). If you want to protect the partition with a password, enter the password and be sure

If you forget the password assigned to a partition you will not be able to retrieve any data stored in it.

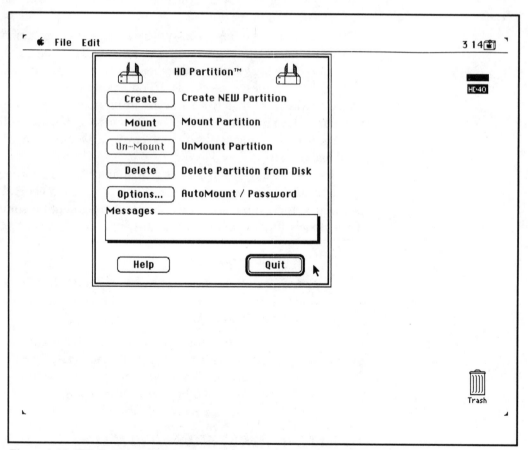

Figure 4.13: HD Partition initial screen

that the password box is checked. When you are ready, click on the Create button to create the partition. You will then be prompted to choose the volume on which the partition should be created. You can create partitions on any hard disk or floppy, but you cannot create a partition within another partition.

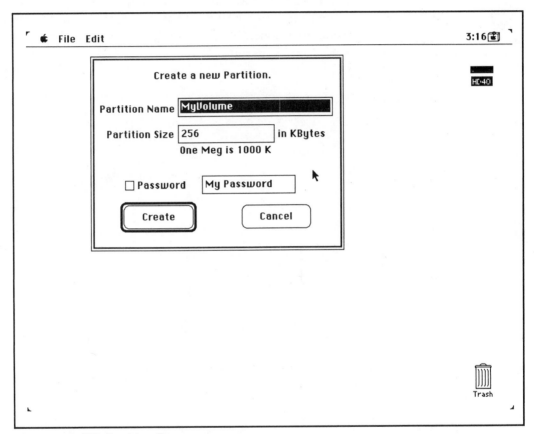

Figure 4.14: HD Partition Create screen

Once a partition has been created, it must be mounted before it will show up on the desktop. You do this by selecting the Mount button and then selecting the name of the partition in the list box. You can use the Drive button to select the appropriate disk.

SUM can also mount selected partitions automatically every time the Macintosh is started. To make a partition mount automatically, select the Options button and then the button labeled Add Partition to AutoMount List. You will then be presented with the dialog box for selecting partitions to mount. After you select all of the volumes that you want to have automatically mounted, select Save Auto-Mount Changes and Done. When you start your Macintosh, the specified partitions will appear on the desktop as disk drives.

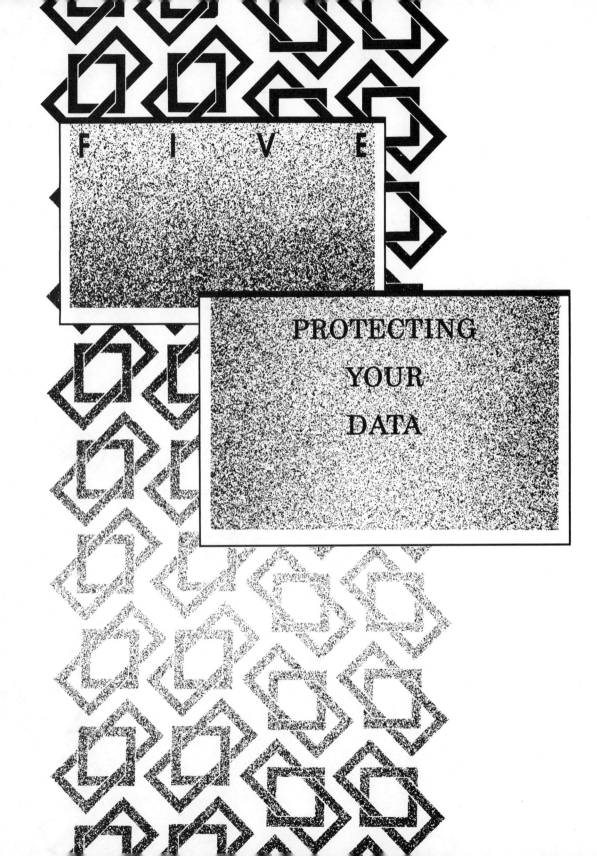

F I V E

PROTECTING

YOUR

DATA

In this chapter, I turn to the issue of data preservation and security. You'll see how to ensure that your data is safe from accidental loss, unauthorized access, and corruption by viruses and other damaging software.

I'll begin by looking at how to use floppy disks in conjunction with your hard disk, both as a means of preserving your software and of backing up your complete work environment. I'll survey different preservational approaches and evaluate some of the more important features of backup software.

Next, I'll discuss viruses and other rogue software: how to detect them, how to guard against them, and how to remove them from your system. Then I'll turn to the issue of human intrusion, an even thornier subject. I'll cover the strategies and psychology behind choosing and using a password, and look at access-limiting software. Finally, I'll talk about using hardware security systems to protect your hard disk as well as its contents.

ARCHIVES, BACKUPS, AND THE INEVITABLE

It's important to note the distinction between archiving software and backing up your hard disk. Archiving consists of simply making sure that all files exist in duplicate form in a location other than the hard disk. The goal of archiving is to make your files available in the event of a mishap, not to duplicate the structure of your hard disk's contents—that's what backups are for. Backups ensure that all functional aspects of your hard disk are preserved along with the data: System File setup, hierarchical organization, folder formats, etc. Archiving requires no special software but does require a systematic, disciplined approach to the job; backup programs provide a more automatic, straightforward procedure.

Which is the right tactic for you? For the most part, it depends on the tasks for which you use your Macintosh. You may not need to invest in backup software if you work on only a handful of documents—book manuscripts or a single set of spreadsheets— during the course of a month. But if you produce numerous new or updated documents during that period, chances are you'll find a backup program worth investing in.

No matter what your needs, there's a hard truth that can't be overemphasized: preserving data is an important part of owning a hard disk. Preserving data is as important to using a computer as adding oil and brake fluid is to the function of a car. The hard disk is not a solid-state technology. At some point in its career yours is going to stop working, even if you've used it for years without incident. It's not a matter of odds, but of time.

Preserving your data takes time, it takes money—if not for special software, then for floppy disks—and it's hard to see the benefit of doing it. All of this would seem to add up to a wasted effort. Frankly, preserving your data can be a hassle. And isn't that why you bought a hard disk in the first place, so you wouldn't have to juggle dozens of floppies?

But take a moment and consider how much effort you put into creating the data stored on your hard disk. Unless you can afford to do the work all over again (if that's even possible), you can't afford to do without a data protection scheme. At the risk of sounding pessimistic, I recommend that you think of it as insurance against the inevitable.

WHEN AND HOW OFTEN?

Stopping to preserve your data should not interrupt your work schedule. Still, the rule of thumb is "if you can't afford to lose it, save it." Following is some advice about saving documents.

In most programs, you press ⌘-S to save your work. Save your work whenever you are interrupted or you have to leave your desk.

- Save the document you are working on to your hard disk whenever your work is interrupted for more than a few minutes or if you need to leave your desk. In most programs you press ⌘-S to save documents, but some also have auto-save options that automatically copy all changes and additions after a specified period of time. If you work under MultiFinder, you can take the added precaution of saving a document every time you switch from one launched application to another.

- Save an important document onto a floppy disk as soon as it's completed. Do this as an extra measure independent of your regular data preservation plan. I recommend this specially for documents that you have to submit on a deadline, since problems have a way of occurring when you don't have time to deal with them. A good way to make sure you save your important work to floppies is to take a single floppy, designate it "Current Work," and keep it in your floppy drive whenever possible.

- Schedule a weekly preservation session for a time when the task won't have to compete with other, possibly more pressing duties. Many people plan to do it on Friday as the last agenda item of the work week—but best intentions aren't quite enough, and the task is put off in favor of last-minute obligations. The best time to preserve files is in the morning on whatever weekday is your least hectic.

ARCHIVING WITH FLOPPIES

Most floppy-disk-based archives consist of two parts: commercial data, which include applications, DAs, and the like, and personal data, your documents, folders, and custom resource files. This distinction is a practical one to make, since commercial and personal data present separate challenges. A commercial file tends to take up more storage space, but it usually needs to be archived only once. Personal files are usually modified more often and therefore require more frequent archiving.

COMMERCIAL DATA

The best way to start an archive is to gather the master floppies that store your commercial data—the disks the software was packaged on—and run them briefly in the Mac to ensure that none have been damaged or inadvertently erased. Next, make disk copies of all your software that does not have a source disk—programs downloaded from bulletin boards, shareware programs, and so forth. Once you have all your commercial data copied, start labeling and arranging it in some sort of useful order. You could arrange it alphabetically or by order of importance. It also helps to note which disks contain startup files.

The System file can be reduced by using Font/DA mover to remove fonts and DAs.

Finally, copy your System Folder, configured to your preferences, to a fresh disk. Remember, though, that most System Folders (and even System files) are too large to fit on a single floppy. You may have to split the contents of the System Folder over more than one disk. To do this, reduce the size of the System file itself by making a copy of it on the hard disk, then use Font/DA Mover to purge it of Fonts and DAs, and copy these separately to another floppy. Don't forget to throw away the System file duplicate on the hard disk when you're through.

PERSONAL DATA

How you approach the archiving of your personal data depends on three factors: how much data you'll be dealing with, your organizational choice, and whether you have a file compression utility. Each of these factors can affect the others, so a bit of careful consideration is in order before proceeding. The better your archiving plan fits your needs, the easier it will be to live with and maintain your archived files.

The most obvious strategy for archiving would simply be to copy every folder onto a floppy. But in a time of crisis you would find yourself frantically juggling dozens of disks while you try to find a vital file.

Another option is to categorize your data by dedicating specific floppies to each subject, client, or project with which you're working. This option probably offers the greatest ease in locating files, but it requires significantly more floppies, some of which won't be filled to capacity, and it is very time-consuming to have to update not one disk, but many. If categorizing by floppy disk is the most viable approach for your data, be sure to use the compression utility feature to cut down on floppy consumption.

The best way to organize your floppies in an archive is by the dates you create them.

For most users, the most efficient method is to organize floppies according to their date of creation. That way, you need to add only one new floppy at a time to the archive and you won't need to update the others. This takes a little more time to set up at the start, but it's usually worth it; combined with file compression, organizing floppies by date probably represents the best use of your time and resources.

Before you establish a date-based archive, consider just how difficult it will be to organize the archive file and how structured your archive needs to be. Placing 50 occupied megabytes into files in strict chronological order is far more daunting than placing only 15. You may also be able to organize on the criteria of this distinction: every file created up to now, as opposed to all files created in the future. Using a librarian utility such as DiskQuick can also make location tasks easier. Librarian utilities are described later in this chapter.

As you organize your archive files by date, be sure to organize your files according to when you last modified them, not according to when you created them.

To set up a date-based archive, start by ploughing through the folders on your hard disk, temporarily changing each one's view format to View by Date. Take care to organize by date last modified, rather than by date of creation. Next, copy your personal data to floppies, giving each disk a name that reflects the date when it was made.

After that's done, you need to decide on a means of updating your archive. The best way to do this is:

1. Move each new (or newly modified) file to a special folder on the hard disk.

2. Copy it to a floppy at the appropriate time.

3. Move the files from the special folder to their ultimate destination.

When you transfer a date-based archive back to the hard disk, copy your earliest version of the files first and work your way up to the most recent version.

If you need to restore your hard disk's contents from your date-based archive, be sure to load the floppies strictly by order of date, from earliest to latest. That way, modified files will be automatically replaced with their most current version (expect the frequent appearance of the Replace existing file? dialog box).

No matter what approach you take, sorting through, shuffling, and copying a myriad of files is tedious and likely to lead to oversight, error, and neglect. That's why I recommend archiving only when you have a small number of files or a large amount of discipline and free time. For the rest of us, streamlining the process with backup software or hardware is the practical path to take.

USE LIBRARIAN UTILITIES

Whatever strategy you decide on for preserving your files, you'll probably find it useful to have a catalog to help you find the resting place of your software and the contents of your floppy disks. Librarian utilities such as DiskQuick automate this process, providing a useful written record of the contents of a volume.

DiskQuick and similar programs can display the contents of a volume in a number of formats. Examples are what folder a given file is in, its size, creator ID, or RAM demands (see Figure 5.1). Disk-Quick can keep track of your hard disk's contents as well as your floppy-based archive. It can tag certain files for regular updating. If your archive files are spread across a multitide of floppies, a volume librarian is well worth the expense.

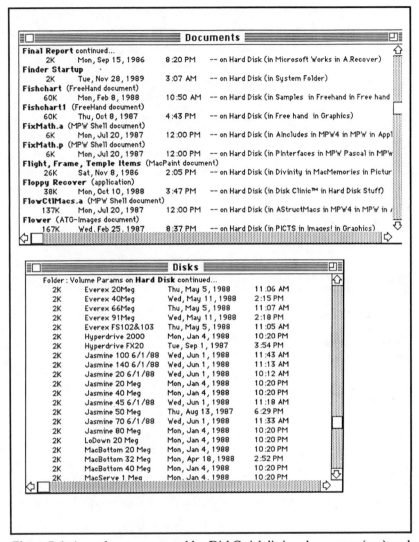

Figure 5.1: A catalogue generated by DiskQuick listing documents (top) and one listing disks (bottom)

BACKUPS

Archives don't require specialized software, but their usefulness is decidedly limited. For clear, unambiguous, hassle-free data preservation, backing up beats archiving hands down. Not only does backing up preserve more than archiving in terms both of volume structure and file contents, it's accomplished with an automated process. Backup files also let you restore lost data with a minimum of fuss and effort.

There are two classes of backups: floppy-based, which rely on floppy disks to be the preservational medium, and hardware-based, which safeguard the hard disk's contents with another mass storage volume. It costs little but takes a lot of time to use floppy-based backups. Hardware-based backups, on the other hand, are expensive but efficient. Choosing a backup strategy depends on a number of factors—your budget, the value of your data, your work habits, and your degree of dedication to preventative maintenance.

FLOPPY-BASED BACKUPS

If you've chosen to back up your hard disk with floppy disks, take these precautions before you plunge in:

When backing up your hard disk with floppies, allow one double-sided floppy for each 700K on your hard disk.

- Calculate the number of floppies you'll need. Allocate one double-sided floppy for each 700K of data on your hard disk. A full 20-megabyte disk would need 30 floppies, a full 118-megabyte disk would need 88 floppies.

- Use fresh disks if you prefer, but used ones will do nicely as long as they are reliable and properly formatted for a double-sided HFS drive.

- Don't bother to reformat a previously used floppy, but take care to delete its contents. Also be sure to rename and relabel it appropriately.

- Make sure that the floppy is not write-protected.

- Test each floppy for the unintended or unexpected. Do this by keeping a watchful eye while you copy, open, and delete documents in the floppy's directory. It's tempting to retire marginal floppies to backup duties, but your files will only be safe if your floppies are dependable.

Backup software comes with a range of performance features. Many manufacturers bundle their hard disks with a free backup program. Apple, for example, offers an adequate one with each System package. But it's often a case of getting what you pay for—a careful choice will help make the backup process easier. Look for these features when you evaluate backup software:

- Volume management. A good backup software program will calculate how many floppies are necessary to perform a backup. It will prompt you to mount or unmount the right volume at the right time. It should evaluate each backup disk and halt the proceedings when something is amiss. It may also rename and reinitialize floppies when the need arises, and perform minor desktop and directory repairs automatically.

- Selective protection. A competent program will identify all files that you have modified since the last backup and duplicate them according to criteria that you specify. It will have a similar flexibility when it comes to restoring files from the backup: a good backup program should specify where and how individual files will be resurrected. You should be able to specify precisely which files should be backed up, and in what fashion.

- Copy verification. The utility shouldn't just make copies, it should test copies and confirm whether the new version is an accurate reproduction and can itself be accurately reproduced. If a file is too big to fit on a single floppy, the utility should let you divide it safely into smaller pieces and resplice them later easily and accurately.

- Speed and versatility. Some backup software packages are feature laden but slow, whereas others are swift but stripped down. Most programs work at a pace between 100K and 300K per minute, but claims of up to 1 megabyte per minute have been made. Many backups also offer the option of saving files in various formats, from text-only to full compression and encryption. This option can be useful when disk space or file security are concerns.

Backing Up the First Time

Your first backup will probably take a while, but if you do it right your subsequent backups will be quick and easy, so approach backing up with all the thoroughness you can muster.

If your backup program gives you the option of excluding files, you may want to exclude much of your commercial data, since it's already stored on its original floppies. Be sure to run these floppies first, though, before you rely on them—you want to confirm that they're functional and intact. Also slide their write-protect tabs to the open position so they won't be unintentionally tinkered with.

As you decide which data should go in the backup, remember that your startup System Folder and many of your applications may have been modified to your preferences, and you want to preserve them in their current incarnations. And don't forget the software that may not have a proper source disk—the shareware and public domain programs, the INITs, fonts, DAs, and other marginalia that most Macintosh owners acquire almost without knowing it. You want to preserve this software too.

Unfortunately, the only sure and complete way to test a backup is to use it to recreate the contents of your hard disk. This task is recommended only for those with ample spare time and a spare hard disk. Others might compare files on the floppies with those on the hard disk, watching for omissions and irregularities. If your backup application is capable of partial restorations, perhaps you should reconstitute a file or folder for practice and self-assurance.

⊙ Don't add or
remove files or
folders from a backup
floppy (except as specifically allowed by the
backup software).

When your complete backup has been compiled, label the floppies clearly, set them away from your other disks, and let them be. Don't change any volume, file, or folder names on those floppies. Don't attempt to open the backup files with any application other than the backup utility. Unless the utility allows otherwise, don't add to or remove any of the floppies' contents; a seemingly innocuous change could boggle the program and render your data reserves unreadable. You can, however, safely make direct disk-to-disk floppy copies of your backup volumes, for an extra measure of security.

Backing Up After the First Time

Once you've established a basic backup storehouse, you should update it at appropriate intervals. The backups you do after the first one are called *progressive* or *incremental* backups. Progressive backups add new files to the storage, but they also update the preserved files to which you have made changes. If a file hasn't been modified since the date of the last backup, it won't be disturbed.

Incremental backups, because they usually involve modifying previously backed up files, give rise to a new set of problems. If the new version is corrupted or if the updating process is incorrectly executed, the file can be garbled and unusuable. Nonetheless, incremental backups are more convenient than starting from scratch every time.

RESTORING BACKED UP FILES TO THE HARD DISK

No matter what your backup strategy, the moment of truth comes when you have to retrieve a file because of a data loss or other malfunction. A full-featured backup application should offer three file options: mirror restoration, second-volume restoration, and file-specific restoration.

- A mirror restoration recreates the contents of a volume as completely as possible. Correctly executed, it's as if the hard disk never malfunctioned in the first place: all files are recreated in their original location, and the directory structure is intact. Use a mirror restoration when damage or data loss is relatively major and the disk itself has been satisfactorily repaired.

- A second-volume restoration makes the contents of a backup accessible in a modified form as the subdirectory of another volume. For instance, you could place the backup of a 20-megabyte hard disk on an 80-megabyte drive, and what was originally its root level would become a folder. This allows you to use your data while the 20-megabyte drive is being repaired and eventually transfer it in mirror form.

- A file-specific restoration lets you select files or groups of files for reconstitution and save them to another hard disk or to a floppy. It's the best approach when time is short and only a few files need to be accessed.

Keep in mind that none of the options are mutually exclusive. You should be able to perform them in any combination, and at any time after you've compiled a backup.

PLAN FOR MAXIMUM SECURITY

Whether you archived or backed up your data, you now have a collection of floppy disks on your hands. Since the safety of your data rests in large part on the safety of these disks, take these steps to guarantee a minimum of mishaps.

- Isolate them from other floppies. If you have a miscellany of floppies and you're shuttling them between computers or using them for various tasks, don't keep them in the same area as your preservational disks. If you do, you run the risk of accidentally using a preservational disk, especially if you're not the only one working with your Macintosh.

- Write-protect the disk. In the upper right-hand corner of every $3^{1}/_{2}$-inch floppy is a sliding square of plastic called the write-protect tab. Use your fingernail, a pencil, or a paper clip to slide it up and down. When the tab is slid down and you can't see through the square window, the disk drive will both read and write to the floppy. On the other hand, when the tab is slid up and you can see through the square window, the drive will read only. This means you can copy from the floppy disk to the hard disk, but you can't introduce changes directly to the floppy yourself. The protection tab is a useful safeguard against accidental erasure. You can restore a disk to either read and write or to read-only status at any time by sliding the protection tab up or down.

- Store them away from the workplace. Perhaps you have to guard your floppies against not just mechanical malfunctions, but against fire, theft, or other catastrophes. If your data is that valuable, consider stashing your preservational disks in an entirely separate location—your home, another office, or even a safe. Some people assign a briefcase case just for floppies and carry it back and forth whenever an update is in order. Although floppy disks are remarkably tolerant of temperature and circumstances, be sure to keep them away from heat and moisture when you transport them. Magnetic fields like those generated by refrigerators or other major appliances can also ruin a floppy disk. If you decide to purchase a safe for storing your floppies, make sure you buy a model especially suited for storing magnetic media.

HARDWARE-BASED BACKUPS

Even with the best backup utility, transferring the contents and essence of a hard disk to a stack of floppies is a cumbersome, tedious process. If budget allows, you may want to take a look at the numerous hardware units that can make backing up easier and faster.

One obvious but expensive hardware solution is simply to buy another hard disk of the same capacity and add it to the SCSI daisy-chain. A less expensive solution would be to purchase a *removable-media mass storage device*. These devices preserve data on a high-capacity replaceable unit of one sort or another—a type of cassette, a megafloppy-like disk, a CD, or an ordinary VCR tape. Each method has its own critics and champions, so it's hard to declare any one format clearly superior to the others.

The issues involved in removable-media technology are discussed in Chapter 10.

Some removable-media mass storage devices are designed especially for backup purposes, others are stand-alone alternatives to the hard disk, and a few are the forerunners of devices that may replace hard disks in the future. You can use any or all of them to enhance your current system. The cost, features, and performance of mass storage devices must be weighed in the balance when you go shopping for one.

VIRUSES AND OTHER ROGUE SOFTWARE

Before 1988, the threat of misleading, mischievous and malicious programming was virtually unknown to Macintosh users: viruses and related programs were obscure subjects in software engineering classes or occasional topics for computer professionals. Although they had been reported on mainframes and other systems, viruses and rogue software seemed more a part of folklore than reality.

Then, almost overnight, their reality became all too apparent. Within a few weeks of dissemination, a virus spawned in Canada began to appear on Macintoshes in several countries. At the same time at least one other damaging program caused considerable grief among users in the U.S. The ensuing furor produced a lot of indignation, a little bit of nervousness, a few court cases, and the realization that personal computing would never be the same. Few people have been significantly affected by illicit Macintosh software, but even fewer can afford to ignore the issues this software raises.

WHAT IS A VIRUS?

The term ''virus'' is often used to describe any code created with devious intent. Actually, the concept of viruses has been around since the earliest days of computing. A virus is software that can, like its biological equivalent, spread by infection from one host to another. Most viruses are invisible programs that install themselves on a system without the user's knowledge. Viruses quietly place copies of themselves on any storage volume they come into contact with, either hard disks or floppies. They reproduce themselves when a volume on which they're hiding is connected to another computer.

But a virus can do more than just reproduce itself; just about any command can be incorporated in a virus. Often, after a task has been achieved, the virus is instructed to self-destruct and wipe out all evidence of its existence. This would make viruses seem very dangerous, but the format has its limitations. For example, the code must be kept small in order to remain unobtrusive and invisible. Also, the program must be designed to anticipate and modify itself to every operating system to which it may be transferred.

Viruses began as an intellectual exercise, a conceptual demonstration to prove that the computer's health, like a human's health, exists as a function of an ecology. Creating viruses eventually proved an irresistible challenge for a few programmers, and system administrators soon incorporated testing for rogue software into their regular functions. But for decades it was believed that viruses would remain a rarity, a phenomenon occurring only in mainframe and other large-scale systems, where the sheer bulk of processing tasks occasionally allows a virus to slip through.

Why are viruses now afflicting microcomputers? There are two reasons.

- With the personal computer boom has come a flood of new programmers, many of whom, as much as their predecessors, relish the challenge of creating a virus. Sophisticated programming languages have made it possible to pack more code than ever in increasingly tinier packages.

- The success of a microcomputer relies in large part on how much third-party software is available for it, and manufacturers have given programmers more access to specialized information about circuitry and design than ever before.

The Macintosh has been especially hard hit. This is due, in part, to the Toolbox architecture, which lets a small, illicit program get a big job done simply by issuing commands to the ROM. On other PCs, an illicit program has to include all the code necessary to do the job itself. Another factor is the Mac user interface. Besides making some applications easy to use, it makes it easier for users to pass along shareware, public domain software, and pirated software. Another reason viruses have hit the Mac so hard is the number of Mac networks—user groups, local area networks, and electronic, modem-accessible bulletin board systems.

By and large, the Macintosh community responded swiftly and effectively to the first outbreak of viruses. A number of free or shareware utilities to combat viruses were created and distributed by individual programmers and by Apple Computer alike. The custodians of bulletin boards started policing their contents more carefully. Commercial products began to incorporate tools for virus detection and removal.

But the battle isn't over yet, and it's unlikely to be over in the foreseeable future. Even the most effective virus-fighting resource can only find what it has been taught to look for; it may be helpless against programs designed and behaving on a new set of principles. At present, almost all antiviral software addresses only one or both of the two most prevalent types of virus, classified as nVIR and Scores. (These will be explained later in this chapter.) Experts have cracked the secrets of these, but viruses belonging to entirely new categories may yet appear.

SHOULD YOU WORRY?

Viruses and their ilk have received a lot of attention, some of it bordering on the alarmist, but viruses are a cause for concern, not for worry or for panic. It's best to view them as just another factor to be addressed in your overall data protection strategy. The problems you may encounter are more likely to originate in the mundane, not in a virus. With a little preventative effort you can rest assured that your system is, and will remain, virus-free.

Whether you know it or not, your Macintosh belongs to a vast, interconnected network. Just about every software source has been found to be infected at one time or another—electronic bulletin boards, shareware, even commercial programs fresh from the manufacturer. Only the most isolated units can be considered immune from viral contagion. Unless your Mac has not come into contact with new software or storage devices since 1986 or earlier, it's best to consider yourself at risk; even a seemingly blank floppy used only to copy from your system could carry a virus.

What sort of threat do viruses represent? So far, most of the viruses that have affected the Mac have been more or less benign. Often they do nothing more than announce their presence and promptly self-destruct. But even these represent an unanticipated presence in the system—they can cause problems ranging from minor performance slowdowns to no performance at all. And a well-written virus can take command of the system or any online volumes. Only restraint on the part of the programmer can keep a virus from causing lasting damage.

WORMS, BOOBY TRAPS, AND TROJAN HORSES

Besides viruses, there are three types of rogue programs—software designed to wreak havoc on the unsuspecting—to watch out for. *Worms, booby traps,* and *Trojan horses* aren't self-replicating like viruses are. Instead, they use other means of transmission. The three are found in the Macintosh far more rarely than viruses, but their potential for destruction is just as great.

- A worm can be written as a kind of virus. In fact, a worm is very similar to a virus, the difference being that a virus reproduces itself only in the interests of infecting another system, but a worm produces a rapid population boom. Once set in motion, a worm can quickly occupy all storage space and overwhelm the computer.

- A booby trap masquerades as an especially enticing piece of software. Typically, it will appear as a file with a title calculated to titillate, such as "Sex Survey," or to convey confidentiality, such as "Corporate Espionage Report." Then, once it is launched, a booby trap shows its true colors, often triumphantly declaring the nature and extent of the damage it has inflicted. Some are benign but others have been known to cause irreversible harm. Either way, by the time a booby trap goes off, it's often too late. If you're suddenly faced with an unusual or ominous screen display—or other evidence that something's amiss—don't just wait to see what happens, cut off the power as fast as you can by flicking the power switch or by pulling the cord out of the Mac or the wall socket. You can experiment with the suspect file further, but only if you're running from a floppy and all your other volumes (including an internal hard disk) are safely offline.

- A Trojan Horse is more subtle. Instead of merely pretending to be something else, it actually functions as advertised—but at the same time it carries out another, covert task. Trojan horses have taken the form of spreadsheets, word processing documents, and HyperCard stacks. Their unauthorized results have included everything from a simple message ("Gotcha!") to the erasure of a hard disk's entire contents. Because of their innocuous image, Trojan horses can be especially insidious, quietly engineering changes that don't appear until days, weeks, even months later. Like booby traps, Trojan horses can in fact have even greater malicious potential than viruses, since they do not need to be small in order to remain hidden.

Fortunately, booby traps and Trojan horses usually don't spread as far as viruses and worms. They are disseminated only by intentional copying, and when one copy betrays its true nature the bad news usually travels swiftly. The threat from a booby trap or Trojan horse can usually be nipped in the bud simply by trashing the file.

Some antivirus utilities will check for booby traps and Trojans horses as well, but the best way to guard against them is to test new software before placing it on your hard disk. (You probably don't have to worry about brand new, professionally produced software on an official master disk.) Testing techniques for finding booby traps and Trojan horses are discussed later in this chapter.

Scores Viruses

The Scores virus, so called because it often places an invisible file by that name in the System Folder, is the most common form of virus. The Scores virus behaves unpredictably. Some Macs infected with it display no ill effects; others display a severe degradation of performance. Common symptoms of Scores are problems in using the Set Startup option and problems in running or printing from MacDraw. It is also blamed in particular for frequent system crashes and for damage to MacDraw and Excel files.

The easiest way to check for a Scores virus is to open your System Folder and examine its contents under the View by Icon format. Look at the Scrapbook and Notepad resource files to see if their icons look like miniature Macs or like documents (Figure 5.2). If they look like documents, your system is likely infected. But looking at the Scrapbook and Notepad file icons is not the only way to detect the presence of the Scores virus. There are two ways to probe even deeper. The easiest way is to use a special utility such as Virus Rx specifically designed to target Scores viruses. The other method is to use ResEdit to examine the invisible files on your system.

> Using ResEdit is explained in Chapter 7. The Virus Rx utility is described in the "Detection/Removal Utilities" section of this chapter.

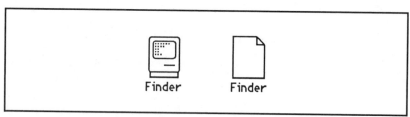

Figure 5.2: Viruses of the Scores variety often change System resource files from custom icons (left) to default document icons (right).

If you're familiar with ResEdit, you can use it to open and examine the System Folder. You may see a number of invisible files, but you should be concerned only with ones named Scores, 2 Virus

ResEd, or Desktop—these are symptoms of the Scores virus. Don't confuse a Desktop file nested in the System Folder with the file of the same name on the root level of your volume; the one on the root level is supposed to be there and should not be disturbed.

If ResEdit or a detection utility has diagnosed Scores, radical surgery is the only treatment. You must replace all applications on the infected volume. Advanced users thoroughly familiar with the inner workings of the Mac, however, may be able to use ResEdit to eradicate the virus.

To remove Scores, start with the System Folder and dispose of all its contents; you can use Font/DA Mover to remove installed fonts and desk accessories if you want, but everything else should go. Next, delete all applications (not your documents, just the applications), taking care to ensure that all are removed. The Scores virus tries to hide not just in the System Folder but in every application. A single untrashed application could reinfect the volume.

Once the System and all applications have been eliminated, install fresh versions on the volume and proceed as usual. But before you consider the crisis passed, check again for a possible recurrence of Scores—the copy you used to restore an application may have been the original source of the infection.

nVIR Viruses

The second most common type of viruses belong to the nVIR genre. Though much less prevalent than Scores, the nVIR virus is more difficult to detect. Fortunately, it's also not as disruptive or destructive.

Like Scores, nVIRs attach themselves to the resource files of an application, creating a unique resource with the identifier "nVIR." An nVIR places an INIT of its own in the System Folder, and this INIT is accessed whenever an infected application is launched. In most cases, the INIT does no more than cause the Mac to emit a beep during launching, but if you have the MacinTalk speech synthesis software, you may hear a calm voice say, "Don't panic."

The voice is right—there is no need to panic. The nVIR virus is more of a nuisance than a menace. Rehabilitating your system is a simple matter of removing and replacing the infected applications and System Folder. Some utilities, such as Interferon, may even be

The use of Interferon is discussed in the "Detection/Removal Utilities" portion of this chapter.

able to remove the virus without erasing your files. After you've removed an nVIR, you'll need to check periodically for its recurrence; the nVIR virus is exeptionally tenacious and can pop up again even when you thought you already removed it.

Detection/Removal Utilities

Almost as soon as a virus hits the Macintosh community, a utility is written to detect and combat it. Virus-detecting utilities are provided by prominent programmers more or less as a public service. Most of them are free or shareware. Virus utility software falls into two categories: some detect viruses, and others search for and destroy them. Some utilities tackle only the Scores or nVIR virus, while others handle both.

Apple Computer's contribution to the antiviral war is Virus Rx (Figure 5.3), a free program that targets Scores. Instead of detecting the virus directly, it compiles a list of files that show unusual, inappropriate, or suspicious modifications. Virus Rx then recommends a course of action; it may give the volume a clean bill of health or recommend some files for removal. Files that are decreed ''dangerous'' should be replaced at once, as should those decreed ''fatal'' (they may not be infected, but they won't work at all). Although Virus Rx

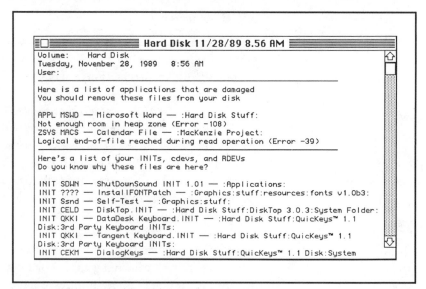

Figure 5.3: Apple Computer's Virus Rx utility checks for suspicious alterations to files.

won't always give you a definitive diagnosis of Scores infection, it's fast, easy to use, and accurate.

Interferon, more potent than Virus Rx, is a shareware utility that patrols for Scores, for nVIRs, and for a few obscure virus types as well (Figure 5.4). What's more, it eradicates viruses without your having to make manual deletions or restorations.

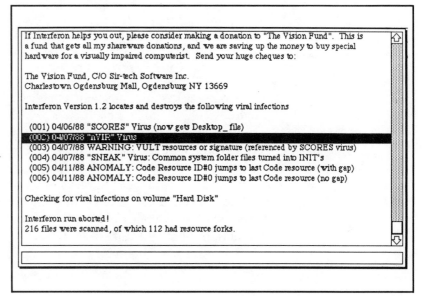

Figure 5.4: Interferon searches for and destroys the most common viral strains.

To use Interferon, copy it to a startup floppy, then enable the write-protect tab (this will keep it from becoming infected itself). Interferon scans all online volumes to look for irregularities that indicate the presence of a specific virus. The names of the files being checked flash at the bottom of the screen. The checking process cannot be stoppped once you start Interferon, so give yourself enough time to carry out the operation. A 20-megabyte hard disk will take about six minutes.

If Interferon finds what may be an infection, it displays a message in the scrolling panel. The message includes a number indentifying the type of infection—001 for Scores, 002 for nVIR, and 003 to 006 for other viral types. You can remove these files yourself or select the Eradicate command, which deletes the virus automatically.

Interferon, Virus Rx, and most other utilities may be useful against viruses, but they are not the cure-all. They were written to attack certain types of viruses—they can't anticipate new kinds that might appear. Besides, most of them were written rapidly and under a small budget, so they are not bug-free, nor do they have as many features as they should. Many, such as Virus Rx and Ferret, are one-time-only releases and will not be improved or upgraded in the future.

ONLINE BUT OFF LIMITS: ACCESS LIMITATION

A hard disk is the equivalent of a file cabinet—it is a compact storage device. But unlike a file cabinet, which can be locked, a hard disk can be easily accessed, tampered with, or even stolen. Therefore, access limitation is a must for work requiring security. It's also useful for anyone who just wants to keep some parts of a system out of certain peoples' reach. Macintosh users in the Pentagon use the technology for access limitation that I'm going to describe, and so do parents who want to let their childen play on the computer but don't want important files to be tinkered with.

The three main approaches to access limitation are *password protection, data encryption,* and *physical security devices.*

- Password protection, the most straightforward and limited of the trio, refuses to mount a volume (or sometimes, to complete the startup process) unless the right password is given.

- Data encryption uses a variety of mathematical methods to scramble a file's contents, unscrambling it only when the right commands are given.

- Physical security devices employ the brute force strategy, limiting hardware and software access simply by locking the unit away.

Of the three, which access limitation is best for you? Depending on the circumstances and the actual products available, the solution may incorporate one, two, or all three of them.

Even though it makes no changes to the data it protects, password protection is generally considered an effective security technique. Theoretically, an expert system cracker, given ample equipment and time, could copy password-protected files to an unprotected disk, but that would be quite a feat. Most password-protected hard disks are so secure that if the password is forgotten, there is no recourse except to erase its entire contents with a magnetic field and start over.

Password protection is convenient, usually adding no more than a few seconds to the startup process. But it is inflexible—it protects all the data on the volume.

For people who need more flexibility in their security, data encryption offers a better solution. You can transfer and transmit an encrypted file just like any other file—you can copy it to a floppy, post it on a network, even download it with a modem. But unless the person possessing a copy knows the key words required to unscramble it, the copied file will amount to nothing more than a waste of storage space.

Encryption, like password protection, also has a few drawbacks. It takes time to process the file during both the encoding and decoding process. Also, a secured file usually takes up more hard-disk space than its unprotected counterpart. Users may be a little disturbed by the fact that encrypted files can be duplicated freely, but there's no need to worry about this. Even the most brilliant Mac programmer with another copy of the encryption program can't fathom the scrambling scheme.

To keep your hard disk in your possession, you might consider installing a physical security device. Some, such as cabling systems, do little more than anchor your equipment to another, bulkier object; others have metal bars and bands that make the system impossible to use when you lock it up.

These devices may foil the typical thief looking to make a quick getaway, but that doesn't mean they're foolproof. Usually the locks are no more complicated than those an experienced picklock would encounter elsewhere, and chains and cables need only to be cut. Given time and determination, a person could probably overcome such security—especially if they don't mind mutilating the Macintosh in order to take its internal hard disk out. Still, there's no safer alternative, save locking the system away in a safe.

Whether it's hardware or software, keep in mind that all access limitation products currently in the Macintosh marketplace share one limitation: they can't be counted on to keep the elements or a strong magnetic field from destroying your data. All it takes to blank out a hard disk or any magnetic media device is a sufficiently strong magnetic field. Extremes of heat or cold will also destroy your hard disk by buckling the platters or melting their coating. If you are concerned about the possibility of such a catastrophe, either accidental or deliberate, your best insurance is an up-to-date, safely stored backup.

PASSWORD PROTECTION

When evaluating password protection software, there are a number of features to look for.

- A versatile program will accommodate many authorized users, as well as many passwords.

- It should be compatible with all other user-customized aspects of the startup process (especially MultiFinder's ''Set Startup'' options).

- It should feature a way to override the program, usually by means of a special floppy, in the event that the volume starts malfunctioning or the password has been lost.

All software-based methods of access limitation have a weakness that can't be eliminated, no matter how sophisticated their programming: each relies on passwords or other kinds of user-defined codes to determine when to lift its defenses. That means even the fiercest protection strategy can only be as secure as the password that controls it, just as the most elaborate burglar alarm is only as safe as the place where its key is hidden.

When working with a password program, your biggest challenge will likely be the password itself—how to choose it, when to change it, where to record it in case it's forgotten. As you'll soon see, the subject of passwords belongs not to the realm of technology, but to the realm of psychology.

Selecting a Password

You'll want a password that's easy to remember. Still, phrases that strike you as appropriate may strike others as obvious. If you're an avid golfer, for instance, keep clear of words like "fore" or "birdy." There's nothing wrong with a password that has a connotation for you, but your co-workers may be thoroughly familiar with your interests and affinities, and your password may evoke a subject that others associate with you. On the other hand, it's unlikely that they know the name of the boy who sat at the desk directly in front of you in your seventh grade math class.

The ideal password is this: a word, term, or phrase that is personally meaningful and thereby memorable, but so far removed from its original context as to place it beyond the reach of the educated guesser.

Below is a list of the most popular password types. Some password-cracking programs are instructed to try the terms that fit into these categories. When choosing a password, stay away from the following:

- Common names such as "Bill" or "Margaret." Also avoid middle names and maiden names, since many people use them.

- Obscenities, especially the four-letter variety. Most password crackers will try them early on.

- Science fiction terms, especially those made famous by science fiction writers: "Spock," "Hal," and "I, Robot."

- Common objects found in households and offices. Steer clear of "file cabinet," "spider plant," and the like. Resist the temptation to take refuge in the obvious—"computer" or "Macintosh."

- Common phrases, especially those pertaining to getting down to work, such as "wake up," "hey, you," or "get going," and those that offer a greeting, such as "good morning."

Preserving the Password

No matter how strong your memory or how memorable your password, too much is at stake with a password to trust your recollection. Once you've decided on a password and entered it in your Mac, the password should be written down in a safe and unobtrusive place. Which can pose a problem, since you might find it easier to remember a password than a set of directions to a secreted piece of paper. Besides, you're relying on the same memory to retain both pieces of information. That's why both password and hiding place are usually products of personality and force of habit, and why most would-be security crackers employ psychology as well as computer expertise.

Here's a trick that often works: hide the access code in a place that's not hard to find, but in a form or context that makes it all but impossible to identify as the password. One sterling example of this was devised by one user with a thoroughly undependable memory, who employed as passwords only seven-digit numbers. These numbers were even harder for him to recall than they'd be for most people, but this didn't concern him; when the password slipped his mind, he would simply turn to the address book on his desk, just inches from his Mac. There, entered under the name of a mythical Mister Strubinski, he would find the seven-digit password disguised as a phone number.

If your memory isn't up to even as simple a plan as this, find someone you can trust to keep the password both safe and confidential, and enlist their help. If you give the password record to, say, your spouse for safekeeping, all you'll need to remember is that you've done so. If you forget who you gave it to and forget the password as well, you're covered: when your spouse learns of your plight he or she will tell you what your password is.

Changing Your Password

Some people manage the task of password retention by painstakingly remembering a password, then sticking with it indefinitely. But circumstances do arise in which a new password is appropriate. In fact, some Mac users change passwords as a matter of routine. Don't become a creature of habit, and don't hesitate to replace your password whenever it seems like the right thing to do. Although there's no need to be paranoid, anything that leads you to suspect a breach of security is probably cause for a new code.

If your workplace is situated so that others, even from a distance, can watch the keystrokes you make, you may want to change your password as a precaution against the possibility of someone detecting the access code from your finger movements.

With systems that are used by more than one person, passwords should probably be changed whenever someone who knows the current one will no longer be using the system—even if the person is utterly trustworthy and such a change is inconvenient for other users. It's not a matter of trust, it's a matter of human nature: your password remains very important to you and others who rely on the system it protects. But to a person who'll no longer need the access it provides, the password is now just a useless piece of information and will likely be handled by both the conscious and unconscious mind with too little care.

In this light, the policy of automatically changing passwords when someone stops using the system should not be seen as a sign of mistrust, but as a courtesy to those departing: the password becomes a piece of trivia that they won't have to worry about inadvertently divulging. And you won't have to worry about temptation striking in times to come.

DATA ENCRYPTION

Most encryption programs employ a methodology similar to that used by compression utilities—some applications offer both features in one package. The contents of a file's data and resource forks are broken down, analyzed, and substituted with a representational code; to reconstitute the file, the process is reversed.

Whereas compressors perform this task in the same manner every time, encryptors make up a new set of rules for each file, coding and decoding accordingly. The codes are not simple ones based on the substitution of one letter for another, and they allow for a vast number of possibilities and very complex coding schemes.

Just how complex? Well, some Mac products offer Data Encryption Standard (DES) as an option—the same method used by governments to protect top secret data. DES was considered the ultimate, unbreakable coding system until a team of specialists recently succeeded in breaking it. But the task required weeks of calculations on one of the most powerful mainframes in the world, so your encrypted data is probably safe.

If you're interested in data encryptors, you may want to look for one offering encoding standards suitable to your needs. Remember, the more elaborate the encryption method, the more time and storage space will be required. For example, Sentinel offers three: SuperCrypt, BlockCrypt, and the formidable DES. SuperCrypt is fast, space-efficient, and simple only in comparison to DES; both SuperCrypt and the more complex BlockCrypt will provide sufficient security for most Macintosh users.

Like password protectors, encryptors require that you establish and maintain passwords and user authorization lists. This entails the effective use of psychology as well as software. Encryption requires you to keep track of another topic as well: multiple passwords for multiple files (although you could apply one password to them all). If you send encrypted files to someone else you'll need to safely convey the password too.

HARDWARE SECURITY DEVICES

Macintoshes are compact, relatively lightweight, and easy to unplug and disconnect. Even the bulky Mac II isn't much bigger than the average TV or VCR. These features make the Mac easy to use, but they also make it easy to steal. Every computer theft represents a significant monetary loss, and that loss is compounded when your hard disk is among the missing; valuable if not irreplacable data may be gone for good. And if that's not frustrating enough, it's very likely that the data so priceless to you will be useless to the thief— most of it will end up deleted from the disk.

Computer theft is a grim occurrence, but it can be avoided. Small as it may be, the Macintosh can actually be secured more easily and thoroughly than most computers, thanks to its insightful design. Apple realizes that big value in a small box appeals to pilferers, so a *security slot* is included in the casing of all Macs. Although they look simple from the outside, security slots have internal spines that distribute weight across a large surface area; when a cable or chain is inserted, it can't be pulled out with anything short of a power winch, which would tear out a large part of the case as well.

There are a variety of anchoring packages. Some use hard-to-pick locks, some metal rods instead of cables, and others use especially strong adhesives to supplant the slots. Adhesives are useful when you don't want to drill holes through your furniture. The Mac II doesn't have the slots, so adhesives are the only option for Mac II owners.

Muzzle Your Mac

You can also use a hardware device to prevent others from inserting a floppy in a floppy drive (and perhaps thereby introducing troublesome software to your system). Ergotron sells a product called the Muzzle that covers the slot of a floppy drive—it could be handy if you are unable to lock away your entire computer.

PART THREE

WHEN SOMETHING GOES WRONG

Maybe you'll be lucky, and you'll never have a major hard disk problem. Or if you do, perhaps it will strike just moments after you've safely duplicated your data elsewhere.

Maybe you'll be lucky, but the odds are against it. Even the best-engineered, best-maintained hard disk is susceptible to Macintosh mishaps, software bugs, and wear and tear. Preventative measures will go a long way, but they're only part of the picture. You need to know how to identify and rectify a problem when it occurs.

In this section, we'll discuss the skills and tools necessary for doing just that. Chapter 6 shows how to diagnose and contain both software- and hardware-based malfunctions and how to ensure that they don't create complications throughout your system. Chapter 7 takes you through the steps of retrieving, repairing, and replacing your hard disk's contents.

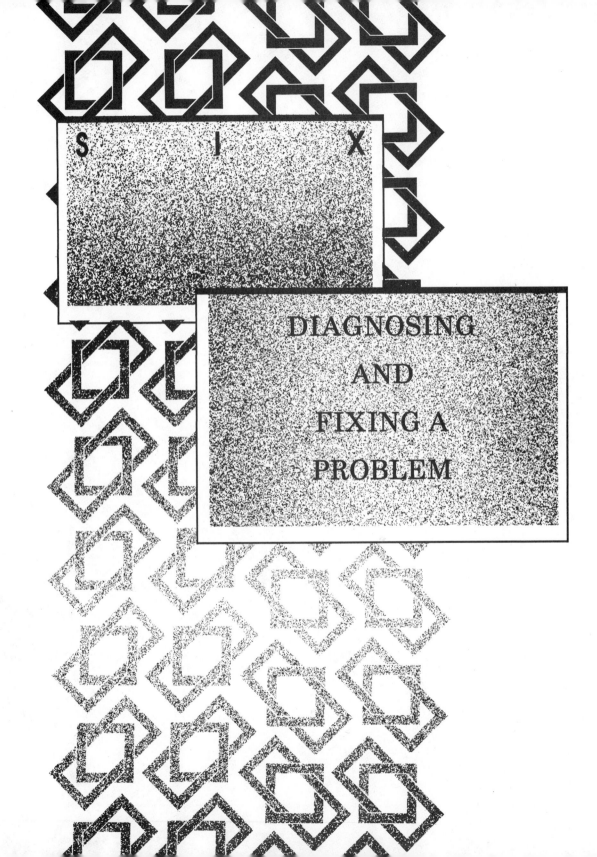

S I X

DIAGNOSING

AND

FIXING A

PROBLEM

To a Macintosh user, few things inspire more frustration and fear than a hard disk that isn't working right or not working at all. If your hard disk isn't working, this chapter should help you isolate your problem. And, even if you're certain you have diagnosed your problem, take care to read this chapter before moving on to Chapter 7.

You should read it even if you're not in the midst of a crisis—you'll be much more calm and confident when disaster does strike. It's easier to learn about tools and techniques under stress-free circumstances.

DON'T PANIC

When working with a damaged hard disk, the cardinal rule is don't panic.

First of all, a calming note of encouragement is in order. As long as you've taken the proper precautions, you can usually recover most, if not all, of the data from even the most severely malfunctioning hard disk. It's extremely difficult to accidentally damage or delete information. Besides, hard disks are safer than floppy disks because the storage media is more durable and it's very hard to completely erase the platters. Even intentionally erasing the platters may not obliterate all your data. If your hard disk is a lost cause, its contents are likely to be recoverable, although it may take time. Whatever you do, don't panic.

Instead, view the situation as an exercise in deductive reasoning. Tracking down and remedying a problem can be a valuable exercise, one that can make you feel more in control of the technology. And if your quest is unsuccessful? Then you'll have all the more motivation to be conscientious about data preservation in the future.

APPROACHING THE PROBLEM

In this chapter, you'll find step-by-step troubleshooting procedures for problems under these categories:

- Software-centered problems are those that appear in software. The term's ambiguity is intentional: although it appears in software, the problem may either involve or have originated in hardware.

- Hardware-centered problems are those that appear in hardware. Like the previous category, however, problems in this category may have originated elsewhere.

- Nonspecific problems are those that can't be attributed very clearly to either hardware or software. This category is more complicated than the others; problems here likely involve both hardware and software.

The troubleshooting procedures in this chapter aren't comprehensive, but they will help you track symptoms at least to the point where expert help is needed. Read through the whole of a procedure before following it. And don't proceed if you're unclear about any instructions. You may also want to read the other procedures in a category, since many have methods in common, and a step may be better explained in one procedure than in another.

THE BIG PICTURE

Although hard disks are our primary subject, effective troubleshooting requires looking at Macintosh technology as a whole: computer, peripherals, wires and circuitry, programs and other data, as well as the standards and assumptions by which they all operate.

Effective troubleshooting takes more than the ability to identify problems. It also takes an understanding of the factors behind those problems—the conditions in which they arise and the elements they may affect. Your computer system is an interdependent, interactive environment capable of functioning to a high degree of complexity. Hardware problems can trigger software problems (or vice versa), and secondary effects can beget still more repercussions. Some problems are neither hardware- nor software-related—they arise instead from an incompatibility between the two.

Incompatibility problems between software and hardware occur in all computer systems, but especially on the Macintosh, where the line between hardware and software (or cause and effect) is blurred. Its operating system is a hybrid of firmware and software. Even basic operations require the cooperation of a number of separate elements.

Given these conditions, even a clear-cut problem can have a number of causes, a number of consequences, and more than one avenue of treatment. The best approach to finding and defining a problem is to proceed by experimentation and exclusion, take nothing for granted, and start from the general and proceed to the specific.

With the right grasp of concepts as well as specifics, you can ferret out many more problems than could possibly be anticipated and addressed in this chapter. You can also spot and eliminate potential trouble before it occurs, or recognize one problem as a symptom of another, greater one.

Finally, your attitude and approach may make the difference between success and failure. Try to set aside the time to do the job right. Some improperly applied cures can cause further problems. By the way, don't be afraid to investigate the obvious. Is everything plugged in? Is the wall socket supplying current? Does that disk have a valid System Folder? Is a missing file really missing, or just mislaid? You'd be surprised how many seemingly major problems have a simple solution.

WHAT CAN GO WRONG

The technology that goes into a working Macintosh hard disk system can be grouped in three categories, mechanical, electrical, and software, each of which presents its own set of problems:

- Mechanical components, such as disk spindles, read/write heads, keyboards, monitors, and indicator lights wear out with use and the passage of time. Some of these, such as the power supply or the flyback transformer, have no moving parts but wear out nonetheless. Noticable changes in use—eccentric operation or an unusual noise—may signal an imminent malfunction, but some parts fail without warning.

   With few exceptions, most mechanical problems are beyond the skills of the average Mac user. Only expert technical know-how and authorized replacement parts can fix a mechanical problem, which is why these problems are among the most expensive to fix. The good news is that problems of this kind rarely cause a complete data loss. With the help of a specialist, even the contents of a ready-for-the-junk-heap hard disk can often be recovered.

- Electronic components won't wear out, but they can be damaged or disconnected. Electronic components include hard disk controllers, the Mac's CPU, the RAM, the ROM, the rest of the system's circuitry, and all the wires that connect these things together. Although an informed user can diagnose many electronic problems, in most cases only an expert can administer the cure. Most electronic components are solid-state and extremely small-scale, which means they are more likely to need replacing than repairing.

- Software is the most common cause of malfunctions. This is because even the simplest piece of software must thread an intricate course, interacting with the operating system, the Finder, and other software. Fortunately, software problems are the ones that lend themselves most easily to user solutions. Unfortunately, they're also most likely to involve data distortion or loss.

WHEN HELP IS NEEDED

In general, turn to the expertise of others after you've done as much to pinpoint a problem as you possibly can, and before you resign yourself to what seems to be a permanent problem. An Apple-authorized technician may not be necessary when your problem is related to software. Hardware problems are another matter—even the most brilliant and experienced Mac enthusiast may find a hardware dilemma beyond his or her reach.

When you have a problem, take advantage of the product or software manufacturer's customer service or technical support staff. Call them up—they are the best qualified and prepared to help you. Most companies rely on their customer service departments not only to please customers, but to detect bugs that eluded discovery in-house. Software companies in particular pay special attention to support services, and will likely treat you as a field tester as well as a customer. Be sure to find out if the troublesome product in question is still covered by a warranty.

Experts can tell you what needs to be done, but only you can decide if the data that stands to be rescued is worth the time, effort, and cost involved. Some documents are vital, unique, and irreplaceable; the loss of others may be a minor inconvenience or repetition of effort. As you make your decision, take stock of the resources you might use to recover the missing information: your archive or backup, miscellaneous floppies, the storage volumes of a co-worker, even printouts or a noncomputer source.

Finally, whatever you do, don't make matters worse by adding an ego problem to your computer problem. Don't let pride or fear of ridicule make you afraid to seek help. Whatever happened wasn't your fault. It was either an accident or a product flaw. And even if your problem resulted from an action you took, you're not to blame. An engineer or programmer should have seen to it that the action was impossible to take in the first place.

THE DYSFUNCTIONS: CRASHES, BOMBS, FREEZES, AND HANGS

Let's get underway by defining some of the terminology of malfunction. In general, a Macintosh problem is most likely to be a crash, a bomb, a freeze, or a hang.

Crashes   A crash is the most serious sign of a dysfunction. The term refers to a condition in which the computer is misbehaving profoundly and is essentially no longer a computer—a crashed Mac might display only a blank or garbled screen, or it may not work at all. Crashes are caused by a hardware or a software problem, or by a combination of both.

Head crashes are explained in Chapter 1.

If your screen suddenly shows the chaotic behavior characteristic of a crash, power down the Mac at once, even if it means flicking the off switch or simply pulling the plug. Don't concern yourself with unsaved data—it has probably been lost already. Most likely, a software error has profoundly confused the computer, or a crucial component has failed. Crashes of this sort shouldn't be confused with head crashes, which occur on the hard disk when a read/write head touches a platter and damages its surface.

Bombs   A bomb is when a variation of the dreaded bomb box appears on the screen. A bomb box may signal a problem as catastrophic as one that accompanies a crash, but a bomb box is also a sign that things are still under control. Bomb dialog boxes, part of the firmware portion of the Macintosh operating system, appear when the machine cannot interpret instructions it's receiving from the System or from an application.

When a bomb box appears, you really have no option but to select the OK button. This will automatically reboot the computer. Meanwhile, any unsaved data is lost to the ages. In some cases, you'll be lucky enough to see a different button, usually labeled Resume. Selecting this button is worth a try even though its effectiveness is a function of the application that was running when the bomb appeared. If things do return to normal, check for data loss before you proceed.

Not all bomb boxes are alike. The two-digit number in the lower right-hand corner, a code generated by the firmware, describes the circumstances that caused the bomb box to appear. This code is an important diagnostic tool, but don't rely on it to find out exactly what went wrong. The two-digit codes mean more to programmers than to users. Some applications also use the codes in other, specialized dialog boxes. In this case, the codes are usually preceded by a minus symbol.

The meanings of the more prominent codes in the bomb box are listed in Appendix A.

Freezes A freeze is when all of a sudden nothing happens. Everything on the screen, including the mouse cursor, freezes in place. When a freeze hits, check your mouse and keyboard connections, the usual culprits. If that doesn't work, borrow a mouse you know is operational. If that fails to unfreeze things, it's time to flick the switch or pull the plug.

Hangs A hang is when the screen refuses to change, although you can move the mouse cursor freely. A hang usually signals a failure by the active application or the System—either the System doesn't know how to carry out a command, or the application has begun a task that it can't complete. Look at the mouse pointer before you decide how to respond to this condition: if it's the standard pointer arrow or text-insertion beam (on the left in Figure 6.1), it's time to reboot. But if the cursor is one that indicates a wait is in order (a watch, a beach ball, or an hourglass), give the computer fifteen minutes or so before shutting down. Waiting cursors usually mean that the Macintosh is reading to or writing from memory, and a variety of circumstances can slow either process down to a crawl.

Figure 6.1: Common cursor forms

Crashes, bombs, freezes, and hangs are by far the most common signs of a crisis on the Macintosh; each announces unambiguously that something has gone awry. It's often convenient to refer to the four collectively because any of these symptoms may result from a given problem. That's why I use the term *dysfunction* only for circumstances involving bombing, crashing, freezing, and hanging.

USING DIAGNOSTIC PROCEDURES

The diagnostic procedures described in this chapter apply to floppies and other storage devices as well as hard disks. For the sake of clarity and conciseness, however, I will assume that you have at least one SCSI hard disk connected to your Macintosh, and that you are using the hard disk as your startup volume.

If you have an internal hard disk, you may not find the following as helpful as you would if you had an external hard disk. It's not that the principles explained here don't apply, it's that they may prove impossible to apply. A nonworking internal hard disk often means a nonworking Macintosh, and vice versa. Most internal hard disks have special built in or bundled problem detection resources. Check your user manual or contact the manufacturer's technical support staff if your hard disk isn't working.

One final proviso: the technology involved in diagnostic procedures is quite complex. You might find yourself at the end of a procedure with still no answer in sight. I will explain the most useful ways of tacking down a hard disk problem, but I can't anticipate and address every possiblity. If a problem remains elusive, don't give it up as a lost cause. Look at other troubleshooting information in this book and elsewhere. Remember, sometimes the answer doesn't come because the wrong question is being asked. Be sure you understand the nature of the problem and you can identify the symptoms.

TRANSPLANTING THE SYSTEM WITH INSTALLER

One remedy is often prescribed in these pages: replace an unusable or unreliable System with a fresh one. You may not relish the task of replacing the System, since yours probably contains customized features such as fonts and desk accessories, but it's well worth it if your hard disk isn't working.

Fortunately, you can perform a System transplant without losing your customized features: since 1987 Apple has included a utility called Installer on all System disks. Not only does Installer automate the process of System replacement or installation, it can do so without disturbing your customization. It will also optimize the new System to suit the model of Macintosh that you use. Here is how to use Installer.

1. Launch the program. Installer works on any mass storage device or floppy, but only when the volume's current System is not presently in use as the startup file.

2. Installer presents a single dialog box (Figure 6.2). Click to select the entry that corresponds to your Mac. If you have a

512K and 128K Macs can't use the Installer to change the System.

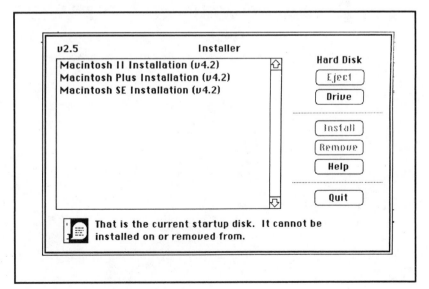

Figure 6.2: The Installer dialog box

512K or 128K Mac, however, your model is not listed. That's because Apple recommends sticking with an earlier version of the System. It's probably best to heed their advice. Trying the Plus option may work, but it won't produce any changes in performance.

3. Specify the target volume by clicking the Drive button and wait while Installer calculates the potential impact of a new System. If it determines that the volume has enough room for installation, you are then apprised of how much storage space will be taken up and how much will remain.

4. Give it the go ahead by clicking the Install button. You'll be informed when the job is done.

Just how does Installer tailor the system to your Mac model? It eliminates elements you won't need and modifies some dialog boxes so that Mac images will work with your machine. For example, a Mac II will receive display formats and CDEVs that make use of color, but a Mac SE or Plus will not—these extraneous features would only waste storage space.

SOFTWARE-CENTERED PROBLEMS

In order to address hard disk problems rooted in software, I've broken down the pertinent procedures into two categories.

- "Problems Upon Startup" covers the conditions that show up during the startup process, the period in which the computer is turned on and booted up, and all mounted volumes are brought online.

- "Problems with Applications and Documents," which appears later in this chapter, looks at the malfunctions that can occur when you open and launch documents, applications, and related files.

PROBLEMS UPON STARTUP

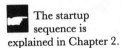 The startup
sequence is
explained in Chapter 2.

The startup sequence is one of your Macintosh's busiest times: the boot blocks have to be read and obeyed, and so does the PRAM. (The PRAM is described later in this chapter.) The System file has to be loaded, INIT commands must be carried out, the Finder needs to be launched, the desktop has to be rebuilt, and the FATs of all online volumes have to be confirmed and at the ready. The more that goes on, the more that can go wrong, and since the Mac is just getting down to work there's not much of a context in which to interpret a problem. The bright side of startup problems is that they almost never involve your stored data. Most announce a System or a hardware malfunction, not a loss of valuable work.

You can't be certain that a startup is successful until you've actually used the Mac for a while without incident. In any case, the first sign that things are proceeding as planned is the happy Mac icon (Figure 6.3).

Figure 6.3: The happy Mac icon

Introducing the PRAM

Numerous problems can plague the startup process, but the parameter RAM, or PRAM, is the culprit in most of them. The PRAM is the Mac's third type of memory. Neither permanent like ROM nor temporary like RAM, the PRAM is a 256-byte storehouse of data that the Mac uses, for consistency's sake, in its clock, calendar, and alarm settings. The PRAM is also used to configure the non-SCSI ports and all custom options available in the Control Panel (see Figure 6.4). Unlike regular RAM, its contents don't disappear when the machine is turned off. A battery located in a compartment in the back of the machine (the Mac Plus or earlier) or deeper within the workings (Mac II and SE) powers the PRAM. The PRAM can be corrupted or damaged.

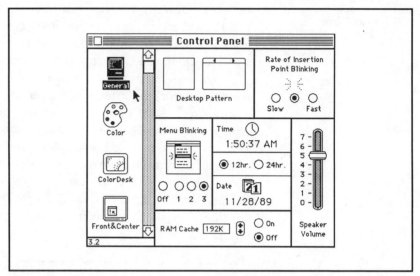

Figure 6.4: The Control Panel displays some of the functions controlled by the parameter RAM.

If a startup problem can't be attributed to any other factor, you can purge the PRAM and see what happens. If you have a Mac Plus or earlier model, your Mac's battery compartment is in the back, so purging is a simple matter; just open the door, remove the battery for three to five minutes, and replace it. Be sure to reset the clock and all your Control Panel preferences when you're through.

The SE and the Mac II's PRAM require a slightly more complicated purging procedure, since the battery is soldered directly to a circuit board and you can't remove it. PRAM purging on these models requires pressing the Option, Shift, and Command keys simultaneously while selecting the Control Panel from the Apple menu. This will trigger a dialog box (Figure 6.5).

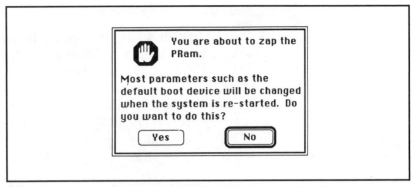

Figure 6.5: Attempting to purge the PRAM summons this dialog box.

This procedure takes a few moments more than most. Even if you choose not to follow through, the dialog box may remain on the screen for a half-minute or so.

No Screen Display

Another problem that sometimes occurs at startup time is that the Macintosh screen does not display the disk requested icon (Figure 6.6) after you turn the power on. If the screen is activated but blank, snowy, or garbled, shut down the computer, disconnect it, and take it to a qualified repair technician for servicing. You probably have a hardware problem in the monitor, in related circuitry, or in the CPU.

Figure 6.6: The disk requested icon means that the Macintosh has not received or recognized a startup volume.

Startup File Not Recognized

Even though a volume with a valid startup file has been placed online, the disk requested icon may either remain displayed or be replaced by the disk rejected icon (Figure 6.7). When this happens, check to see if the question mark in the middle of the icon is flashing on and off. If it isn't flashing, consult a technician. Most likely, there is a problem with the ROM. If it is flashing, shut down, take any SCSI volumes offline (by switching them off or disconnecting them), insert a floppy you know to be a valid startup disk, and try to reboot.

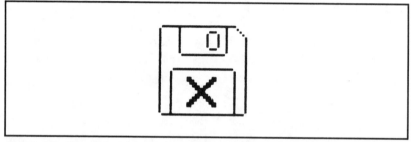

Figure 6.7: The disk rejected icon indicates that the Macintosh recognizes a volume, but not as a startup source.

If that does the trick, it's likely that the startup file on your SCSI volume has been rendered unrecognizable. Replace it, then reboot three or four times from the replacement before resuming business as usual. If a System transplant doesn't eliminate the problem, replace any INITs that may be in the System Folder.

If booting from the floppy doesn't help, or if the disk requested icon is replaced with the disk rejected icon, you'll need expert servicing. The problem may be in the ROM, the RAM, the CPU, or in connective circuitry.

Startup Aborted

What does it mean when the disk requested icon, the happy Mac icon, or the Welcome to Macintosh message box is replaced by the sad Mac icon (Figure 6.8)? The sad Mac icon indicates that a System file has been located, but the Macintosh is unable to read all or part of it successfully. Consult the icon's error code to determine if the problem lurks in the hardware or the software. If it's a hardware problem, call in the pros. If it's a software problem, shut down and take all SCSI volumes offline, then try to reboot from a startup floppy.

Figure 6.8: The sad Mac icon signals that system startup cannot be completed because of faulty or missing bootup data.

If you succeed in rebooting from a startup floppy, it's likely that the System file was somehow corrupted. Shut down again, put your SCSI volumes back online, and reboot with the startup floppy still in the internal drive. If the volume with the suspect floppy subsequently mounts (that is, if it appears on the desktop), replace its System file and see if it will function as a startup source. If not, reboot from the floppy once more, replace any INITs in the System Folder, and try again. If the volume does not mount, you may have a corrupted FAT.

Troubleshooting with the Sad Mac Icon

The sad Mac icon is more than an irreverent image designed to put a whimsical face on a sobering situation. It appears when the System file fails to pass certain diagnostic tests built into the ROM. Unlike the error codes of the bomb box, sad Mac codes can give you useful information about the nature of a problem. Underneath the icon itself is a six-character code (Figure 6.9). Let's look at the more important information it provides.

- The first two characters indicate if the problem is hardware- or software-based. The 0F code means a software failure, the 01 code means a ROM problem, and 02 through 05 mean the RAM is at fault.

- The last four characters are used to define the problem. If the first two characters are 0F, the final four pinpoint the type of

Figure 6.9: Codes underneath the sad Mac icon

software problem. If the first two characters indicate a RAM problem, the others will specify which memory chip isn't working properly.

From a user's standpoint, the sad Mac codes are most useful for determining whether the problem is in the software or the hardware. If it's in the software, a System replacement is in order; if it's in the hardware, you'll require repair services from an expert.

Alternating Icons

What to do when startup is aborted and the sad Mac icon appears is explained in the "Startup Aborted" section earlier in this chapter.

Sometimes during startup the disk requested icon continuously alternates with the happy Mac icon, and startup proceeds no further. This happens because what seems to be a file glitch can sometimes be an error in reading the file instead, and the Mac is instructed to try again. Odds are that your System file has problems, but the computer doesn't know when to give up and display the sad Mac icon. When the disk requested and happy Mac icons alternate, proceed as if the sad Mac icon appeared and startup was aborted.

Redundant Icons on Desktop

SCSI addresses are discussed in Chapter 2.

When five to seven copies of the same volume icon appear on the desktop after startup (Figure 6.10), it doesn't mean that your hard disk has miraculously multiplied. This dramatic quirk is caused by an online device with the SCSI address of 7, the same SCSI address as the Macintosh itself. You have misaddressed a device, and the computer is understandably confused. To clear up this problem, resist the temptation to click on any of these icons. Instead, shut the Mac down as soon as possible. Reset the device's address to a number between 0 and 6, then restart and check for possible data loss.

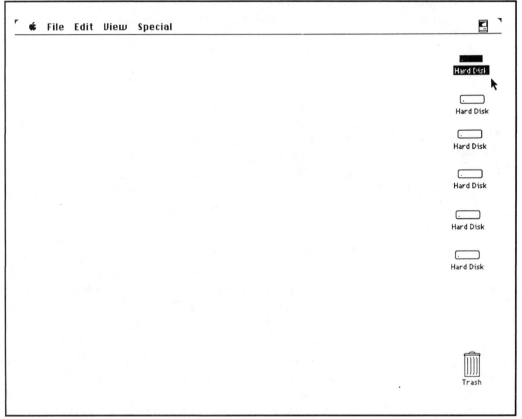

Figure 6.10: An incorrectly set SCSI address can cause the Macintosh to display multiple hard disk icons.

Volume Icon Missing

When the icon of an online hard disk or other SCSI volume is missing from the desktop, it's likely that the problem occurred for one of three reasons:

- The SCSI bus is faulty or disconnected.
- The volume hardware isn't working.

- The volume cannot be mounted by the Mac because it has a damaged FAT or directory.

Bringing a SCSI device online after the computer is turned on can cause crashes and hangs.

First, shut down the Mac and check all related cabling and power cards. Make sure that terminators are in place and that the connectors are firmly seated. Next, reboot and see if the icon in question appears. The computer confirms whether a volume is present on the SCSI bus only during startup. Bringing a SCSI device online at any other time may even cause crashes and hangs.

If the icon is still missing, look for signs of life on the hard disk itself. Is the fan working? Restart the Mac to see if you hear the usual sounds of the read/write heads moving from their parked positions. If your Mac has an indicator light, does it light up even intermittently during startup?

Repair utilities for mounting volumes and replacing directories are explored in Chapter 7.

If the unit is operating normally but the icon still refuses to appear, a repair utility may be able to mount the volume and replace the damaged directory or FAT. Until such a restoration has been carried out, don't use your Mac unless the hard disk has been safely disconnected.

Icon Missing from Directory

If the contents of a folder are normally displayed but the icons of one or more files are missing, first make sure that the file is really missing. Perhaps it was deleted from the volume, moved to another folder, or renamed. Use Find File or another mass volume search utility to see if it turns up elsewhere on the hard disk or on other volumes. If someone else uses your system, inquire if changes have been made unbeknownst to you. If the lost file is a document, browse through other documents of the same type to make sure it wasn't retitled. (Advanced search utilities like GOfer can do this for you.) If it's an application, persue folders under the View by Icon format and look for its distinctive icon under an assumed name.

ResEdit and other retrieval utilities are covered in Chapter 7.

If you're certain that the file has indeed disappeared, all is not lost—the volume directory may have lost track of it, or it may have been converted into an *invisible file*. An invisible file is one meant to be read by the Mac but not by the user, such as the Desktop file. Invisible files don't have icons, but they can be located, opened, and modified with utilities such as ResEdit.

Until you've completed your retrieval work with utilities, don't work with any other file on or add any new files to the hard disk. This will keep the Mac from writing over files that you want to save. If the Mac can't identify a file, it may not hesitate from writing over the sectors that the file occupies.

Changed Volume Icon

Sometimes the icon of a hard disk or other online storage volume is displayed, but its appearance is modified or another icon is substituted for it (Figure 6.11). When this happens, do not open the volume by double-clicking or any other means. Instead, shut down immediately and reboot under another System file. If the icon returns to normal, replace the System you used previously, but if the problem persists, this means the volume is unable to identify itself correctly. Use a repair utility to attempt repairs. At worst, you may need to reinitialize the volume, which obliterates its contents. Still, if you don't have a current backup all is not lost—some utilities allow you to copy the contents of a hard disk without formally mounting the volume.

Figure 6.11: A volume icon (left) changed from its normal appearance (center) and replaced by an inappropriate icon (right)

Changed Application Icon

Sometimes an application can be located in the View by Icon or View by Small Icon display format, but its icon has been either replaced with the generic default icon or modified (Figure 6.12). In the case of the default icon, don't proceed until you're confident that the application really has a distinctive icon. The vast majority have one, but many amateur and public domain programs display the default icon instead.

Figure 6.12: An application's distinctive icon (left) and the default icon (right)

If the application should have its own icon, something is amiss. Don't launch the application unless you're desperate. Instead, shut down and reboot with a fresh System. If this works, replace the first System. If it doesn't, throw away the icon in question and replace the application on the hard disk. If for some reason you don't have a copy of the application at hand and you're desperate to use it, you may want to risk launching it anyway; it's possible that only the code governing the icon has been corrupted.

Still, if you decide to launch, take a few precautions.

- Make sure you're running the Finder rather than Multi-Finder, since the possibility of corrupting other applications is greater under MultiFinder.

- Make duplicates of any documents you wish to use, and work only with them.

- Don't just forge ahead if everything seems normal after launching. Before getting down to business, make sure that the application can open, create, save, and reopen documents without mishap.

Does the application dysfunction when you launch it? Chances are the icon display instruction isn't the only fouled up part of the document's file fork. You might be able to pinpoint the problem with the help of a repair utility, but the inner workings of applications are usually too complex and convoluted for all but programmers and software engineers. You would probably be better off with a new copy of the application.

Changed Document Icon

Just as an application icon can be modified or replaced with a generic default icon, so can a document icon—it can be modified or replaced with the generic document default icon (Figure 6.13). When the default icon appears, it could mean that the document's *creator ID* has been deleted or damaged. This is the part of the resource fork that describes the icon that should be displayed on screen and tells the Finder to which application the document belongs; in other words, which application to launch when the icon is doubled-clicked. The damage is usually light when a default icon appears, but a misdrawn icon usually means that the resource fork has been corrupted.

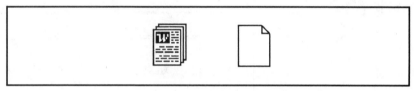

Figure 6.13: The distinctive icon of a document (left) and the default icon (right)

Whether the default icon or a misdrawn icon appears, the next step is to test the document's viability. First, open or create another document of the same type and use it to make sure that the parent application runs normally. Then return to the Finder and make a duplicate of the document in question (be sure to put the duplicate in the same folder as the original). Finally, launch the application and open the document's home folder.

If the Mac cannot open the duplicate document, turn to Chapter 7 for help in retrieving it.

Try to open the duplicate by using the Open... command to inspect it for absences and additions. The Mac might bomb or otherwise misbehave instead of opening the document. This means at least one of its file forks has been corrupted beyond the computer's comprehension.

On the other hand, if you can open the duplicate, inspect the contents. Copy what is worth saving to a brand new document. If the contents appear so garbled as to be unusable, it's still possible that only the resource fork is damaged but the data fork is intact.

Does the document itself show up in the scrolling field of the parent application's Open... dialog box? If not, it means that the program does not recognize it, and so it can't be opened. Some applications have commands such as Import or Open Other that can interpret various document formats; if any are available, they're worth a try.

After all this, if you still can't launch the duplicate, quit the application. Return to the Finder and try to launch the duplicate of the document by clicking on it directly. There's an outside chance that the parent application will be launched and the document opened. The odds are better, though, that a version of the dialog box in Figure 6.14 will appear. Don't let this dialog box discourage you; it only indicates that the document's creator ID is not recognized. The Mac can't launch the application because it doesn't know which one to launch.

If a dialog box now says that application is busy or missing, turn to Chapter 7.

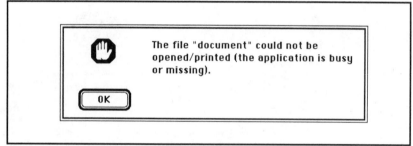

Figure 6.14: Dialog boxes of this type usually mean the application needed to open a document is missing, though the application may actually be present but unidentifiable.

Nonstartup Volume Not Recognized

Sometimes the startup process appears successful, but an online volume other than the startup disk is not mounted by the Macintosh and a dialog box appears asking if you want to initialize it (Figure 6.15). Probably no Macintosh message is more disheartening than this one. Yet, in just about every circumstance, the situation is not as dire as it seems. There's a lot you can do before taking the Mac up on its offer of initialization, and the odds are good that your data is not lost. The box's message doesn't mean that the volume is blank—just that the Mac can't figure out how to read it.

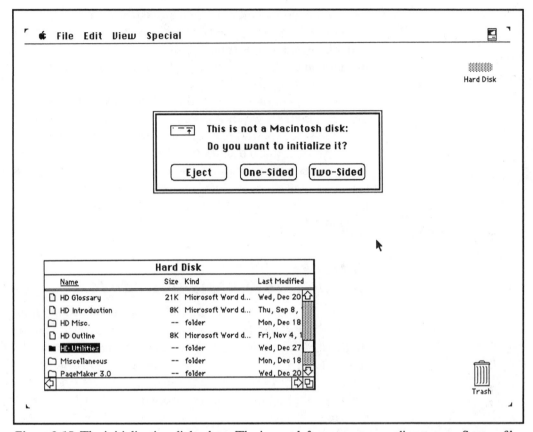

Figure 6.15: The initialization dialog box. The icon at left may vary according to your System file.

Most of the Macintosh user interface is designed to minimize problems—to make it as difficult as possible for you to unintentionally do something that has permanent consequences. That's why the Save Changes? dialog box appears whenever a file is closed, and why you must select Empty Trash after dragging a file to the Trash icon in order for the deletion to be carried out. But the initialization dialog box is one aspect of the interface that can be downright misleading.

The box's message is simple enough. It is triggered when you insert a brand-new floppy or a floppy previously formatted for a different kind of computer. But if it appears when you insert a floppy that you know is already Macintosh-formatted, do not initialize it except as a last resort.

The initialization dialog box creates problems because it presents only two courses of action: you either eject the disk or initialize it.

If the initialization dialog box appears after you've inserted a floppy you know is Macintosh-formatted, do not initialize it except as a last resort.

And initializing it will obliterate any current contents.

In most cases when the Mac asks you to initialize a hard disk you know is Macintosh-formatted, there's a good chance that much of the data on the floppy is still intact, but the FAT or the disk directory has been damaged or obliterated.

One last item of advice on the subject: if you decide to initialize a disk, choose the Two-Sided option only if the floppy is designated as a double-sided (800K) disk by the manufacturer. Single-sided 400K disks can be intialized on both sides, but resist the temptation to do so; the other surface of a single-sided disk is coated but not tested, and can fail at any time. (In fact, some are double-sided disks that didn't pass inspection on one side.) If it's worth saving, it's worth saving on a reliable floppy.

PROBLEMS WITH APPLICATIONS AND DOCUMENTS

Over the years, the Macintosh has garnered a reputation in some quarters for being idiosyncratic and problem-prone. The truth of the matter is, Mac models are extremely reliable but extremely difficult to program. Even a modest application has to conform to the user interface, has to access the right parts of the ROM Toolbox at the right times, and has to reshape its operations to accommodate dozens of variables, such as CPU types, RAM availability, or the presence of MultiFinder. These constraints involve more than mere conformity—they allow the Macintosh to place most of its resources at a program's disposal. That's why programming the Mac means following a boggling set of rules. And the more things need to be done right, the more they go wrong.

Launch-Triggered Dysfunction

Launches are problematic because so much needs to be done. The application must be located and loaded into RAM. Its instructions must be followed, resource files consulted, fonts accessed, windows drawn. Any new or preexisting documents must be displayed. And all this needs to be done smoothly and consistently in as few seconds as possible.

If the Macintosh bombs, crashes, hangs, or freezes when you attempt to launch an application, look to see if you are running under MultiFinder. Some applications that were written when the Finder's RAM management rules applied aren't compatible with Multi-Finder. Try starting up under the Finder and see what happens.

Next find out if the application is capable of running on your computer. The SE and Macintosh II models can run software created for the Mac Plus, 512K, and 128K models, but only if the software is written in accordance with Apple's programming protocols. Unfortunately, many software authors didn't strictly follow the protocols, and their applications make assumptions about hardware that don't hold true for the SE and Mac II. Some of these programs have since been rewritten for full compatibility; if yours is still being supported by the manufacturer, find out if an upgraded version is available.

It may also be that the opposite is the case—the application was written for Macintoshes more advanced than yours. Most software is written to be as compatible as possible, but some relies heavily on the superior computing power of the advanced models, and if this is the case, running your software on a Mac Plus or less would be impractical if not impossible. That's why it's a good idea to determine a product's limitations and system requirements before buying it. And before you choose between throwing away the application and buying a bigger Mac, find out if the program could run on your current model with the help of a hardware upgrade or enhancement; some extra RAM may be all you need.

Next see if the application is compatible with the entire contents of the System Folder. Some applications require a certain version of the System, the Finder, or a printer driver. Others are allergic to INITs and CDEVs. Check your manual or user guide, and while you're at it double-check for any other special requirements that you may have overlooked.

If, after all this, you still haven't found a solution, replace the application with a fresh copy. If your program incorporates lots of options and customizations that you don't want to lose (such as Microsoft Word), you might want to copy the suspect version onto a floppy instead of tossing it in the trash. Either way, before bringing on the new one, first take the precaution of removing the version in question from the hard disk. Don't use the update method that triggers the Replace current version? dialog box. You haven't ruled out the possibility that the fault lies in physical damage to the sectors, and replacing the current version may make the change by directly over-writing the sectors currently occupied by the application.

Does the new application work fine? If you hung on to the previous version in hopes of retaining its customization, bid it farewell and get started customizing the new version. The problem may have been in the software alone. If it was caused by physical damage to the plat-ters, your hard disk should automatically identify and avoid the affected areas in the future.

If the dysfunction is triggered by the new application as well, your System is suspect. Install a new one and try again; if that does the trick, go ahead and bring the vindicated version of the application back out of retirement. Be sure to give it a dry run before considering the case closed.

Application Can't Be Launched

What if you attempt to launch an application by double-clicking and you're unsuccessful, but the Macintosh does not dysfunction as a result. Instead, you see a dialog box announcing the Mac's inability to comply. In rare cases, the command is ignored entirely. If you're in MultiFinder, reboot under Finder and give it another try. If a doc-ument created by the application is at hand, try to open a newly made duplicate of it and see if that launches the application. Lastly, try to launch a few other applications residing on the disk.

Do the other applications launch without incident? Then the Mac considers this one to be damaged; it lacks too much of the necessary data for launching. Follow the procedures to remove and replace it.

If more than one application is unlaunchable, it's likely that either or both the Finder and Multifinder are faulty. If this is the case, a new System is called for. This may solve the problem but not repair the damage, so if the applications remain unlaunchable they should be replaced as well.

If you still aren't getting any results, there may be incompatibili-ties between the software and the contents of your System Folder. Check your user manual or any related documentation for System-related requirements or limitations.

Insuffient Memory for Launch

What does it mean when the Macintosh refuses to launch an application and instead displays a dialog box declaring that available memory is inadequate for the task? This happens when the application requires more RAM than your Mac is capable of supplying under any circumstances. An application's minimum RAM requirements are usually noted in the documentation and also in its Get Info box under MultiFinder. If you're short on RAM, you may want to look into memory upgrades.

See if the application is supposed to run on your Macintosh configuration. It may be that other software is gobbling up a disproportionately large amount of RAM. Maybe your Mac has been looking for more memory than the application actually needs. If you're running under MultiFinder, the quickest solution is to free RAM by quitting one or more of the applications currently open, or by shutting down and rebooting under Finder. But even if these steps work, don't conclude that you'll always need to launch the application under such stripped down circumstances; you might be able to manage the memory allocations instead. Likewise, if you still don't have enough RAM under Finder (or if MultiFinder wasn't a factor in the first place), look into the issue of memory allocation under Multi-Finder (explained later in this chapter).

If it still can't launch, it's time to take a look at the big picture. Select the About the Finder... entry from the Apple menu. Unless you're using an outmoded System, you should see a dialog box like the one in Figure 6.16.

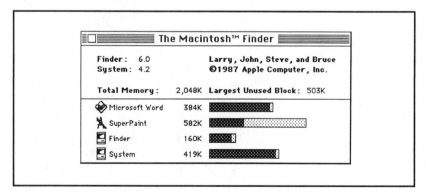

Figure 6.16: The About the Finder... dialog box

This box represents an up-to-the-second snapshot of your RAM: the amount with which your Mac is equipped, the amount currently being used by the System and the Finder (and other applications when you're running under MultiFinder), and the amount remaining in reserve. If the Largest Unused Block figure is less than the application's recommended minimum, your only recourse is to seek a simpler, less memory-hungry situation in which to launch.

The most effective way to free more memory is by cutting frills from the System Folder. If you have a monitor capable of displaying color or gray scales, deactivating those options may make a big difference. Other candidates for deactivating are custom backgrounds, special sound files (for warning beeps and the like), many INITs and CDEVs, fonts, and DAs. Remember, the criteria is appetite, not size: you're looking for software that affects the Mac's general operations and is likely to be kept in RAM. In extreme situations the best solution is to keep a bare-bones System Folder on a floppy, then use it to boot up before launching the application.

Managing Memory Allocation Under MultiFinder Under Multi-Finder, an application's Get Info box displays the minimum memory recommended by the programmers and the actual amount the Macintosh will use. These two figures usually start out the same, but as you use the application the Application Memory Size is increased or decreased. Why do the two figures differ? Because the minimum RAM recommendation is based on normal performance expectations, but the demands you place on the application may be higher than normal.

If you've got the memory to handle it, increase the memory allocation to speed up the application's performance ability. Performance will improve when you're dealing with large, complex, or multiple documents; more RAM means the computer spends less time reading from the disk. You'll want to consider allocating more memory for your word processor if you're writing a book, or for your desktop publishing program if you're working with scanned photographs.

Decreasing the memory allocation may be called for when RAM is at a premium or when you are unlikely to push the application to its limits. Remember, though, that RAM reductions can be risky: memory inadequacies tend to announce themselves with dysfunctions. Nevertheless, most applications can run with an allocation smaller than the official minimum. The threshold varies, however, and the only way to find it is through trial and error.

To change the memory allocation in either direction, just delete and replace the current figure (the box it's in is actually a text field). Remember that your specifications are retained as a part of the file and will be passed along with any duplicates you make.

Dysfunction During Document Opening

The utilities described in Chapter 7 can also help with problems that occur during document opening. The "Launch-Triggered Dysfunction" and "Changed Document Icon" sections appear earlier in this chapter.

When you launch an application by clicking on one of its documents and it results in a system dysfunction, try to find out if the dysfunction is triggered by the document or the application. If you can't open other documents or launch the program directly, treat the problem as though you would a launch-triggered dysfunction. On the other hand, if the problem seems related to the document, see if you can open it from within the application by following the procedures you would use if a changed document icon had appeared.

Application Not Found

Launching an application by clicking on one of its documents results in a dialog box indicating that the parent application cannot be located. But is the application actually present? Use a volume searcher like Find File to make sure. And don't just check the startup volume—look at any other volumes on which the application might reside. If it doesn't turn up, make a fresh copy from your backup stock. If it is present and accounted for, try opening the application directly.

Document Has Been Changed

One common problem is that a document opens as usual, but its contents have been garbled, reformatted or otherwise modified. This happens because system changes can cause some documents—especially text and page layout files—to alter drastically. For example, text created in one font may be displayed in another one. Some programs require separate font installations, so check to see if the original font has been installed in your current System file, and that the document's application can access it automatically. If line spacing and page breaks have also been affected, check the Chooser desk accessory (Figure 6.17) when the document window is open and active. The Macintosh reconfigures page setups for different printers; a document created under LaserWriter will be different from one created under ImageWriter. Selecting the proper printer driver will correct page setups.

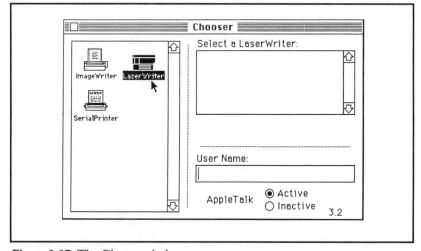

Figure 6.17: The Chooser desk accessory

If system changes aren't the trouble, it may be that the document itself is fine and that the changes are due to the Mac's incorrect reading of its text and resource forks. If you suspect that this is the case, close the document immediately, making sure to choose No in the Save changes? dialog box.

When you've returned to the desktop, make and open a duplicate of the document. If the unwanted changes were transitory, things should be normal, but if the problem persists, the changes are permanent. If you have a backup copy, use it instead.

Dysfunction Upon Command

What does it mean if the Macintosh bombs, crashes, freezes or hangs when a command is given—document saving, opening, cutting and pasting, etc.? In the case of freezes and hangs, the Mac may have unexpectedly run out of RAM in the middle of carrying out the command. Wait a few minutes to make sure that it isn't just taking its time. Next, shut down and try again, only this time take steps to free up memory before launching the application. If you were running under MultiFinder, restart with Finder. If you had multiple documents open within the application, try accessing only one at a time.

To track down the incompatibility that might have caused a bomb or a crash, see the "Launch-Triggered Dysfunction" section of this chapter.

If the dysfunction is a bomb or crash, then an incompatibility needs to be tracked down and eliminated. Follow the same steps you would to treat a launch-triggered dysfunction.

Document Will Not Print

Suppose you attempt to print a document and the Macintosh responds as expected but does not print the document. First, check your printer to see if it is correctly connected to the Macintosh. After you've checked the connection, open the Chooser and make sure the right printer driver has been selected. Does the appropriate printer driver appear in the Chooser? Make sure that the driver is present in the uppermost level of the System Folder.

HARDWARE-CENTERED PROBLEMS

So far, we've been tackling problems in much the same way that a detective unravels a mystery—using deductive reasoning, zeroing in on the answer by methodically looking for clues, then following a trail of telltale signs until it leads us to the culprit.

But some Macintosh and hard disk problems don't lend themselves to the deductive approach as easily as others. Sometimes there's only one symptom: something doesn't work. Perhaps your entire system is inoperative and unresponsive. Or perhaps there are some vital signs—a flickering screen, a fan that sounds different. Maybe the Mac itself, patiently displaying a disk requested icon, suddenly is oblivious to the hard disk that serves as its startup volume.

In these cases the powers of deduction are still useful, but the diagnostic process is much shorter and less enlightening. Problems caused by accidental disconnection or misconnection are easily diagnosed and remedied by the average user; beyond that, there's usually little to do except identify and isolate the malfunctioning unit, then seek qualified help.

If it's your hard disk that's out of order, bear in mind that only the most severe physical mishaps pose a threat to data. Even when data is damaged the loss is usually far from total.

If the casualty is your computer itself, take heart from the fact that all Macintoshes have been designed with few parts, all of which are readily available, easily replaceable, and, for the most part, relatively inexpensive. And just because your Mac isn't working, that doesn't mean your work needs to come to a standstill—almost all serviceable hard disks can be transferred, temporarily or otherwise, to another system.

TRANSPLANTING YOUR HARD DISK

When your Macintosh is ailing but your hard disk is healthy, downtime doesn't have to be unproductive time—you can connect your hard disk to another Mac and resume business as usual.

Transplanting an internal hard disk can be a problem. Some can be removed only by experts, and some cannot be installed in all Macs. Still, any external SCSI device can be attached to any Mac as long as it has the appropriate port, even if the unit is formatted for a model different from your temporary computer.

Internal or external, a hard disk initialized on the Mac II may perform more slowly with a less powerful model. The reverse, however, does not hold true: when a Mac is connected to a hard disk with a slower interleave, it simply conforms to that ratio. The drive may be capable of speedier performance, but only reformatting will tell.

When you hook your internal hard disk up to a new Macintosh, take care to resolve any potential SCSI address conflicts. Make sure that devices already attached are daisy-chained with your new hard disk. Remember, the Mac searches the bus for startup files in descending address order from 6 to 0. If a daisychain already exists, make sure your intended startup volume has the highest address in the daisychain. And when working on a multivolume system, try to avoid later confusion by making sure your files don't accidentally stray onto other volumes.

NOISES

Keep your ears tuned for unusual noises—they're often the first sign that things aren't operating right. Not every strange sound signals an imminent crisis, but a change in the normal repertoire of clicks, hums, and whirs may be a symptom. Here are the basics of sonic diagnosis.

- If the hard disk sounds consistently louder than before, if it emits new noises when you turn it on, something is wearing out. Perhaps it's just the fan, but it could also be the drive's motor, or the shaft and bearings assembly on which the platters rotate. Whatever it is, you need to have your hard disk serviced right away. If the fan is acting up, it can be replaced. And if the noise comes from the main mechanism, that's a sign that it's almost worn out—most are engineered to work quietly for most of their useful life.

- If you hear a strange noise when the Macintosh is reading and writing to the hard disk, there has probably been a loss of function in the mechanisms of the read/write heads. Many external hard disks have an indicator light that flashes when reading and writing are underway, so it's easy to tell when a strange noise occurs during a read or write operation.

  Problems with the Read/Write heads call for immediate servicing. If the read/write heads are hovering a fraction of an inch above the platter surface, any further deterioration will make the heads crash down on the platters, obliterating your files and rendering the entire drive beyond repair.

- If a sound usually made by the Mac or hard disk is absent, but the units themselves continue to operate, it is probably because the fan isn't rotating. You can keep using your system long enough to save your data and shut down, but don't push your luck any further. Get expert servicing before getting back to work.

  Some users intentionally disconnect the fan; in doing so they reduce the life of their equipment. A computer may be able to operate for days or weeks with no visible mishap, but the hard disk is another matter entirely: a lot of moving parts are packed into a tight package, and the combination of closeness and motion creates heat. Fans are so important in hard disks that some manufacturers have designed fail safe mechanisms into their units to make the entire drive stop working when the fan stops.

Mac II Startup Tones

If the Macintosh II does not function when switched on, but emits a brief series of musical tones, this signals a failure somewhere in the RAM resources: the ROM has run a check of available memory prior to beginning the startup process, and it has discovered something amiss. This is a special feature unique to the Mac II. In the Mac II, RAM is stored on *single inline memory modules* (SIMMs), a series of microchip units that snap into place in an array of eight slots. This modular approach makes for easy upgrades: SIMMs can be removed. The ones with more memory can be snapped in their place in less than a minute. But since they're not soldered, they can also come loose. When RAM emits a series of musical tones, it may mean that one or more SIMMs is burnt out or broken. It may also mean a SIMM isn't correctly connected, or one of the eight slots are vacant. Apple recommends you leave memory problems to authorized service sources, but you may want to check first for a simple solution. Opening your Mac II doesn't void the warranty. Look for loose SIMMs, but first make sure you know what to look for.

PERFORMANCE PROBLEMS

Some problems don't announce themselves in a cataclysmic fashion. They arrive gradually and often subtly, so that you don't recognize they are there until months or years have gone by. When a Mac's performance begins to decline, your first reaction might be to take it in stride; it's natural for things to slow down as they get older, so why complain?

Yet, unlike cars and old gray mares, your system should function at the same performance level it had when it was brand new. Mechanical parts may wear out and need to be replaced, but even the most tired component on the Macintosh shouldn't slow down normal functions such as launching applications and opening files. When a slowdown occurs, don't just live with it—solve it.

Slow Startup

Suppose the Macintosh's startup process takes considerably longer than it used to. Most likely, the Mac is taking more time because it's has more to do. INITs, CDEVs, custom screens, and other specialized software add time to the startup sequence; elaborate software can take several seconds to load. Check your System Folder to see if you're loaded with start-up related files. Either remove a few if your system takes too long to start up, or accept the delay.

On the other hand, if a stuffed System Folder doesn't seem to be the problem, it's possible that some part of the data used in the startup process has developed a glitch, one so minor that the Mac handles it without notifying you. Has anything that should have been accessed been skipped instead? If so, replace it; if not, install a fresh System.

If you're still having no luck, check the connectors and addresses of any SCSI devices—something might be sending confusing signals down the SCSI bus, which is read by the Mac during startup. If the slow booting up process is followed by an overall slowness, open the About the Finder box to find out if the total amount of RAM has diminished. If it has, you've got a hardware problem.

Slow Access Time

File fragmentation and its treatment are explained in Chapter 8.

Sometimes basic Finder operations, such as the opening of folders and the launching of applications, seem slower than before. Is the problem confined to your hard disk? Comparisons with other volumes may help you determine if it is, although most floppy disks will run even slower than the most sluggish hard drive. If your hard disk has been in use for a while, the problem could be file fragmentation, which is easily remedied.

Does the Finder work slowly on other volumes as well? Maybe it doesn't have sufficient RAM to work with. If you're running under MultiFinder, open the About the Finder box to see if something else is hogging the memory. If you're running Finder only, check that same box to confirm that the overall amount of RAM is what it should be.

Slow Document Handling

Suppose a command that affects large portions of a file (for example, scrolling or cutting and pasting) takes an unusually long time to carry out. If you're under MultiFinder, look in the About the Finder box for signs of cramped memory conditions. You may need to quit other applications—and possibly even MultiFinder itself—in order to free up RAM. If there isn't a RAM crunch, perhaps the application's memory allocation has been set unnecessarily low. Check this figure in the application's Get Info box, and reset it if necessary.

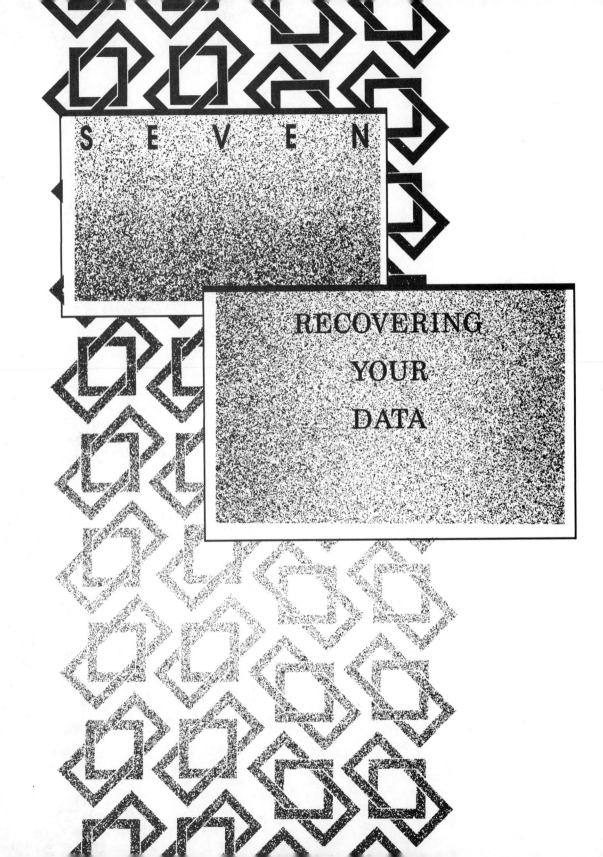

SEVEN

RECOVERING

YOUR

DATA

In the previous chapter, our concern was the general principles of troubleshooting and treatment. But sometimes a problem can't be fixed. Instead, it has to be coped with, and its permanent effects have to be minimized as much as possible. That's the concern of this chapter.

If you're reading this in order to find the solution to a crisis you're having, don't proceed until you've followed the diagnostic instructions in Chapter 6. The procedures and resources detailed in this chapter are of a more drastic variety. You probably shouldn't undertake them until you've exhausted the simpler recourses from the previous chapter. Still, if the simple methods fail, the information contained in this chapter may save your data.

THE FOUR TYPES OF DATA LOSS

Unfortunately, the Macintosh offers about as many opportunities to lose data as it does to preserve it. Whether stored on a hard disk, a floppy, or other media, Macintosh files are vulnerable to heat, strong magnetic fields, and just plain human error. In general, incidents of data loss fall into the four categories described below.

DIRECTORY DELETION

A file is considered "deleted" whenever it has been expunged from your Macintosh system, whether intentionally or by oversight. Deleting is usually achieved by dragging a file icon to the trash and selecting Empty Trash from the Finder's Special... menu.

But putting a file in the trash is not the only way it can become missing in action. The Mac doesn't always wait for the Empty Trash command to delete a file you have disposed of. Even if you place a file in the can without selecting Empty Trash, the Mac may delete the file automatically when it needs the storage space occupied by the trashed file. Likewise, the contents of the trash are purged whenever you launch a new application or shut down the Macintosh.

If you have inadvertently trashed a file, your first step should be to open the trash by double-clicking on the trashcan in the lower right-hand corner of the desktop. (The trashcan is a file folder like any other, albeit one with a unique icon.) If the trashcan is bulging, this means it still contains the files you jettisoned. You can drag them back onto the hard disk if you want to. On the other hand, if the trashcan is not bulging, this means either no files have been thrown away during the current work session or files placed in the trash have been deleted.

The Mac will delete a file placed in the trash if it needs the extra storage space occupied by the file. So files can be deleted from the trash even when the Empty Trash command is not activated.

Some applications give you the option of deleting files without placing them in the trash. This option, when it exists, is usually accessible from the File menu. When you delete a file directly from the File menu you do not have a chance to reverse your decision. As soon as you select OK, the file is removed from the disk.

In most cases, a file deleted from a hard disk is not actually expunged from the drive's magnetic-media platters. Instead, the file's entry is removed from the FAT (file allocation table). This is why it cannot be displayed on any level of the volume's directory. The actual data remains in the platter's tracks and sectors until the space it occupies is needed to store a new file. Only the information needed to locate the file and display its icon—what is contained in the FAT—is removed from the hard disk when you delete a file.

DIRECTORY DAMAGE

The second most common way data is lost is due to directory damage. This happens when the information needed to locate, display, and manipulate a file is mangled or misplaced and the file simply disappears from the Mac's directory. The file itself is not really lost—it continues to occupy tracks and sectors on the volume's storage medium. But because the computer cannot access it appropriately, neither can you.

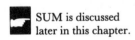 SUM is discussed later in this chapter.

Still, directory damage can be counteracted with full-featured utilities like SUM (Symantec Utilities for the Macintosh). The key to minimizing loss is to act swiftly and take steps to restore a file as soon as you note its absence. When you notice that directory damage has occurred, don't save another file to the same disk. If you do there is a good chance you will not be able to recover your missing data.

FILE OVERWRITTEN

Overwriting means that a file has been deleted from a directory and that one or more of the tracks and sectors it used to occupy is occupied by other files. Overwriting happens when the information needed to locate a file is lost but you save a new file to the hard disk anyway. The reason you should try to recover a missing file at once, and not save any other files in the meantime, has to do with overwriting: if you save a new file it may occupy space that holds data from your missing file.

A completely overwritten file cannot be reconstituted by any utility. All the information it stored disappears once it is overwritten. But in some cases, when the entire file has not been overwritten, the remaining sectors can be gleaned for content and meaning (especially with text-only documents). For the most part, however, an overwritten file is permanently lost. Even if you can recover part of the data, it may not include the critical information that the application needs to open and use the file.

HARDWARE CRASHES

The final and most profound type of data loss is caused by a physical problem. Data is lost when the magnetic storage media of a hard disk are stressed or corrupted or when intricate mechanical parts collide. A head crash or disk crash occurs when a Macintosh is dropped from a table or subjected to similar strains and the drive's read/write heads come into contact with the platter surface.

Head crashes and disk crashes have significant consequences. Usually the data in the affected sectors is obliterated. Moreover, the sectors themselves usually become unusable. Fortunately, most hard disk drivers will identify damaged sectors and automatically avoid using them.

WORKING WITH DISK FIRST AID

Disk First Aid, Apple Computer's recovery utility, has been included in the System software package since Version 5.0. Although it's not as effective or capable as some third-party programs, it's worth using if you have it on hand. At the very least it's a good step to take before resigning yourself to reinitializing a volume and losing all the data on it.

Disk First Aid has a limited scope. It addresses only volume-level problems, not file-level ones. Although it is useful when you cannot mount a volume or when the directory has been damaged, it won't help you recover a corrupted application or a deleted document. Use

Disk First Aid when you attempt to mount or open a volume and a Reinitialize? dialog box appears. It may provide the solution when your system won't boot from the hard disk.

Using Disk First Aid is a simple matter of launching the application and designating a volume for testing (Figure 7.1). The default choice is the floppy disk in either the internal or external drive, but if

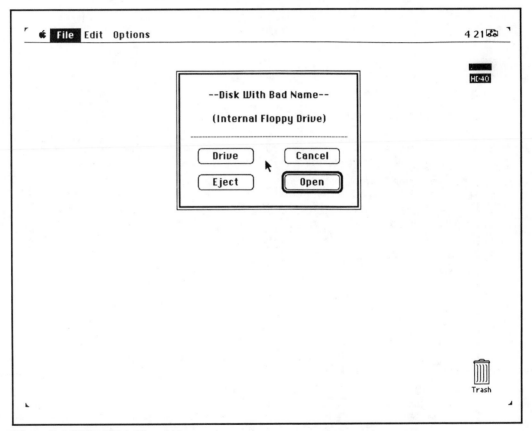

Figure 7.1: Using Disk First Aid

there isn't one, Disk First Aid selects the current startup volume. To choose another drive, click the Drive button until its name appears in the dialog box. You can select and test a volume even if the Mac cannot mount it on the desktop. If the disk drive with the unmountable disk is connected and operational, this means that your problem lies with the disk, not the drive, and Disk First Aid will tell you so by announcing a "Disk With Bad Name." This usually means that the disk is not readable by Disk First Aid.

Make sure that the volume you're testing was not used as the startup and is not write-protected. Disk First Aid can examine a startup or write-protected volume and verify any damage, but it can't make repairs. If you need to run Disk First Aid on your hard disk, copy it to a bootable floppy and start the system with the floppy.

To use Disk First Aid:

1. Click on the Start button (Figure 7.2). This puts Disk First Aid through its paces.

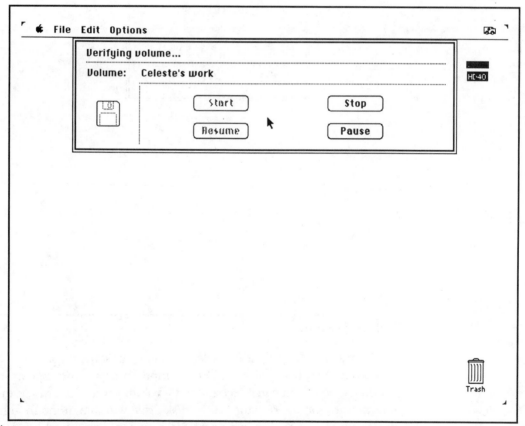

Figure 7.2: Testing a volume with Disk First Aid

2. The Ready to Start message is replaced by the Verifying volume... message. It takes Disk First Aid a couple of minutes to check a hard disk. The program does not display the wristwatch or other wait cursor while testing is underway. You can abort, pause, or resume testing at any time by clicking the appropriate button.

3. When Disk First Aid is finished checking, a diagnostic message appears.

Here are the primary diagnostic messages:

Disk First Aid does not work on volumes formatted under the MFS standard. Since the Mac uses MFS standard on most 400K disks, Disk First Aid might not work with them.

- "Finished. No repair necessary." This is supposed to mean that the volume is normal, but often it means that the volume needs repairs beyond those Disk First Aid can offer.

- "This is not an HFS disk." This message can be misleading. Disk First Aid doesn't work with volumes formatted under the earlier MFS standard. The message might mean you have an MFS volume, but it could also mean you have an HFS volume whose formatting has been garbled or corrupted. The Mac uses the MFS standard on 400K disks unless you hold down the Option key during the format operation. This means that Disk First Aid will not work on the majority of 400K disks.

- "Verification completed, but cannot repair system disk." This ambiguous message doesn't seem to recommend making repairs, but that's what it really means. It appears when the startup volume is the one that's been tested. When you see this message, reboot from a floppy or other volume that contains Disk First Aid, relaunch Disk First Aid, and go through the steps again. This time, you should get the "Disk is in need of repair..." message.

- "Disk is in need of repair..." This one appears in its own dialog box and means that Disk First Aid thinks it has identified and can fix the problem. You have nothing to lose by clicking the Repair button—there's no danger of losing any data on the volume. At worst, Disk First Aid will do nothing; at best, it will mend your disk. In a minute or less, Disk First Aid will say if the repair was successful or unsuccessful. If it declares a success, don't assume that all your troubles are over. Quit the application and see how the volume functions from the Finder. Open some files to be sure that all of their contents appear correctly. If Disk First Aid was unsuccessful, it's time to try another utility.

WORKING WITH SUM

By far the most potent tool for data recovery is SUM (Symantec Utilities for the Macintosh). SUM is one of the most useful acquisitions a Mac hard disk owner can make. Not only is it effective in retrieving lost data, it can also provide preventive protection against further loss.

SUM is not a single utility but a group of programs and files controlled by the Disk Clinic application (Figure 7.3). Each program can be used individually, but Disk Clinic is the hub from which the other programs are initiated.

A glance at the Disk Clinic main menu shows the numerous features Disk Clinic has to offer.

- QuickCopy makes high-speed duplicates of floppies.

- HD TuneUp tests and repairs file fragmentation to speed up hard disks.

- Symantec Tools offers another set of specialized utilities with which to recover text files.

In this chapter we'll concern ourselves with Disk Clinic's data recovery capabilities.

RECOVERING DELETED FILES

With the Recover Deleted File(s) command in SUM's Disk Clinic (Figure 7.3), you can resurrect many of the files missing from a volume, even those that you intentionally disposed of. The program works as well on floppies as on hard disks, and on SCSI as well as non-SCSI drives.

It's important to note that the Recover Deleted File(s) utility can only treat files missing from the directory, not damaged files still

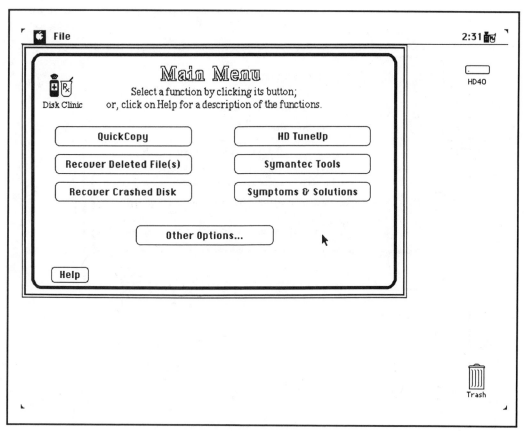

Figure 7.3: Disk Clinic controls the Symantec Utilities for the Macintosh (SUM).

present in useless form on the disk. Still, if the tracks and sectors of a deleted file have not been overwritten yet, Recover Deleted File(s) will try to retrieve all or some of them. The utility has an extremely high success rate in doing so.

File Restoration with Guardian Installed

After you launch Recover Deleted File(s), the first question Disk Clinic asks is whether you installed SUM's Guardian feature previously on the target volume (Figure 7.4). If you did, retrieving your files will be much easier. That's because Guardian doesn't have to search the tracks and sectors themselves. It has a file in which it stores the relevant information.

What to do if you didn't previously install SUM's Guardian feature is discussed later in this chapter under the heading, "File Restoration Without Guardian Installed."

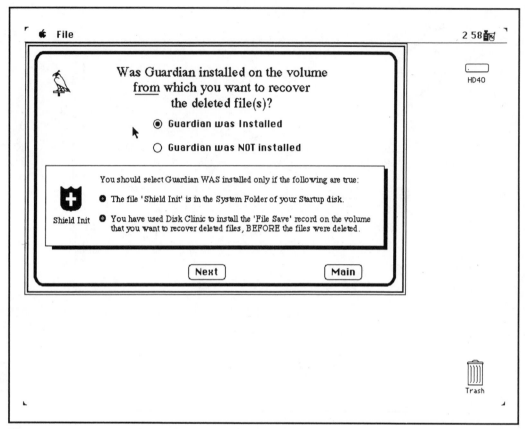

Figure 7.4: The initial screen of SUM's Recover Deleted File(s) application

Selecting the Next option quickly produces the UnDelete Window (Figure 7.5). In the center of the window is a scroll box that lists all deleted files that can still be identified as files. The Size, Date, Time, and Status columns list as much information as can be gleaned about the deleted files.

Note two different type styles in the UnDelete Window. Files in roman type can be recovered but files in italic type have already been overwritten and can't be recovered. The Status column also indicates if a file is lost: *Y* means the file is recoverable and *N* means you're out of luck. Another important column is Size—a 0 in this column may indicate that a file is recoverable but devoid of data.

To restore a recoverable file listed in roman type, select the file and click either Un-Delete File or Un-Delete All Files. After a minute or

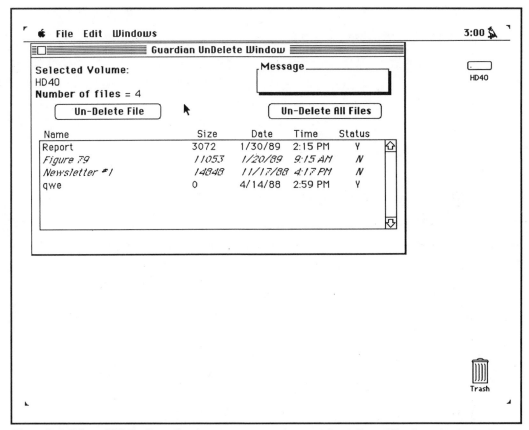

Figure 7.5: When SUM's Guardian is present on a volume, deleted files will be listed in the UnDelete Window.

two, depending on the size of the file or files you want to recover, the utility will inform you when the restoration process is complete.

Restored files are placed in an automatically generated folder on the volume's root level. The first is named "A.Guardian Recovered Files" (Figure 7.6). All subsequent files placed in the folder will have the same designation but the next available alphabetical prefix, which in this case would be "B.Guardian Recovered Files."

File Restoration Without Guardian Installed

If it so happens that you didn't install Guardian and its companion INIT, Shield, on the volume whose deleted files you wish to restore,

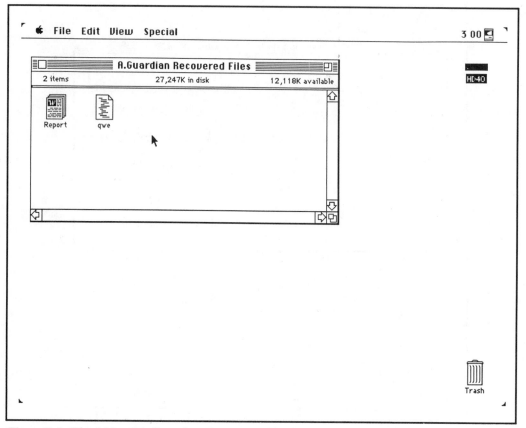

Figure 7.6: The folder "A.Guardian Recovered Files" generated by Recover Crashed Disk(s). Note that some restored files now display generic icons.

SUM may still be able to save the day. SUM can search the surface of the hard disk platters for deleted but identifiable files. The search takes longer than it would if you had installed Guardian. Moreover, SUM will only tally files that can still be retrieved, not files that have been overwritten.

Guardian has a file containing all the information about deleted files on the hard disk, but since you don't have the Guardian feature you have to provide the information yourself so SUM will know how to recover the deleted files. SUM needs to know which drive you want to recover the files from and what type of drive it is. If the files you want to recover are stored on a hard disk, SUM needs to know whether it is a SCSI drive.

After you supply SUM with the needed information, you have two choices for recovering files (Figure 7.7).

- Scanner makes a fast, cursory search for deleted files. Allocate approximately ten minutes per 20 megabytes.

- Signature Scanner makes an in-depth search that consequently is slower—about twenty minutes per 20 megabytes.

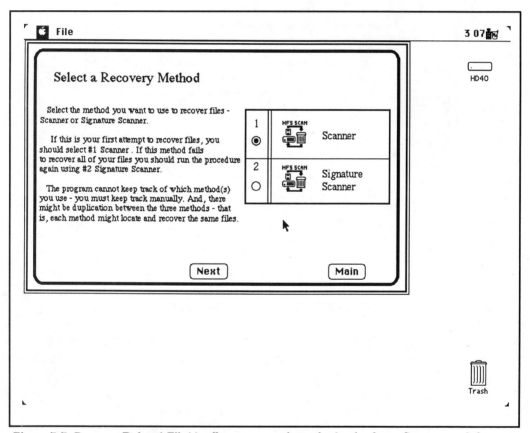

Figure 7.7: Recover Deleted File(s) offers two search methods, the faster Scanner and the more thorough Signature Scanner.

⊙ Be careful not to store recovered files on the same volume from which they were deleted.

Try Scanner the first time around, then Signature Scanner if you didn't get the results you wanted.

Recover Deleted File(s) also asks you to select a destination volume for storing recovered files (Figure 7.8). I strongly suggest that this

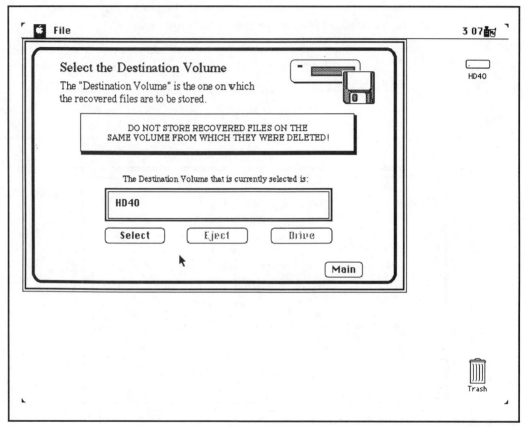

Figure 7.8: SUM asks you where to store the recovered files.

volume not be the one from which the recovery effort was made.
When you retrieve and store on the same volume and file corruption
is present, you'll only make things worse. You're better off saving
elsewhere, such as on a floppy. Files recovered from a volume are
placed in a root-level folder labeled ''A.Recover.'' When the actual
recovery is underway, a display on your screen keeps you apprised of
its progress (Figure 7.9).

RECOVERING ENTIRE VOLUMES WITH SUM

SUM also offers a method for recovering entire volumes which
have become unusable—volumes that Disk First Aid cannot repair.

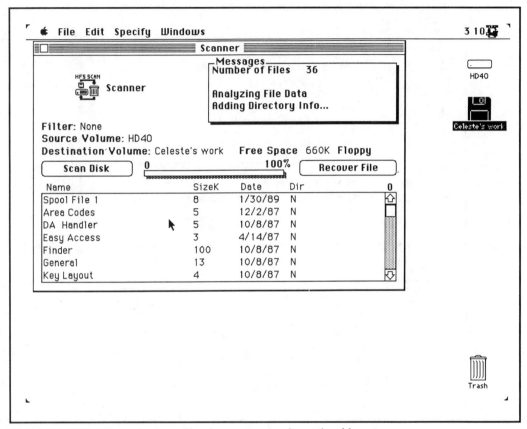

Figure 7.9: SUM lists only those files that are presently retrievable.

If Guardian is installed on your System Folder, you can use SUM's Recover Crashed Disk button to reclaim data in many cases. You can use it even if Guardian was not installed—SUM will scan the disk and try to recover as many files as possible (Figure 7.10).

Volume Recovery with Guardian Installed

Recovering volumes without Guardian installed is discussed later in this chapter.

If Guardian was installed on the system before the hard disk crashed, you need to answer only a few questions before using SUM to recover your deleted volume. This is because, when Guardian is installed, SUM knows where to look for all the information it needs to recover the disk. Tell SUM that Guardian was installed by selecting the Recover Crashed Disk button (see Figure 7.3).

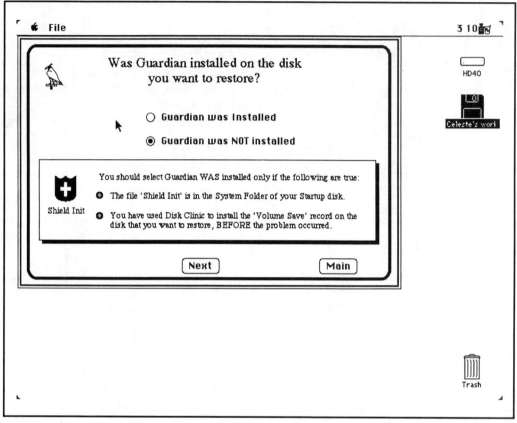

Figure 7.10: SUM can recover crashed hard disks whether or not Guardian was installed.

Next, SUM asks what type of device you are trying to recover. SUM can recover crashed floppy disks, hard disks, or partitions. SUM should be able to recover partitions made with its own partition driver and partitions made with drivers from hard disk manufacturers.

Besides knowing the type of device from which it is recovering data, SUM needs to know how the device is connected to the Mac. If the device is connected with the SCSI port, that is all SUM needs to know. On the other hand, if the device is not a SCSI device, you need to tell SUM exactly what type of disk drive it is. A list of the drivers that SUM knows how to access is displayed; select your disk drive from the list. If your drive is not on the list SUM may not be able to recover data from it.

Next, select which physical drive it is. After the drive has been selected you need to tell SUM whether Guardian's information is stored on the drive you are trying to recover or on another disk drive.

Now that SUM has all of the information it needs to recover the volume, you are presented with the Guardian Restore Window (Figure 7.11). From here you tell Guardian where to locate the volume restore file—the file with the information SUM needs to restore the volume. It can be located either on the crashed hard disk or on a different disk. You specified its location when you first installed Guardian. To restore your hard disk, click on the Restore button and make SUM go to work. If everything works right, you will get a Done, Quit and Reboot message in the message box in the upper right-hand corner of the Guardian Restore Window.

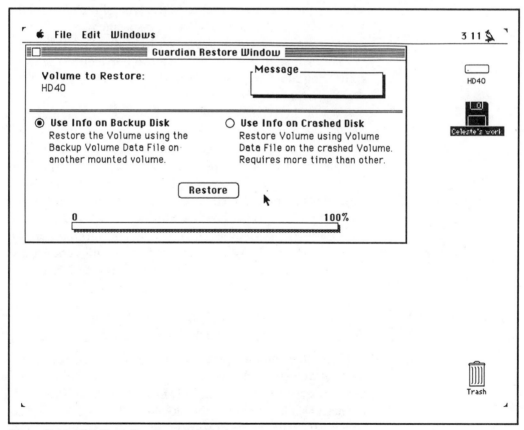

Figure 7.11: The Guardian Restore Window

Volume Recovery Without Guardian Installed

Even if you didn't install Guardian on the volume, SUM's Recover Crashed disk feature can scan a disk and attempt to copy files to a healthy volume. It takes more time than it would take with Guardian, and you need to give SUM more information before proceeding. Also, the operation won't be as thorough as it would be with Guardian installed. Still, you may be able to save vital files from a crashed volume. Even without Guardian installed SUM should be more successful at recovering crashed disks than Apple's less sophisticated Disk First Aid application.

Once you tell SUM that Guardian was not installed, SUM asks you a series of questions similar to the ones it would ask if you had installed Guardian. The big difference between SUM alone and SUM with Guardian installed is the type of retrieval method used. With Guardian installed, SUM has a specific place to look for all the information that it needs to recover from the disk. But when Guardian is not installed, you must choose between three methods for recovering files from the crashed volume—HFS Recover, Scanner, and Signature Scanner (Figure 7.12).

Two of the recovery methods, Scanner and Signature Scanner, are the same ones you use for recovering deleted files without Guardian installed. Scanner makes a quick, cursory search and Signature Scanner makes a slower, more in-depth search. The third method for recovering files, HFS Recover, is the one you should select the first time you attempt to recover a volume. Afterwards you should try using the other two methods. As the files are recovered, they are copied to a working volume, such as another working hard disk or to floppy disks. Each method should recover different files, although some files will be recovered twice or three times, once by each method.

RECOVERING TEXT DOCUMENTS

If you have a word-processed file that you cannot open with the application you used to create it, you may still be able to recover the file by converting it into text-only format. Although you will lose any formatting information you included in the original, and some garbage may appear in the document, all of the text should remain in the

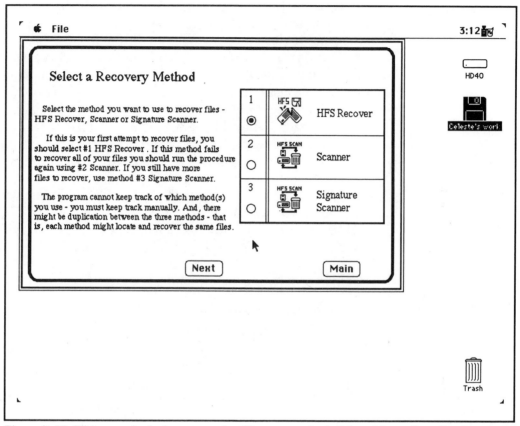

Figure 7.12: Three methods for recovering files on crashed disks without Guardian installed

file. In any case, cleaning the garbage text out of the file is a lot easier than retyping the entire document.

You can convert a document to text-only with any program that allows you to edit the application type of a document. What we are going to do is take the file and make its document type into a text-only file. Once you have converted the file to text-only, you should be able to open it with almost any word processor or with a text editor such as Apple's Teach Text application. The Symantec Tools part of SUM will allow you to change document type to text-only, as will the MacTools program. A number of public domain programs are also available for converting the document type to text-only.

To use SUM to recover a text file, either select the Symantec Tools button from the Disk Clinic application (see Figure 7.3) or launch the Symantec Utilities application from the Finder.

When Symantec Utilities displays its menu bar, select Edit File from the File menu. Now specify the copy of the file that you are trying to recover. If a dialog box appears mentioning End of File or Nothing in Fork, ignore it and select OK. Next, you need to tell Symantec Utilities to make changes to the file on disk. The default setting is not to make any changes to the file. You should select Write Lock from the Edit menu. After you select it once it should not be checked anymore. This is what you want, for Write Lock to be activated.

Now it's time to change the file type. Select Edit File Attributes from the File menu. In the Type field, enter the word *TEXT* (Figure 7.13). This tells Symantec Utilities that you want to change the file type to text-only. Select the Change button and the new file type should be written out to disk. All that is left is to quit the Symantec Utilities by selecting Quit from the File menu.

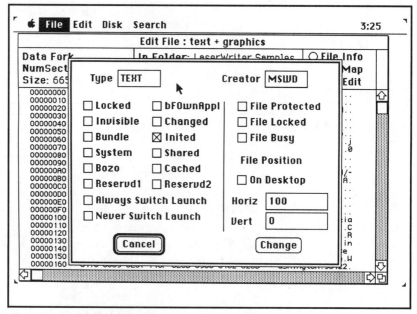

Figure 7.13: The Edit File Attributes dialog box

Now your file can be opened from any word processor or text editor. All you need to do is open it, remove any extra characters that were inserted, and reapply whatever formatting you want. Be careful in case any passages you deleted from the text have reappeared in the document. Some word processors, such as Microsoft Word, leave text in the document after you delete it (although the text is marked as deleted so the program knows not to display or print it). After converting to text-only, some of this deleted text may reappear.

USING RESEDIT TO EXAMINE RESOURCE FILES

Data forks and resource forks are examined in detail in Chapter 3.

ResEdit is a powerful utility developed by Apple for examining and modifying the resource fork of an application. Every file on the Macintosh has two distinct components: the data fork and the resource fork. A file may have an empty data or resource fork, but the fork still exists even when empty. Resource forks contain the information that an application needs to operate, such as icons, pictures, text, dialog boxes, menus, and computer codes. Data forks hold the data that you create with an application. This is not always the case, however. It is possible to store applications in the data fork and documents in the resource fork. Sometimes a file is stored on both the data and resource forks. An empty file might be stored on both an empty data and empty resource fork.

Only use ResEdit to examine duplicate copies of applications. You don't want to damage the originals.

Using ResEdit to modify the resource fork of an application or document can be dangerous—you might make the application nonfunctional. Only use ResEdit to examine duplicate copies of applications. Before you launch ResEdit, select the document that you want to examine from the Finder, then select Duplicate from the File menu. Now, when you pick a file from ResEdit, be sure to pick the duplicate of the application that you want to examine.

ResEdit also provides an easy way to locate hidden files that are in the directory but do not show up from the Finder. In its file list, ResEdit includes hidden files along with the others. For example, when you look at the root level of the hard disk you should see the Desktop file. Desktop is a hidden file that the Finder uses to assign documents to the appropriate applications.

When you launch ResEdit you are presented with a window listing all the files at the root level of all mounted disks (Figure 7.14). To move into a folder, just double-click on the one you want. This will open a new window listing all the files in the folder (Figure 7.15). To move towards the root, click the close box on each window until you are at the desired level. Once you have the file you wish to open in a window, double-click on it. ResEdit will show another window listing all of the resources in the file (Figure 7.16). (A complete list of resources appears in Appendix A.) To examine a resource, click on its name. Either the resource or a list of resources will appear. If a list of resources appears, click on one of them and the resource itself should be displayed.

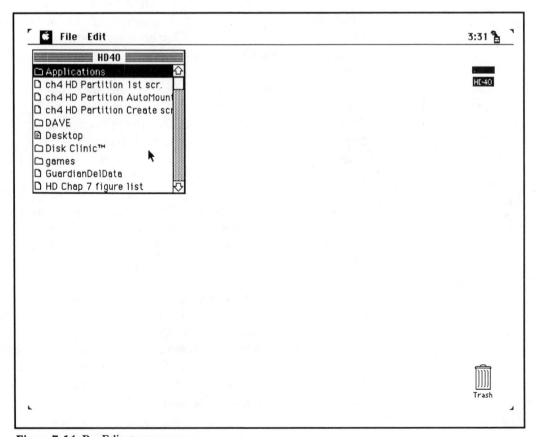

Figure 7.14: ResEdit startup screen

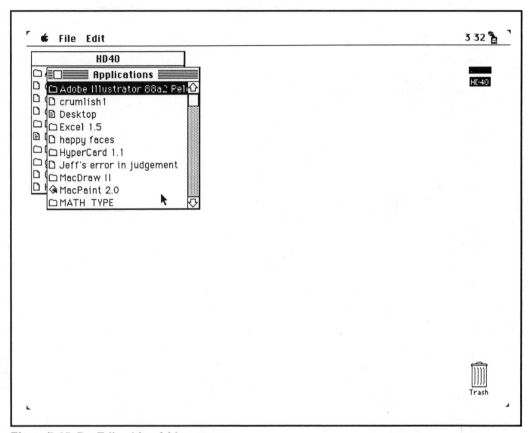

Figure 7.15: ResEdit with a folder open

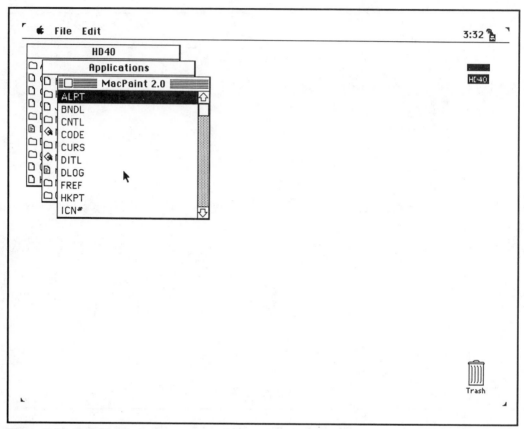

Figure 7.16: ResEdit displaying resources in MacPaint

P A R T   F O U R

MAXIMIZING

HARD DISK

PERFORMANCE

Even an excellently organized hard disk can become sluggish over time. What was once an eminently logical directory layout can become a morass of file clutter and folder confusion. I'll show you how to remedy these matters in Chapter 8, which has advice on streamlining tactics such as reformatting and eliminating file fragmentation. Chapter 9 details a number of the fringe benefit functions made possible by your hard disk—macro keys, printer spoolers, and applications that augment or replace the Finder. Chapter 10 looks at system growth and how to incorporate new hard disks or other devices in your SCSI setup. Chapter 11 looks at the various issues raised when you hook up your Mac and hard disk to a network.

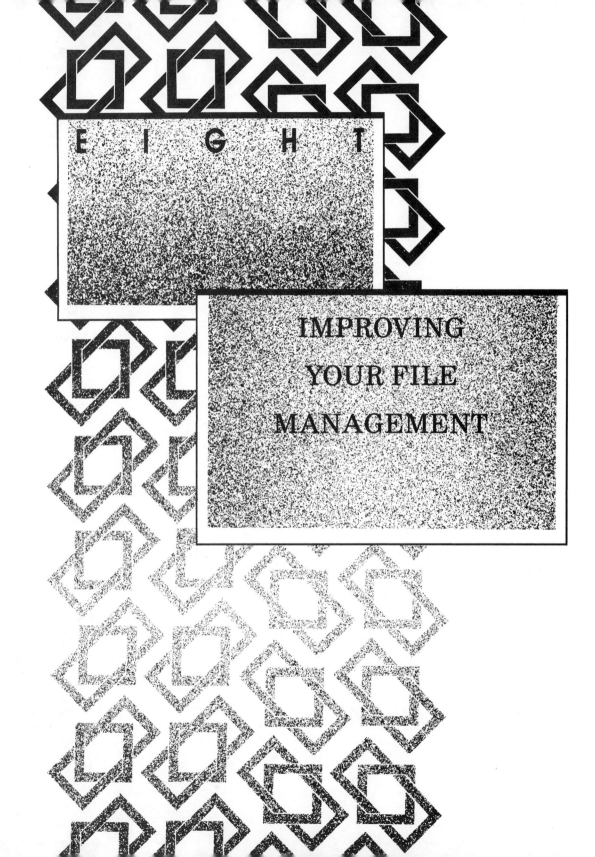

EIGHT

IMPROVING YOUR FILE MANAGEMENT

Organization is merely the first step in getting the most out of your hard disk; the next step is maintenance. Keeping your hard disk optimally useful is an ongoing process that requires you to make critical evaluations of your file and folder organization and the performance of your computer.

When necessary, you will have to make adaptations.

Time changes things, and your hard disk is no exception. A directory structure that once suited your needs perfectly may become antiquated and awkward to the point where you stick to it only by force of habit. Files and folders that were once in logical locations may soon languish in out-of-the-way, undeserved obscurity. And all hard disks exhibit signs of impaired performance at some point—they slow down noticeably as the hours of use take their toll.

Fortunately, symptoms of computer slowdown and poor organization are easy to identify and remedy. With the proper techniques and tools, you can keep your hard disk tuned and in shape for years to come.

EVALUATING ORGANIZATION AND PERFORMANCE

When it comes to file management, the first question you should ask youself has to do with clarity and convenience: is your organizational setup still easy to use and understand? You may find yourself misplacing files or plowing through an excessive number of subfolders. The second question is about capacity and capability: is the hard disk sluggishly taking taking more and more time to carry out basic operations? Perhaps it is filled to the brim or overloaded with little-used files. Because organization problems tend to evolve gradually, many users don't identify them so much as acclimate to them. You should make a habit of evaluating the organization and performance of your Mac. Keep a running critique in the back of your mind while you're at work.

WHEN TO REORGANIZE

In most cases, file management is a matter of refinement, not renovation. In general, your hard disk's organization should change when your needs change, a process which can be slow or sudden depending on your circumstances. A modification can be as subtle as placing a much-used application directly on the desktop while consigning another to a folder, or as radical as completely reformatting the disk and starting afresh. Changes should be based on need, not on crisis. In other words, update your setup when it becomes more of a hindrance than a help, instead of waiting for it to become a complete handicap.

A good time to address file management issues is during your backup or archiving duties. This way, you can inspect your files and preserve them at the same time. If you use a cataloging utility, check for little-used files by scanning the date last modified field. Some mass volume search utilities can also compile a list based on the date last modified.

Here are a few rules for managing files:

When you move an application, be sure to move its resource files as well.

- Relocate currently used files and applications if they are three or more folders down the directory hierarchy—in a folder nested in a folder nested in a folder. If you want your file at hand, place it directly on the desktop; if you need it for a current project, place it in a new, specially named folder on the hard disk's root level. And if you expect to be working with it regularly, give it its own folder. For instance, MacDraft may currently be in your ''Graphics'' folder nested in if your ''Applications'' folder, but if you find yourself using it often you'll want to create a root level ''MacDraft'' folder instead.

- Create a new folder only when there isn't an easier way to group related files together. It's easy to create and populate new folders, but if you overorganize, your files will be tidy but hard to locate. Remember, each new folder will be on another level of the hierarchy, which means another set of mouse-clicks and keystrokes to execute.

  In general, you don't need to create a new folder if you have only one or two files to place in it. If you want your files to be grouped in some way, use the view formats. If the folder displays icons or small icons, arrange the files in a row or in a cluster. Add special prefixes to the file names to see them in the View by Name format. An easy way to place a file at the top of the file dialog box is to use a nonalphabetical prefix, such as an exclamation point (!) or an asterisk (*). (See Figure 8.1 for examples). If you have a color monitor, you can use the View by Color format to identify related files at a glance (but you must then be sure to keep the colors current).

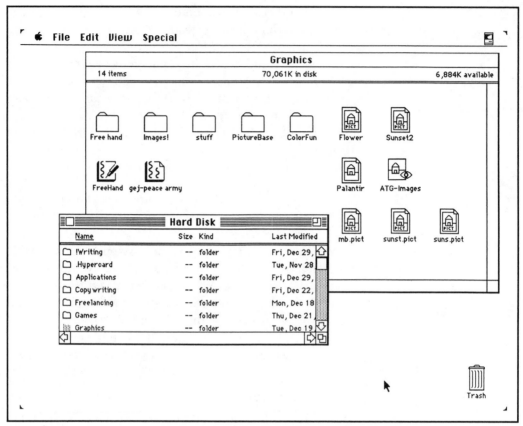

Figure 8.1: Clustered icons (above) and specially prefixed file names (below)

- Remove files from the hard disk when you need more space or when you're confident you won't need to access them very often. When a file clearly belongs in your archive, simply make a floppy copy and delete it from the hard disk, perhaps compressing it first.

When is a hard disk full? In general, a hard disk performs fine until the drive is filled to more than 75 percent capacity. You'll know it's time to clean house when your disk reaches the three-quarters mark. And even if you need to use more than that amount, don't worry. Performance is really a matter of directory size, not of how much storage space is occupied. For example, a drive containing a few very large files will run faster than one with many small files that add up to the same size. You can, in theory, fill up your hard disk right down to the last byte; in practice you should start looking for a new storage device when your hard disk approaches 90 percent capacity.

FILE FRAGMENTATION

Probably the biggest correctable factor affecting hard disk performance is *file fragmentation*. File fragmentation, a natural result of consistent use, occurs when the Mac cannot store a complete file in congruent sectors on the hard disk. Instead, the file is divided among several sectors throughout the platter. A fragmented file takes longer to access because the read/write heads have to move several times in order to carry out an operation (Figure 8.2).

Files are usually read into consecutive sectors when a hard disk is newly formatted. As the hard disk fills up, however, sectors vacated by deleted files become the most convenient locations for new data. This is because single available sectors rarely match the storage needs of a new file, so a conglomeration of them must be compiled in order for the new file to be read to the disk. As you remove and add more and more files to your hard disk, the bulk of the platter surface becomes a haphazard patchwork of files in scattered segments.

DETECTING AND TREATING FRAGMENTATION

The first sign of file fragmentation is slower performance, but it's possible to identify and eliminate file fragmentation long before it starts affecting your work. A number of diagnostic utilities can detect and eliminate file fragmentation. They can also provide useful information about the state of your hard disk's performance.

Using HD Tune Up

HD Tune Up, a part of the Symantec Utilities package for the Macintosh, is accessible either directly through or by way of the Hard Disk Clinic application. The utility tackles fragmentation in two steps. First it analyzes the need for optimization, then it carries it out. In the analysis procedure (Figure 8.3), HD Tune Up reviews the locations of current files, calculates how much sector space is available, and produces an overview of track and sector efficiency.

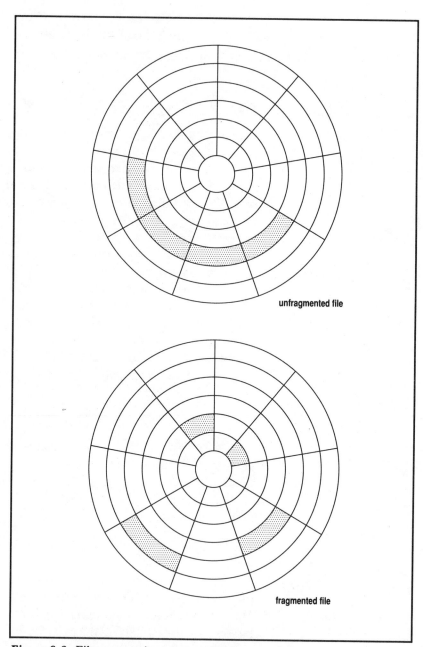

Figure 8.2: Files occupying consecutive sectors (above) can be accessed
quickly; fragmented files (below) take longer to access.

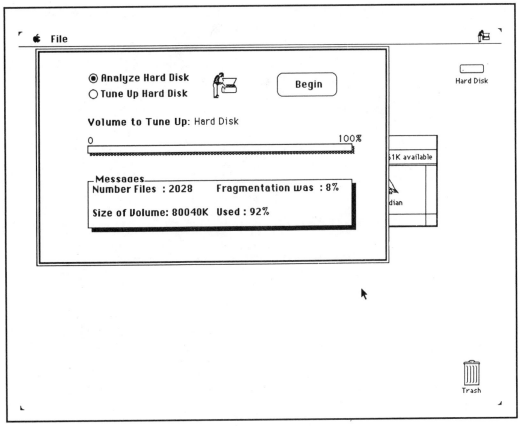

Figure 8.3: Analyzing file fragmentation with HD Tune Up

If HD Tune Up or a similar utility reports that more than 2 percent of your total files are fragmented, it's probably time to defragment your files. Up to 10 percent can be fragmented before the drive's performance becomes noticeably slower, although it's best to play it safe and defragment at 2 percent, especially since the often-used System and desktop files are usually fragmented first.

Optimizing with HD Tune Up takes a while—about three minutes for every megabyte of occupied space on your hard disk. Don't run the program under MultiFinder, as you want to give HD Tune Up as much RAM as possible. It will rearrange, copy, and regroup as many files as possible to free up contiguous tracks and sectors.

The dialog box (Figure 8.4) keeps you apprised of the defragmenting progress and identifies files that cannot be defragmented. Hit the

Don't run HD Tune Up under MultiFinder because the utility needs as much RAM as possible.

Stop button at any time if you decide not to complete the entire task. (HD Tune Up may take a few moments to finish what it's doing.) The newly defragmented files will stay in their new locations, and the other files will remain where they were. You can return and finish up at any time; there is no danger in leaving the hard disk in this state.

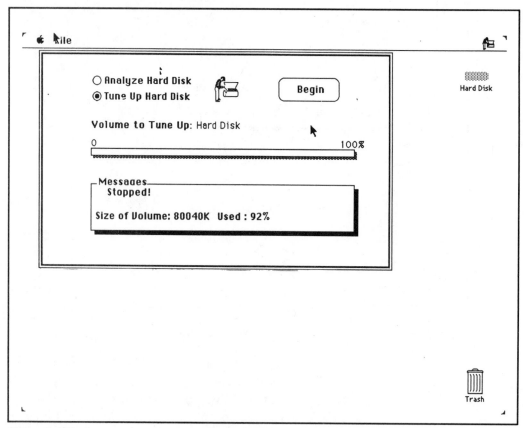

Figure 8.4: Defragmenting files with HD Tune Up

HD Tune Up has a few significant limitations. It can't move locked files. Locked files are those with the box labeled Locked selected in their Get Info windows. You might want to unlock them temporarily before proceeding. Also, partitioned volumes of 600K or less usually can't be optimized, although most partitioned volumes can.

Defragmenting Without a Utility

Another, more drastic way to defragment your hard disk involves reinitializing. This method doesn't require a special utility. If you've made a complete backup of your files, you can select the Erase Disk command from the Finder's Special menu and reinitialize your hard disk. You'll have to boot from a floppy disk, though, since the Mac will not erase a startup volume.

Once the hard disk is purged and reconfigured, the tracks and sectors will be blank and the fragmentation will be eliminated. Now you can use the backup software's restoration capabilities to replace your files. Most programs will copy the files in consecutive fashion. However, most people prefer a defragmenting utility to reinitialization. Restoring from a backup requires a lot of time and floppy shuffling. Besides, you're gambling on the soundness of the floppy copies when you reinitialize.

MAKING FORMAT MODIFICATIONS

You can attend to organizational concerns casually and gradually, but performance changes require more radical methods, most of which involve format modifications. Don't undertake format modifications lightly—they take time and they often involve completely replacing the contents of the hard disk. In fact, you probably shouldn't reformat unless it's clearly necessary. And even if file replacement isn't called for, don't proceed without making a complete backup of the drive. Here are the circumstances under which you should reformat:

When using the same hard disk on different Mac models, configure the hard disk for the more powerful one.

- Reformat when you transfer your drive to a different Mac model. If you are transferring to a more powerful Mac, reformatting will produce a notable improvement in performance. On the other hand, if you are transferring to a less powerful Mac, reformatting may avoid degradation in performance. Don't forget to check SCSI addresses, and change them if a conflict arises, when you move a hard disk from one Macintosh to another.

  Many people shuttle their hard disk between their home and their office Mac. When this situation involves different

Mac models, configure the hard disk for the most powerful one. The operational speed will automatically adjust when you work with the slower CPU.

Before you plug in a PC SCSI drive, make sure it has drivers for the Mac.

- Reformat when the unit was previously configured for a different computer. Do this even if the drive appears to behave normally. And don't just delete its contents—carry out a complete reinitialization. Macintoshes aren't the only computers that use SCSI devices, and the Mac may at least recognize a hard disk from another system as a legitimate volume. Nevertheless, Apple's SCSI standards deviate enough from the norm to cause confusion and severe problems somewhere down the line.

- Reformat when the hard disk was previously configured for purposes other than conventional mass storage under the Hierarchical File System (HFS). This applies to units that were used as file servers on a network, those broken up into unwanted partitions, or those used as downloadable font storehouses for laser printers (that is, directly connected to a laser printer). In these cases, you'll also have to reinitialize before proceeding.

- Reformat when the current driver is not the appropriate one. If a driver from one manufacturer is used to format a hard disk from another, the drive may not perform as well as possible. In this case, the drive should either have a new driver installed, or be reinitialized. The driver is the software that controls the hard disk, and most drives are supplied with a custom version specially designed for the product.

  How do you determine driver types? Check your user manual or other documentation—it should tell you the recommended driver choice. Another way is to look at the volume's icon; many models have distinctive icon designs. If your model's correct icon doesn't appear on the desktop, try to find the appropriate formatting software and make the necessary changes.

Using HD SC Setup

HD Disk First Aid is discussed in Chapter 7.

Besides using it as a troubleshooting tool, Apple's HD SC Setup utility, included in the System Disk software, is useful for general performance evaluation purposes. It should be part of your regular utility arsenal. With it, you can detect potential problems before they erupt. Select the Test button, and HD SC setup will examine the unit—the driver, the platters, the read/write heads, and the SCSI cabling—for hardware-based problems and inconsistencies. It will not analyze or affect the data on the disk itself. If a problem is found, the dialog box will display an assessment of its nature and extent. You may need to reinitialize the drive, but before you do so give HD Disk First Aid a try.

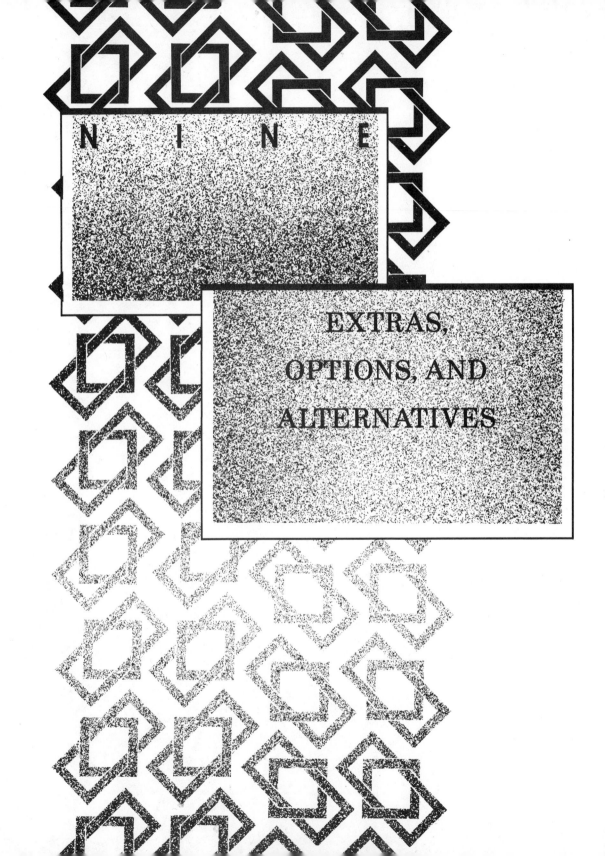

N I N E

EXTRAS,
OPTIONS, AND
ALTERNATIVES

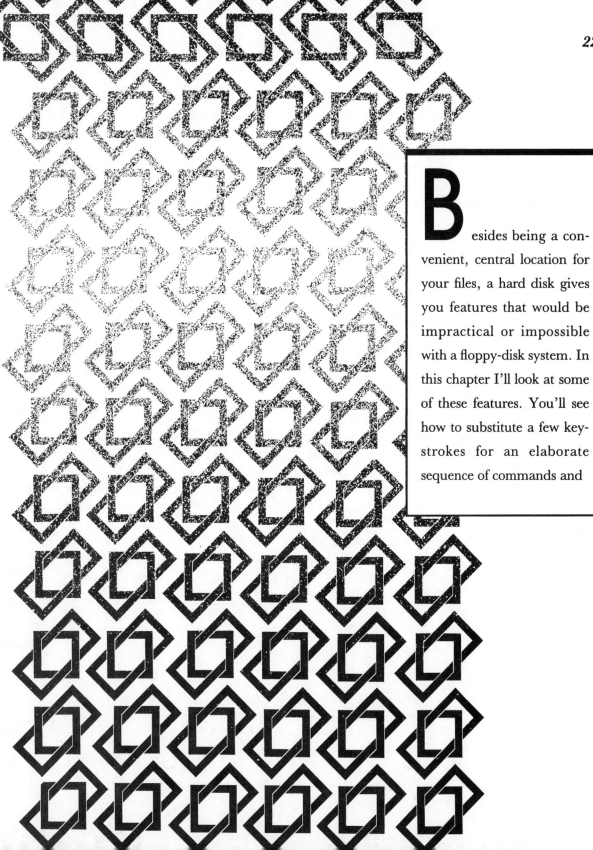

Besides being a convenient, central location for your files, a hard disk gives you features that would be impractical or impossible with a floppy-disk system. In this chapter I'll look at some of these features. You'll see how to substitute a few keystrokes for an elaborate sequence of commands and how to continue using the Mac while a print job is in progress. Then I'll turn to alternative approaches to file management and directory navigation. Specifically, I'll examine programs designed to augment or replace the Finder. Some are simply stripped down or customized models of the Finder; others create an entirely new work environment. I'll weigh their benefits and shortcomings and give pointers on their installation and use.

WORKING WITH MACRO UTILITIES

Typical Mac users find themselves performing certain tasks and procedures over and over again. Examples might be opening an application, a particular document, or selecting options for printing a file. A *macro* utility can automate and consolidate these steps into a single command.

> The Set Startup feature of MultiFinder is discussed in Chapter 4.

The Set Startup feature of MultiFinder can open selected files and desk accessories automatically during the startup process. Macro programs perform a similar function, except they do more than just locate and launch files. A single macro, for example, could create a new document, format it according to business correspondence standards, import a letterhead design, and type in the date and salutation. Another macro could save a document, make multiple copies, print some and send others through a network or modem to specific destinations.

Creating, storing, and using macros is a complicated process, however. You must remember a whole new set of command sequences. And even a simple macro doesn't always work flawlessly under every condition. But if some aspects of your work are systematic enough to warrant automation, macros can offer you a real increase in efficiency.

USING MACROMAKER

> You can only use a macro in combination with the application that was active when you created it.

MacroMaker, an INIT included in the System software package since Version 6.0, is Apple Computer's macro utility. Although it doesn't have as many features as other macro utilities, the program looks and functions like a cassette tape player, which makes it easy to understand and use (Figure 9.1). Keystroke macros—they can incorporate mouse as well as keyboard actions—are recorded, filed, and loaded as cassettes. These macros, however, can only be used in combination with the application that was active when you created them.

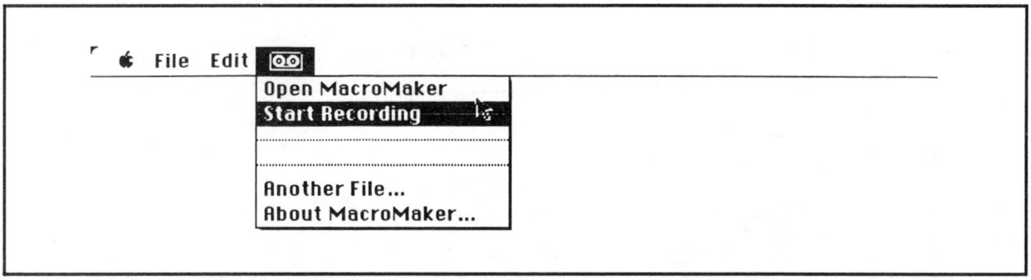

Figure 9.1: Apple's MacroMaker

When MacroMaker is placed in the startup System Folder, a cassette tape icon, actually a menu item, appears to the right of the menu bar. To create a macro:

1. Open MacroMaker (see Figure 9.2).

2. Choose a name for the macro "tape." You can also add descriptive comments if you want to. Both the name and the comments should remind you exactly what the macro does.

3. Move the cursor to the Keystroke field and type the key combination for the macro. You are not recording the macro now—just writing down the keystrokes to help you identify the macro later. MacroMaker displays the keystroke combination, including special symbols for noncharacter keystrokes.

4. Click on the Record button.

5. MacroMaker disappears, but its menu icon blinks on and off to signify that recording is in progress. Perform the steps you want included in the macro—the same ones you entered in Step 3. If you make an error, click the close box and try again.

6. Select the Stop Recording command.

7. When you're ready to save the macro, hit the Store button. The macro you just made will be loaded automatically whenever the application is running. You can select this macro either from the MacroMaker menu or with the keystroke combination you specified. You can add comments about the

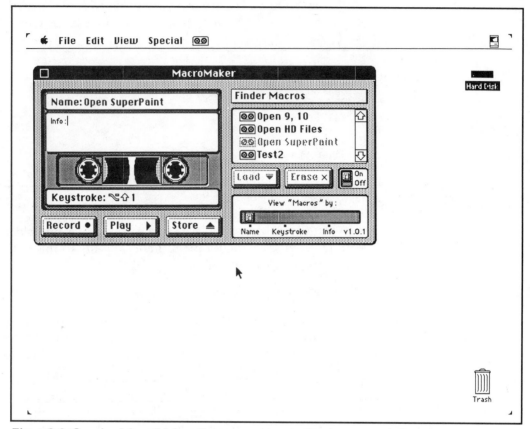

Figure 9.2: Opening MacroMaker. Current macros are listed as menu choices.

macro by clicking in the Info: field and then entering text. Your comments will be displayed in the field whenever the macro is loaded.

You cannot copy a macro from one application to another with MacroMaker. Also, when using the program, limit yourself to keystroke macros since they're not position-specific.

MacroMaker isn't perfect. You can use it to erase macros, but not to edit or modify them. And it can't copy macros, not even simple ones, from one application to another. Since you can't instruct it to wait until certain conditions exist, it won't work with programs that require you to wait before issuing a command. The problem with MacroMaker is it doesn't recognize the actual steps incorporated into a macro—it simply goes through the motions. For instance, if you record a macro that includes opening a folder and you later move the folder icon as much as an inch, the macro won't find it. And if another folder happens to be in its place, the macro will open that one instead. Even worse, if the place is now occupied by an application or document and MacroMaker attempts to treat it like a folder, the Mac may crash or bomb. The solution to working with MacroMaker is to compile macros that include keystrokes only. If you must use mouse movements in a macro, take pains to make sure the icons are in the right places.

USING QUICKEYS

QuicKeys (Figure 9.3) is an INIT and DA combination billed as a "keyboard enhancer." Besides producing multistep macros, it lets you

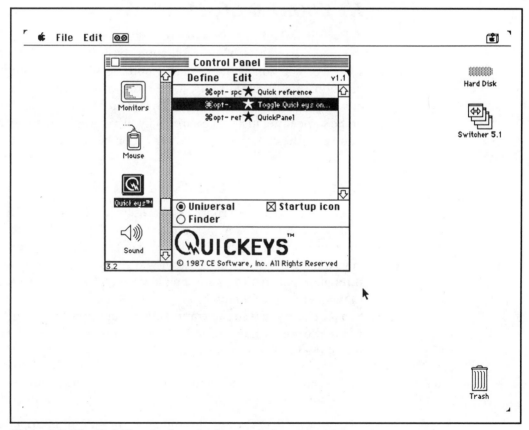

Figure 9.3: The QuicKeys keyboard enhancer desk accessory

create new data-entry configurations. If you favor a layout other than the traditional QWERTY keyboard, QuicKeys can rearrange the key functions for you. Likewise, you can create and install special foreign language characters or mathematical symbols with QuicKeys.

QuicKeys is superior to MacroMaker in a number of respects: the same macros and layouts can be used with several applications; macros can be recorded as a precise sequence of actions to be duplicated "player piano" style, or as a set of commands to be carried out; macros can be instructed to pause between steps; and one macro can be incorporated into another's functions.

MACRO-LIKE KEYBOARD COMMANDS

Even if you don't have a macro utility, you can take advantage of the macro-like keystroke combinations built into the Mac's System software. You don't have to master and use all of the keystroke combinations, but it doesn't hurt to be familiar with them. When using any of these keystroke commands, you don't have to enter both keys at the same time; just make sure that you've pressed the special function key—the command, Shift, or Option key—first.

COMMAND-KEY COMBINATIONS

Most keyboard alternatives to using the mouse require you to press the command key (⌘), the one to the left of the space bar (it's sometimes called the clover or Apple key). You can view command-key equivalents in the application you're using simply by browsing through its menus: the command key equivalents are displayed next to the menu items themselves.

You can use keystroke commands at any time; it doesn't matter where the cursor happens to be or if any text is selected. Here are a few of the most common command-key commands.

- ⌘-C copies a selected area to the Clipboard, without deleting it from the current document.

- ⌘-N opens a new document from within an application or creates a new folder from the Finder.

- ⌘-O begins the process of opening a preexisting document, presenting a dialog box with which to locate the file.

- ⌘-P summons the Print dialog box and gets the printout process underway.

- ⌘-Q closes the currently active application and any open documents belonging to it.

- ⌘-S saves changes made to the document.

- ⌘-V places the Clipboard's contents (generated by ⌘-X or ⌘-C) at the cursor's insertion point. It can be used repeatedly to make multiple copies.

- ⌘-W closes the currently active window. In the Finder, it closes the currently open folder.

- ⌘-X removes (or *cuts*) a selected text or graphic, saving it on the Clipboard (until something else is cut) for placement elsewhere.

The majority of Macintosh applications use these command-key equivalents, but watch out for departures from the norm. In Super-Paint, for instance, ⌘-W simply changes the window display size. In WriteNow, the print dialog is opened not by ⌘-P, but by ⌘-T.

OPTION-KEY COMMANDS

Whereas the command key usually invokes the keyboard equivalent of a mouse function, the Option key opens other possibilities. For example, you can use the Option key to copy an item and place the duplicate in a new location on the same volume. To do this, hold down the Option key and select a file or folder with a single mouse-click; then, with the Option key still pressed down, drag the file to another folder. Instead of relocating the original, the Mac will create a copy with the same name at the target destination.

Option-Key Characters You can also use the Option key to expand keyboard functions. The Mac's System software assigns each key a second character which you enter by pressing Option first. Option-key characters include general-purpose graphics, specialized symbols, and foreign language characters.

Option-key characters vary according to which font you are currently using. The best way to keep track of them is with Key Caps (Figure 9.4), a desk accessory installed on all standard System files. Key Caps creates an on-screen representation of the keyboard. To try it out, open Key Caps and press Option. You'll note that most keys now display a new character. While the DA is open, any key you press will appear in the text window above the keyboard map. Use this feature to practice Option-key alternatives before adding new characters to your text documents.

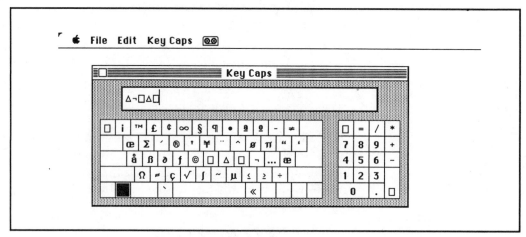

Figure 9.4: The Key Caps desk accessory displays Option-key character alternatives.

You use *dead keys* to access another class of special characters. Dead keys do not produce new characters by themselves; instead, they modify the keystroke that follows. Like Option-key characters, dead-key characters vary depending on the font you're working with. Dead keys are usually used for writing foreign languages or mathematical equations.

Experiment while the Key Caps DA is open to see how the dead keys work. Some dead keys modify any subsequent keystroke, others function only when followed by the appropriate character. Here are a few of the more common dead keys:

- Option-' and Option-e produce the French grave accent (`) and the French acute accent (´) respectively.

- Option-i produces a circumflex (^).

- Option-n places a Spanish tilde (˜) over the letters o, a, and n.

- Option-u places a German umlaut (¨) over vowels only.

Function-Key Combinations

Function keys, also known as FKeys, are actually three-key combinations that work no matter which application is currently running or which activity is underway. To use the Function-key combinations, you press the first two keys simultaneously and press the third one shortly afterwards. Below is a summary of the Function-key combinations.

- ⌘-Shift-F1 ejects the floppy disk in the first internal disk drive (the right one on the Mac II, the top one on the SE). The floppy's icon remains on the desktop, however, and the Mac may ask you to reinsert it during the shutdown process. If you want to exclude the floppy from the current work session, drag it into the trash instead. It will be ejected (but not erased), and the icon will disappear.

- ⌘-Shift-F2 performs the same ejection function as ⌘-Shift-F1, but for the external drive (or the second internal drive on the Mac II and SE) instead of the internal one.

- ⌘-Shift-F3 takes a snapshot of what is on the screen and saves it in a MacPaint file, although you can open, convert, and modify the file with most graphics programs. The file is automatically stored on the root level of the startup volume; the first one is labeled Screen0, and all subsequent screen shots are saved as Screen1, Screen2, etc., up to Screen9. After that, the images will not be saved unless you rename the earlier screen shots. The command is useful for illustrating the steps and procedures of working on the Macintosh, but it can cause dysfunctions in some circumstances and it can't always take an accurate picture of what is on the screen. For example, you can't capture a menu item being selected or a watch cursor indicating a delay because the computer waits until all commands are carried out before it takes a screen shot. If you need an accurate representation of a command being carried out, use an image-capture utility such as Camera.

- ⌘-Shift-F4 takes a snapshot of what is on the screen, but instead of saving it as a document it generates a printout on an ImageWriter or other dot-matrix printer. If you want a copy from a laser printer instead, press ⌘-Shift-F3, and print the resulting MacPaint file.

The other ⌘-Shift-FKey combinations (5 through 0) are there for you to add your own commands. You can add commands with a macro program such as QuicKeys or with special FKey installation utilities such as FKey Manager.

WORKING WITH PRINTER SPOOLERS

One of the biggest fringe benefits of having a hard disk is being able to use *printer spoolers*. If you've ever stood by for minutes or hours while your Mac printed a file, you'll appreciate the advantages they provide.

With a printer spooler, you can continue with your work while printing is in progress. You can send a multitude of files to the printer and rearrange the order in which they're processed. You can even order the Mac to print out a lengthy document at a certain time, such as overnight or during your lunch hour. How can spoolers do all this? By taking advantage of the fact that printers work more slowly than computers.

When you issue a print command, the Macintosh starts compiling a set of instructions for duplicating the pages of the document. These instructions will be sent to the printer. If you are using LaserWriter or a similar laser printer, the instructions are given in PostScript, a printing code which interprets text and images in terms of lines. If you are using an ImageWriter or other dot-matrix printer, the instructions are given in *bitmaps*, a printing code which breaks text and images down into sequences of dots or bits.

Once the Mac has compiled these page descriptions, it sends them to the printer. But it takes the printer much longer to act on the page descriptions than it took the Mac to compile them; instead of being given all at once, the Mac transmits the print job bit by bit in quantities the printer can handle. The printer needs to translate the page descriptions into physical actions. Meantime, the Macintosh (and your work) is put on hold.

This is where spoolers come in—they do the waiting on behalf of the Mac. They intercept the page descriptions so the Mac doesn't have to waste time laboriously feeding them to the printer. Instead, the page descriptions are saved as a document in their own right, and the spooler, not the Mac, passes the print document to the printer. The Mac is still a part of this process: the spooler relies on the Mac to help send the print document to the printer. But the spooler waits for the times when you're not using the Mac—the seconds between keystrokes, the moments when the screen doesn't need to be updated to display a mouse movement—to do its work. Once the print job is done, the spooler deletes the print document and deactivates itself automatically.

Spoolers have their drawbacks: even the best spoolers take longer to print a document than it would normally take, and operations on the Mac can become sluggish when a spooler is at work (although the lost time isn't always noticeable). Moreover, incompatibilities between the spooler and other applications can spoil both the printout and the work you're doing on the Macintosh screen. Some spoolers will not let you use all the features your printer is capable of. Still, spoolers provide greater control over the printing process and greater access to the Mac itself.

USING PRINTMONITOR

PrintMonitor included as part of the system software package since Version 5.0, is Apple's spooler utility. It works with PostScript-compatible laser printers only, only under MultiFinder, and only when the printer is connected via Apple's network (called Apple-Talk). PrintMonitor is especially useful with printers that are being shared on a network, since it can control the traffic flow from several Macs into one printer. Each file to be printed is logged in a *queue window*, which arranges them in order of precedence (Figure 9.5). The first files placed in the queue are normally the first out of the printer, but you can change file order by shuffling or canceling print commands. You can also print at specific times with PrintMonitor. If you have a large document but don't want to tie up the printer during regular business hours, you can leave your equipment on and have PrintMonitor process it overnight.

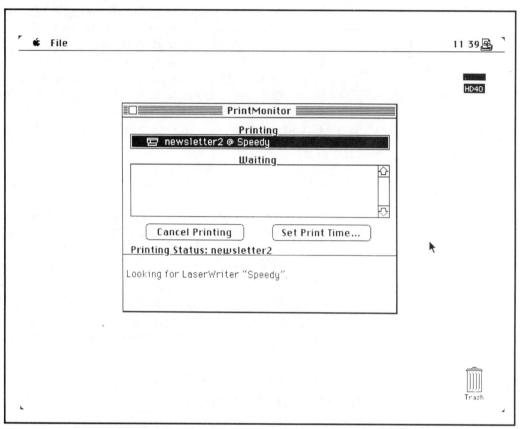

Figure 9.5: The queue window of PrintMonitor, Apple's spooler for PostScript laser printers

A SPOOLER FOR SYSTEMS WITH LESS RAM

SuperLaserSpool is an alternative to PrintMonitor that works on systems with less than a megabyte of memory. It comes in two parts: a DA (called LaserQueue) and the main application (SuperLaser-Spool).

After you have installed the DA with Font/DA Mover, you can launch the SuperLaserSpool application. If you want SuperLaser-Spool to run every time the Macintosh is started, select the SuperLa-serSpool icon and Set Startup from the Finder's Special menu. Be sure that the box next to SuperLaserSpool is checked, and then select OK. SuperLaserSpool will now be launched whenever the Macintosh is started.

SuperLaserSpool does not change the way you print documents from other applications. Instead of going straight to the printer, the documents are placed into a folder at the root level of the hard disk called SLS Spool Files. SuperLaserSpool will then automatically detect their presence and start sending them to the printer without interrupting whatever else you might be doing. By selecting the LaserQueue DA, you can preview and reorder documents that are waiting to be printed, remove documents from the print queue, or deactivate SuperLaserSpool.

DEDICATING A HARD DISK TO A LASERWRITER IINTX

Macintosh-compatible laser printers are renowned for their ability to produce high-quality text in a dazzling variety of typefaces, sizes, and styles. But the downloadable font files they use to produce this text are quite large, so they take up a lot of disk space and are time-consuming to read. While the data is shuttling from the system's hard disk to the printer, the Mac (and its user) are caught in the middle.

This situation can be improved if you use Apple's top-of-the-line laser printer, the LaserWriter IINTX. You can connect a SCSI hard disk directly to this printer and then use the hard disk as a dedicated storehouse for downloadable font files. This accelerates printing and prevents the Mac's performance from being impaired while the printer is working.

The LaserWriter Font Utility software (provided with the printer) formats and controls the dedicated hard disk. Unfortunately, you must commit the entire hard disk to the printer because the formatting erases any previous contents. You can't solve this problem by partitioning because the printer won't work with partitioned volumes. You can return the drive to normal service at any time.

Some SCSI hard disks may not work when dedicated to a LaserWriter IINTX. Be sure to test this arrangement before you buy a hard disk for this purpose.

FINDER ALTERNATIVES

For most people, the Finder is the program that makes the Macintosh what it is. The Finder runs more often than any application, it supplies the familiar elements of the Mac's user interface, the desktop, and the folder display formats. All these benefits are products of the Finder.

Yet for some people the Finder in an unnecessary frill. The same features that make the Macintosh easy for beginners to understand—the graphic icons, the file-cabinet-like directories—require a lot of processing time to manage. Experienced users often would prefer to trade simplicity of function for increased performance. That's why a number of utilities are available that either augment or bypass the Finder for the sake of speed and convenience.

Using Switcher

Switcher (Figure 9.6) is a forerunner of MultiFinder. It's still a useful utility for Macs with less than 1 megabyte of RAM, since they can't use MultiFinder. Switcher lets you launch and work with up to eight applications at once by shifting back and forth between them

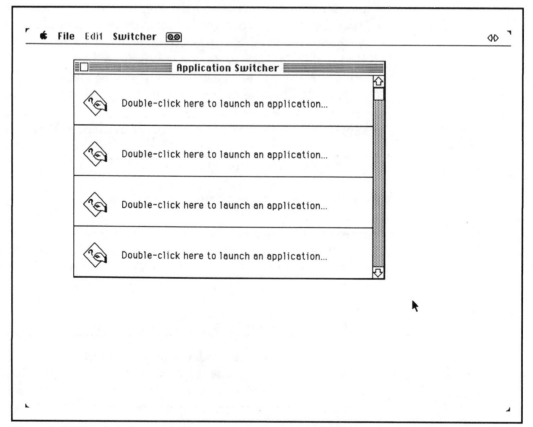

Figure 9.6: With Switcher, up to eight applications can be used at once.

with a single mouse-click. The program isn't as powerful or reliable as MultiFinder, but it can speed up your work significantly.

With Switcher, you designate which file to launch by double-clicking on one of eight default icons; then you double-click on the desired application. Alternatively, to open a specific document, you select the application first, then choose the Attach Document command from the File menu.

When you select a document, Switcher will show you the amount of RAM it occupies. Keep track of these figures and refrain from adding more files when the memory runs low. The Show Info Window command will display an overview of how much RAM each application is using (Figure 9.7) and a picture of each application's current window.

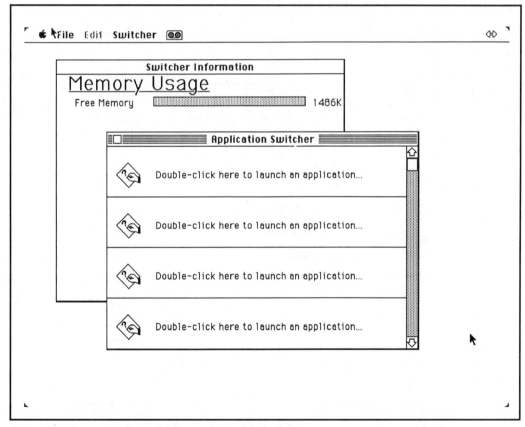

Figure 9.7: Summarizing RAM resources with Switcher

Notice the scroll arrows in the upper and lower right-hand corners of the menu bar. Click on either one and the screen will slide horizontally to reveal the window of another application. Click again on the opposite side of the arrow to return to where you started from. You can close any of the files individually, or you can close all the files at once by quitting Switcher.

Using DiskTop

DiskTop (Figure 9.8) is the Swiss army knife of the Macintosh world, a multipurpose utility packed into the form of a desk accessory. It's one of the more versatile Finder alternatives, since it also

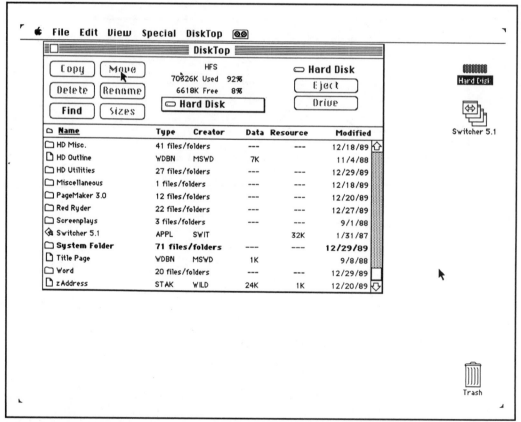

Figure 9.8: The DiskTop utility

functions as a volume searcher, a high-speed copier, and a resource modification tool. You can use it to rename, relocate, create, and delete items, to launch applications, to convert graphic documents from one format to another, and even to create custom menus. Moreover, it's a DA, so you can use it anytime.

DiskTop provides a window that looks and functions much like the traditional desktop, with the icons of all mounted volumes in the upper right-hand corner and the Trash icon below. But it also provides extra information: whether each volume is HFS or MFS, how many bytes are occupied, and how many remain.

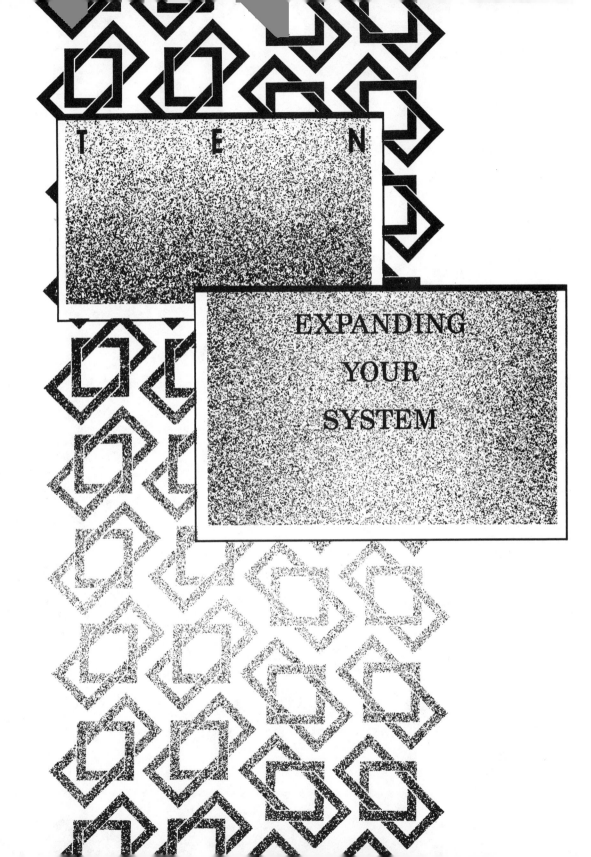

TEN

EXPANDING YOUR SYSTEM

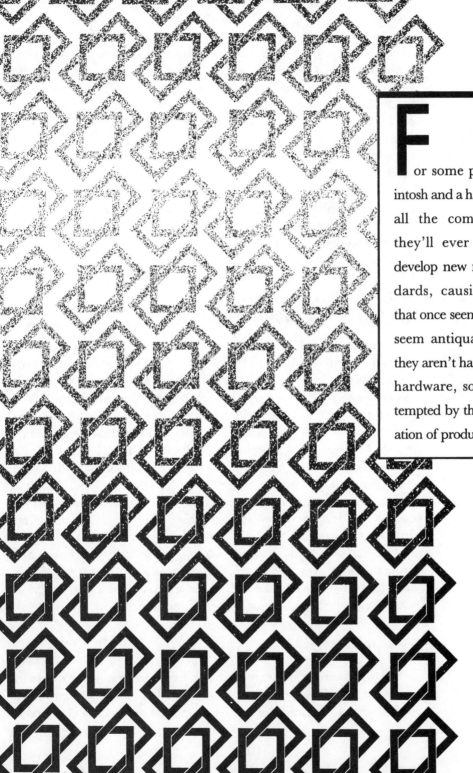

F or some people, a Macintosh and a hard disk provide all the computing power they'll ever need. Others develop new needs and standards, causing equipment that once seemed advanced to seem antiquated. Although they aren't hampered by their hardware, some people are tempted by the newest generation of products.

Fortunately, because the SCSI standard isn't a dead-end street, your Macinosh system can easily accommodate the new and improved. In fact, the Mac will likely be capable of accommodating innovations for years to come. Equipment that isn't state-of-the-art is only obsolete when it no longer helps you work the way you want to.

Expansion is the subject of this chapter. I'll explain how to improve capability and performance while you continue to get the most out of your current equipment. I'll detail the process of adding other devices to the SCSI bus and describe some of the new products that are available—not just additional mass storage drives, but a wide range of products. Then I'll move beyond SCSI to other connection standards, the expansion ports of the SE and Mac II.

WORKING WITH MULTIPLE SCSI DEVICES

The versatility of the SCSI standard is as admirable as its speed. Instead of being a bottleneck, the Mac's single SCSI port can accommodate seven peripherals as easily as one. That's because the bus works as a sort of device-only network to transfer data and administer to transfer needs at the same time. The port serves all seven peripherals because SCSI intercepts, identifies, and evaluates each communication before conveying it further along the bus. Each communication is sequentially placed and removed according to a changing set of priorities.

This smooth and seamless coordinative ability makes building and using a multiple-unit SCSI setup almost as easy as getting your first drive up and running. Each SCSI device requires only a single cable and power cord; configuration matters are rarely very complex. So, while there are precautions to take and pitfalls to avoid, you don't have to worry: any mistakes won't endanger your hardware or software, unless you force connections or ignore problems.

SETTING UP THE DAISYCHAIN

Daisy-chaining and SCSI addresses are discussed in Chapter 2.

Daisy-chaining is the technique you use to add external devices to the SCSI bus. The system avoids potential confusion by assigning each device a SCSI address. All data placed on the bus is prefixed with a SCSI address. If a device doesn't recognize the address as its own, it simply passes on the data.

To establish a functional daisychain, follow the steps detailed below. These will help you build a SCSI setup to meet your current expansion needs and to accommodate further additions in the future.

Connection and Termination

Begin by plugging in the power cord and linking the new unit to the one currently attached to the Mac. You can reverse the order of connection if you want; the address, not the physical position of a device on a daisychain, establishes position on the SCSI.

Every SCSI device should have two ports, and each device employs one of two port designs: the multipin port, which is identical to the one on the Mac, or a larger coupler port, which is interlocked rather than inserted. If the port types on your devices don't fit together, get an adapter cable or coupling from a computer store or the drive manufacturer.

A SCSI bus must have a terminator at its physical end. Otherwise, signals sent up the bus might bounce back down, confusing the Mac and its peripherals and leading to a dysfunction. Terminators absorb bus signals, which means that anything connected to the bus after a terminated device will not be able to access the bus. You should remove or disable the terminators on all but the last device.

Some terminators are hardware units placed between a connector and the port; you can remove these by hand. Others are incorporated into the unit's design; you remove them by flipping a switch or by using a software utility. Still other terminators are permanently installed; you have to move the devices in which these are installed to the end of the daisychain, have them removed by a service technician, or have the unit's manufacturer remove them. Check your user's manual to see how to remove your terminator.

OTHER MASS STORAGE HARDWARE

Most Macintoshes rely on floppies and hard disks for storage needs, but floppies and hard disks are not the only game in town. There is a wide and growing field of alternative drives offering different advantages. For example, floppy and hard disk hybrids combine the high capacity of hard disks with the convenience and portability of the floppy disk. Other mass storage hardware represents a new generation of storage technology, offering you the performance potential of a higher magnitude entirely.

CARTRIDGE DRIVES

Cartridge drives save files on half-inch or quarter-inch tape cassettes that are similar to those used for audio recording. Like floppy disks, the cassettes encode data magnetically, but they hold much more data than a floppy disk can—a cassette can hold as much as 60 megabytes. Some systems contain a cartridge drive and a hard disk in the same unit; other cartridge drives stand alone. Either type can back up any volume on the SCSI bus—some cartridge drives even work with several Macs connected to a network.

Cartridge drives have their limitations, however: the tape can be broken or tangled, and data can't be accessed quickly enough on a cassette for it to serve as a real-time volume, that is, one that supplies and stores data while you are working. But cassettes make backing up easier because they eliminate the need to stockpile and shuffle floppy disks. The process is even easier with drives that allow you to make backups automatically at specified intervals.

HIGH-CAPACITY FLOPPY DISKS

A *high-capacity floppy disk drive* is another removable-media storage alternative. You can use it as a backup, as an individual volume, or as both. A high-capacity floppy disk is a beefed up variation of the standard floppy disk, with larger platters and greater density; current versions can store up to 10 megabytes per disk.

In general, a high-capacity floppy disk works slower than a hard disk but faster than a non-SCSI floppy. The disks are more expensive than cartridge drive cassettes but are more durable. Unlike most cassettes, you can use a high-capacity floppy as an online volume (even as the startup volume) as well as using it as a backup. High-capacity floppy disks are a good choice for anyone who has to deal with very large files—they can be mounted and unmounted quickly. A graphic artist could use them for storing scanned images, a musician for loading sound files.

DISK PACK DRIVES

Disk pack drives, like hard disk drives, use metallic, high-capacity platters, but the platters are contained in removable and interchangable casings. Disk pack drives are not as fast as conventional hard disks, but they offer the highest storage capacity of any removable-media drive—up to 120 megabytes in a single module.

Disk packs are about the size of a paperback book. Like floppy disks, you can transfer them between similar drives. They're also very durable, much more so than tape cartridges or floppies. In fact, disk pack drives are rugged enough to be sent through the mail. Such performance doesn't come cheap, and unless you need high capacity, high performance removable-media storage, you may find other storage devices a better investment.

OPTICAL DISK DRIVES

The laser beams used to *read* data in optical drives are not sufficiently intense to alter the data.

Like hard disks, *optical disks* have rotating platters that are organized in a track and sector system. All optical disk platters have shimmering, mirrorlike surfaces, but the actual composition of a platter depends on the specific technology used by the system. In all cases, a laser beam is reflected off the platter, and the resulting reflections are interpreted as bits.

In many respects, optical disks are a superior storage medium. One can contain copious quantities of data: a 5¼-inch platter holds as much as 550 megabytes, an 11-inch platter up to 4000 megabytes. Unlike hard disk platters, optical disk platters are not affected by dust and magnetic field problems—you can remove and transport them freely.

CD-ROM and OROM Drives

The first optical storage adaptation made for the Macintosh was *compact disk read-only memory* (CD-ROM), also known as *optical read-only memory* (OROM). This technology employs 5¼-inch platters identical to the ones used in audio compact disks. In fact, some optical drives can also function as high-fidelity CD players. A CD-ROM platter contains billions of microscopic indentations and flat spaces called *pits* and *lands*, respectively. When a laser beam is focused on these, it is reflected by the lands and scattered by the pits, which the computer then interprets as 1 or 0, that is, bits.

A CD-ROM disk is not unmodifiable. Though this keeps them from being a complete storage solution, CD-ROMs can provide huge directories and databases in a convenient online form. For example, one disk can contain a complete set of encyclopedias, an unabridged dictionary, and a half-dozen major metropolitan area phone books.

For all their storage ability, CD-ROM drives are slow; it takes about a second to open a file, whereas a hard disk can do the same task in a matter of milliseconds. Because it stores permanent, unmodifiable documents, CD-ROM's greatest potential is in publishing. The medium can be used for preserving and presenting not just documents, but high-resolution sounds and images.

WORM Drives

More flexibility is offered by the *write once, read many* (WORM) optical drive. WORMs allow you to write to an optical disk, although you can't erase or change the data once it has been written there. The files are inscribed with a high-intensity laser and read with another, weaker beam.

WORMs generally run faster than CD-ROMs, and though their contents can't be deleted, they're useful for keeping extensive permanent records. For example, multiple versions of a document can be stored on a WORM drive for retracing mistakes or restoring deletions.

At present, WORM drives are limited by a lack of standardization and flexibility. Different models have different platter sizes (from 5¼ inches to 19 inches) and different organization systems. This means that disks from one model can't be used on the others. WORM drives are also unable to read CD-ROM platters.

Magneto-Optical Drives

The latest generation of storage devices combines the erasability of magnetic media with the storage capacity of compact disks. *Magneto-optical drives* employ both magnets and lasers to read and modify files. When heated by a relatively high-intensity laser, crystals in the platter's substrate align their magnetic orientation with that of a surrounding magnetic field created by the magnets in the drive. When cooled, the crystals retain their new orientation. The specific orientation of the field and crystals depends on whether a 0 or a 1 is being written. When the lower-intensity read beam is focused on the platter it reflects differently off crystals with different orientations, and the computer interprets the reflections as 0 or 1. The read beam does not alter the data, nor do magnetic fields applied in the absence of sufficient heat. The result is a system that allows you to store large amounts of data on a removable platter without sacrificing the ability to modify your data as easily as with a hard disk.

Magneto-optical drives have only recently appeared on the Macintosh market, and their cost is prohibitive: the hardware may cost $3000 or more, and a single disk costs about $250. Yet these figures reflect the newness of the technology more than the cost of production. In the near future magneto-optical drives may become as cheap as hard disks are today.

OTHER SCSI HARDWARE

Not all SCSI peripherals are intended for storage and backup tasks. A growing number of other peripherals are hopping on the SCSI bus, devices such as printers, scanners, and even cameras that produce color slides.

Some devices don't use the SCSI standard because they don't need the speed it provides. Modems, floppy disks, and dot-matrix printers handle data less quickly and in less quantity, so they don't require the SCSI standard—their own ports are adequate for their purposes. Laser printers, file servers, and other network products likewise don't require the SCSI standard, since they are supposed to serve multiple Macs simultaneously or interchangeably and a SCSI setup can work with only one computer at a time.

Printers, modems, file servers and all the products that have traditionally not been on the SCSI bus are usually as easy as hard disks to integrate into a multidevice SCSI setup. Like hard disks, they're usually capable of taking any address or daisychain position.

INPUT DEVICES

The SCSI bus is ideally suited for peripherals that need to identify and process large amounts of data at once.

- Scanners are devices that reproduce printed matter (such as text or photographs) as computer readable data. Some scanners create a bit-mapped reproduction of the original image, that is, they "redraw" the patterns of light and dark that they detect on the page. Other scanners use *optical character recognition software,* which attempts to actually recognize text characters. Once a character is recognized, the computer reproduces it by generating the character's appropriate ASCII code rather than by attempting to redraw it.

- Video and audio digitizers translate moving images and sound into various Macintosh formats.

OUTPUT DEVICES

Some printers can benefit from the greater transfer speed of the SCSI bus. Apple's LaserWriter IISC, for example, uses SCSI to convey high-resolution page descriptions (unlike the other Laser-Writer models, which connect via AppleTalk). Instead of relying on PostScript, the LaserWriter IISC generates printouts based on QuickDraw, the same graphic interpretation standard used to create and update the Macintosh's screen.

Other SCSI output devices include *film printers,* which produce photographic exposures of screen displays and are helpful for slide generation and special presentations. There are also devices that produce large-scale displays for overhead projectors.

OTHER EXPANSION OPTIONS

SCSI is the fastest connectivity standard for all Macintoshes currently sold by Apple, but there's an even more powerful way to tap into the SE and Mac II models—by taking advantage of *expansion slots* and *expansion cards.* Expansion slots let you easily install additional circuit boards or other hardware, which are collectively known as expansion cards.

Expansion cards are more than peripherals sharing a case with the internal floppy and hard disk drives—they're not just connected to the Mac, but integrated with it. This means that expansion cards are as much a part of the computer as any soldered-in component.

Expansion slots are wired into the *motherboard*, the master circuit board that contains the CPU, the RAM, and the ROM. In fact, the multislot Mac II expansion system also functions like a SCSI daisy-chain; any or all slots can be occupied in any order, and cards can be removed and replaced at will.

Expansion slots on the Mac II are administered by a data bus called *NuBus*, a standard developed by Texas Instruments and adapted by Apple. The Mac II's SCSI port can transfer data at a maximum rate of 1.25 megabytes per second, and the SCSI standard itself has been designed to accommodate speeds four times greater than that. But NuBus presents a higher magnitude of performance, reaching transfer speeds of 37.5 megabytes per second. The bus can also be accessed by more than one computer; in fact, control of the NuBus bus can even be handed over to an expansion card, turning the CPU itself into a peripheral.

Theoretically, hard disks could be produced in expansion card form, and just about any type of peripheral could at least be connected by way of an expansion port. But it's unlikely that such products will materialize until they can be engineered to operate faster than the SCSI speed limit. In the meantime, NuBus gives the motherboard additional resources for high-speed communications and for replacing standard functions with advanced alternatives. Below is a summary of different kinds of expansion cards:

Monitors are only as capable as their cards are powerful.

- Video Cards coordinate all visual display functions. Macs before the II model use only the 9-inch black-and-white screen, with all video instructions built into the ROM. But the Mac II doesn't have a display of its own—it was designed to work with a variety of monitors. Instead of anticipating all configurations, the Mac II relies on the expansion cards that accompany individual models.

  A grayscale image requires more resources than a black and white one, and color image still more resources. When it comes to high-resolution color, the video card is often more expensive then the monitor itself. You can pay as much as $30,000 for a video card display package, albeit one that rivals a $250,000 dedicated video graphic system.

- Memory Cards supplement the 1 megabyte of RAM supplied with the standard Mac II. You can install single in-line memory modules (SIMMs) up to a total of 8 megabytes, but NuBus can access even more. The bus is capable of handling up to 4 gigabytes (1024M) at once, although that much RAM has yet to be packed onto expansion cards.

- Bus linkages give two or more computers the ability to communicate and fully access the other's bus. Products such as Bus-Link can build a bus linkage between Mac IIs, or between a II model and even more powerful mini- and mainframe computers. Bus-linked computers don't just send and receive data among themselves: they work together like a single machine to send and receive data simultaneously. The collaborating CPUs can alternate computing chores, working in parallel as needed to process and distribute the data. With a bus-link, a Mac II can access the files of a Digital VAX as swiftly as the files on its own hard disk; likewise, the VAX could control the Mac's screen display with equal ease.

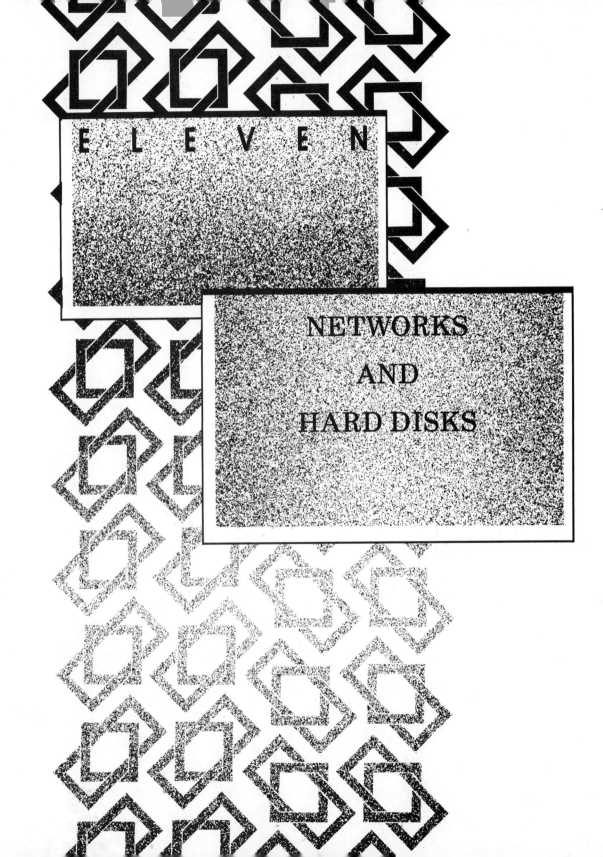

ELEVEN

NETWORKS
AND
HARD DISKS

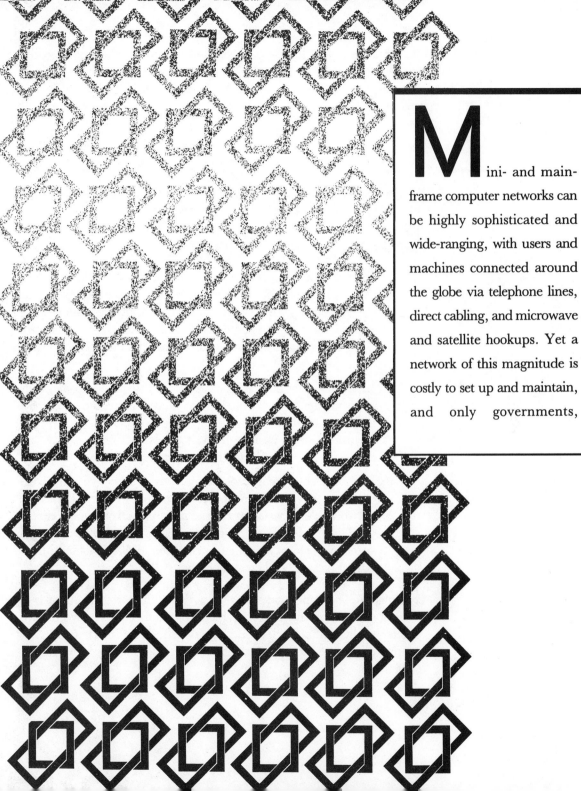

Mini- and main-frame computer networks can be highly sophisticated and wide-ranging, with users and machines connected around the globe via telephone lines, direct cabling, and microwave and satellite hookups. Yet a network of this magnitude is costly to set up and maintain, and only governments, academia, and very large corporations can take advantage of large networks at present. Fortunately, there are microcomputer alternatives to large networks. Networks and how they operate is the subject of this chapter.

NETWORKS AND HARD DISKS

The favored network, and the one that is easiest to take advantage of, is the *LAN*, or *local area network*. Although smaller in scope than full-scale networks, LANs bring the benefits of connectivity into the workplace. These benefits include

- Information access. You can swiftly transmit a file from one computer to another or place it in a location accessible by all users. In many cases, you can share data among computers of different standards—some LANs accommodate Macintoshes, IBM PC compatibles, and computers from other manufacturers as well.

- Interoffice communication. LANs provide an electronic alternative to telephones, intercoms, memos, and other conventional means of communicating in the workplace. An electronic message system, besides delivering messages immediately, lets the recipient confirm that the message was received.

- Resource sharing. Peripherals are more effective (and cost-effective) when they are shared. A number of peripherals are networkable: most laser printers, including all of Apple's except the LaserWriter II SC, some dot-matrix printers, including a special version of Apple's ImageWriter, FAX machines, CD-ROM players, and even modems.

Unlike full-scale networks, LANs can't accommodate thousands of users at once. Also, the need for direct cable connections between computers usually confines a network to a single building. But networks are relatively easy to establish and expand, especially those designed for the Macintosh.

The most popular networks are AppleShare and TOPS. Both use the AppleTalk connectors (located on the back of every Macintosh) to communicate between the various machines. In fact, you can use your Macintosh alone to perform some network functions (for example, sharing AppleTalk devices such as Laser Printers, CD-ROM players, and networked modems); you don't need any additional network software. All you need to do to network an AppleTalk laser printer is install the proper printer driver in the System Folder and connect it with the standard AppleTalk cable. After that, all the Macintoshes on the network can share the printer.

LAN TYPES

Each computer connected to a LAN is classified as a *file server*, a *client*, or both. A file server accesses, locates, and opens files on the hard disks or other storage volumes to which it is attached. It does this when requested to by the client computer. The client is the computer that initiates the access and receives the data.

DISTRIBUTED NETWORKS

Distributed network software allows each Mac in the network to be both a file server and client, either alternatively or simultaneously. In a distributed network, files either belong to one user exclusively or are designated for access by all users. Files, folders, even entire volumes can be made accessible to other users in the network, and who those users are is determined by the system administrator.

Up to nine hard disks can be connected to each Mac, so distributed LANs can make a massive amount of files accessible on a network. But the network software has to shuttle between CPUs for the processor time it needs, which means that hooking up a lot of hard disks to a network slows down processing time.

One way to keep processing time down is to use a *dedicated network*. These make a permanent distinction between file servers and clients, requiring that one Mac be "dedicated" for the sole purpose of file serving. With a dedicated network, the networking software runs exclusively on the dedicated computer, in other words on the file server; only volumes attached directly to the file server can be accessed by the entire network.

WHICH IS BETTER?

Dedicated networks usually work faster than distributed ones. Moreover, it has been argued that the centralized operations of a dedicated network make it more reliable. But you pay a price for using a dedicated network: one Macintosh in the network must always be used as a file server and not for any other purpose. This means, if you want to network more than eight hard disks, the maximum number of hard disks that can be connected to a file server, you need to buy another hard disk and configure it as a file server as well.

No matter whether you use a dedicated or a distributed network, or how flexible and efficient the LAN, working with files on a remote volume isn't as convenient as working with files on your own hard disk. Even the fastest network is significantly slower than a SCSI bus, and transfer speed is reduced when the network's resources are taxed by several users.

WHAT IS SHARED?

How a network works isn't nearly as important as how it can help people work together. At present, there are three ways to share information and work on a network—disk sharing, file sharing, and groupware.

DISK SHARING

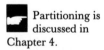
Partitioning is discussed in Chapter 4.

Disk sharing isn't true networking. It's simply partitioning, multiuser style. Partitioning is the process of breaking up a hard disk's storage capacity into separate, or *logical*, volumes. With disk sharing, each partitioned volume is assigned to a particular Mac or user. Typically, volumes may be opened and read by more than one user, but only the assigned user is given the power to modify his or her "personal" volume.

Disk sharing, the earliest form of networking on the Macintosh, has a few limitations. For example, transferring files on a partitioned hard disk is awkward. To make changes to a document stored in someone else's partition, you need to copy it to your own, modify the duplicate version, then request the "owner" of the other partition to make a copy of your copy and replace the original with it.

The only real advantage of disk sharing is that two or more Macs can make use of a single hard disk—a big plus when hard disks were rare and costly items, but not so important an option today. Still, you may want to consider disk sharing if you have multiple Macs and a hard disk with enough storage capacity for everyone on the network.

FILE SHARING

Unlike disk sharing, which merely divides up storage space, *file sharing* allows you to freely exchange data from one computer to another. You can manipulate files on a remote volume as easily as files on your personal hard disk. File sharing's only limitations are those imposed by the network administration.

File sharing works best when access options are exercised—indiscriminate access can lead to unwanted file changes and deletions. Most file-sharing LANs give you the option of "publishing" a file, so everyone on the network can read it, and the option of archiving a file, which stores a copy from which other copies can be made. It is up to the individual users and the network administrator to establish rules and privileges concerning access to files.

GROUPWARE

The ultimate goal of a network is not just connectivity, but interactivity. In other words, the idea is to share the results of the work and the work process itself. Sharing work has become possible thanks to *groupware* programs specifically designed for use by more than one person. Groupware is a rapidly growing part of the Macintosh software market.

There's no hard-and-fast definition of groupware. In general, the term describes an application that can accommodate simultaneous and separate commands. In the past, networked Macs could run the same application at the same time only when each was running an application copy of its own. Now, with groupware, you can collaborate on projects.

Groupware, far from being a frill, is often the only way to go. For example, a large sales staff would use a groupware database to compile client and order information, with each salesperson consulting or updating the database. With groupware, a committee drafting a proposal could incorporate suggestions from many people without having to wait while first draft copies are distributed, commented on, and collected.

WORKING WITH APPLESHARE

To use Appleshare you should have at least the Mac Plus model with an attached hard disk.

AppleShare, the most popular network standard for the Macintosh (in large part because it was created by Apple Computer), is easy to use. It offers file sharing, groupware compatibility, and a wide range of access options. AppleShare, however, is a dedicated system. To use it you need at least a Macintosh Plus with an attached hard disk. In fact, for maximum performance, I recommend a more powerful model—if you buy a Mac II for file serving, at least it won't need its own monitor and keyboard.

Macintoshes on an AppleShare network are linked by way of the AppleTalk port located on the back of each Macintosh. AppleTalk, a connectivity standard much like SCSI, allows you to connect Macintoshes and other AppleTalk-compatible devices in a daisychain. Apple-Talk is much slower than SCSI but it can daisy-chain more Macintoshes than the eight permitted by the SCSI standard. Apple used to sell its cable-connector kit under the product name AppleTalk, but competitors started selling alternative cabling kits, so Apple has changed the product name to LocalTalk.

Alternatives to the cable-connector method are available. Instead of cables, PhoneNET makes use of the wires in the telephone system. This means you can extend your network beyond one room without knocking holes through walls and floors. PhoneNET will work with most phone wiring, so it is worth an investigation if you plan to set up a network. Ethernet, probably the most popular networking standard in the MS-DOS world, can also be adapted to accommodate AppleTalk, as can IBM's Token Ring network.

AppleShare automatically logs you onto the network when you boot up your Macintosh. (If necessary, it will request a password first.) Once you're on the network you can mount any of the file server's volumes by selecting them from the Chooser. A volume mounted this way functions like any other; it has its own icon on the desktop and file directory. To unmount a volume, you drag its icon to the trash.

On the whole, AppleShare is one of the most "transparent" LANs available: file server volumes don't require a special format and the user interface lets you treat networked files like standard files. However, AppleShare's harmonious design has an Achilles heel: the entire security system of passwords and privileges can be overcome by booting from a floppy instead of the startup hard disk (the one containing the AppleShare software). When you boot from a floppy, the file server functions like a typical Mac, which causes the network to come down and makes all file server volumes as easy to access or erase as any volume on the hard disk. To protect the data on the file server, keep it in a secure location where only authorized people have access to it.

WORKING WITH TOPS

TOPS originally stood for Transcendental Operating System, a good description of this pioneering distributed network. In the TOPS network, each Mac is both client and server, and files can be shared almost as easily with non-Macs as they can among Macs. There are versions of TOPS for MS-DOS, OS/2, and UNIX computers; various software and peripherals can be mixed and matched in a single network.

TOPS is unobtrusive. Users aren't logged on automatically during startup; instead they are connected but isolated until they choose the TOPS desk accessory. That done, they can place a file, folder, or complete volume on the network simply by clicking on the icon and selecting the Publish command from the desk accessory.

Sharing Files Between PCs and Macs

One of the difficulties of connecting different machines together is file formats. Different machines often have their own file formats. To deal with this problem, TOPS includes a utility called Translators with its Macintosh version. TOPS Translators must be resident on the disk with the TOPS network software installed. When you run Translators, it presents two choice boxes for changing file formats, one listing Macintosh Formats and the other listing "Foreign" Formats (Figure 11.1). First you select the format of the original file and then the foreign format into which you want to translate it. TOPS Translators will only translate files between similar formats. For example, it can translate WordStar files into MacWrite files or Excel spreadsheet files into Lotus 1-2-3 files, but it cannot translate an Excel file into a dBASE III file.

Once you have selected a Macintosh and a Foreign file format, you have to specify the files you want to translate. This is done by clicking the Select Files box on the upper right-hand side of the screen (Figure 11.2). You are presented with two standard file dialog boxes. The one

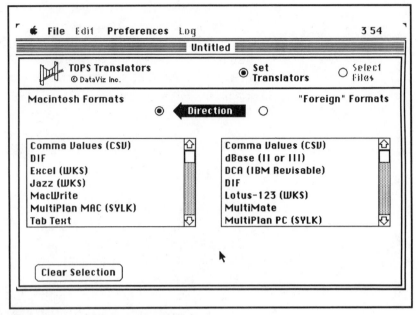

Figure 11.1: TOPS Translators file formats

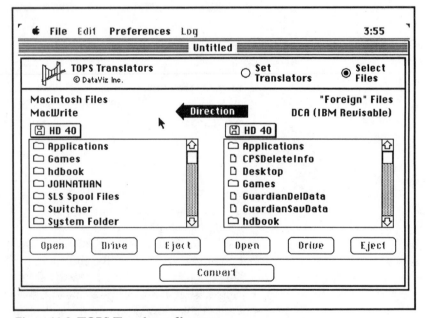

Figure 11.2: TOPS Translators file screen

on the left is for selecting the Macintosh file and the one on the right is for selecting the "foreign" file. Once you have selected both files, click on the Convert button to start the conversion process.

Apple has a utility for translating files between MacWrite and IBM's DCA-RFT format—Apple File Exchange (Figure 11.3). DCA-RFT is supported by many word processors on the IBM, including Word-Perfect 5. Conversions between other formats can also be done with Apple File Exchange, but you need a script file that describes the changes that you want to make. Some software manufacturers provide scripts to convert files created by their programs.

More and more applications are being built to run on both the Macintosh and the IBM PC, so software manufacturers are adding file conversion utilities right into their programs. WordPerfect on the

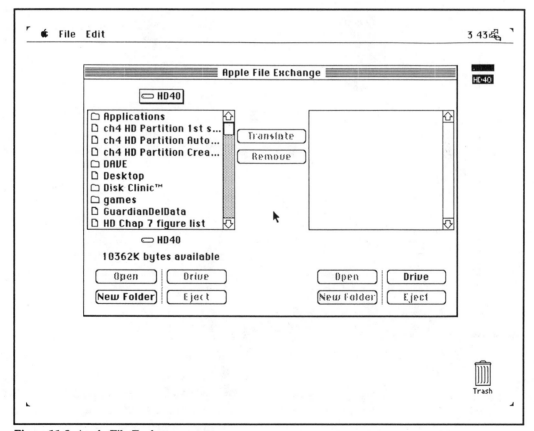

Figure 11.3: Apple File Exchange

Macintosh, for example, can save and read files in the format used by WordPerfect on the IBM PC (Figure 11.4). Microsoft Word on the Mac can also save files for Word on the IBM PC (Figure 11.5). Likewise, PageMaker files can be used on both the Mac and the PC.

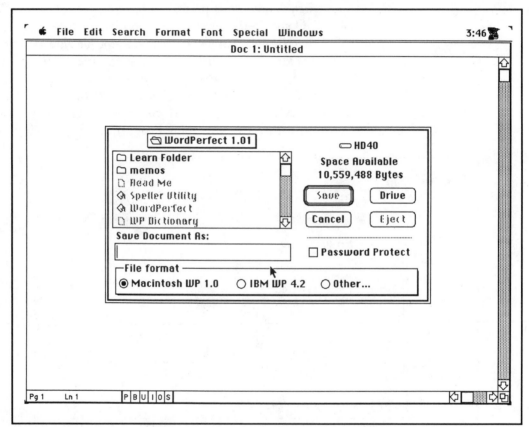

Figure 11.4: Converting WordPerfect file formats for use on the Macintosh

NETWORK ADMINISTRATION

A network, besides being installed and operated, must be *administrated* by a person or group specifically responsible for the job. Administrating can be a full-time job in the case of a large LAN; a small Macintosh network only takes a fraction of the time. Someone must be present who can deal with any problems in case they arise.

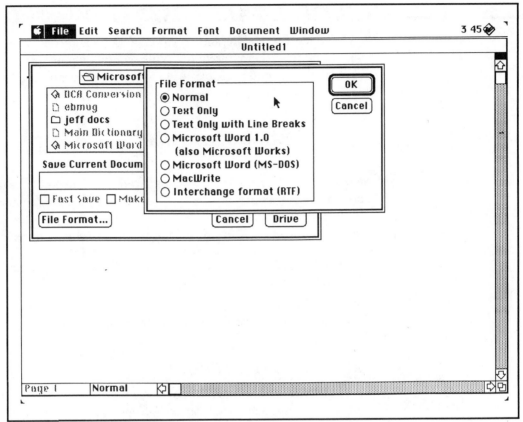

Figure 11.5: Converting Microsoft Word file formats for use on the Macintosh

The job of an administrator is to keep all the hardware elements properly connected, make regular backups of networked hard disks, and establish and keep tabs on the hierarchy of user privileges (who gets access to which files). It's not a good idea to give everyone access to the entire network—a multilevel system is usually best. For example, you would not want everyone with access to a Mac on the network to have access to a database of salaries as well. You might restrict some users to reading files in certain directories and other users to modifying the files as well as reading them. Only a few users should have the administrator's "super-user" status, the ability to change passwords or delete whole volumes at will.

Even if you only have a few Macs networked, you still need to think about security. Design a method for keeping confidential information secure when you set up your network.

NETWORK ADMINISTRATION ISSUES

Networks bring along their own set of topics and concerns, and you should address them carefully. While conditions and circumstances change, the general principles will always prove useful. Let's look at a few of them.

STRUCTURING THE ORGANIZATION

Throughout this book I've stressed the importance of logical and systematic organization in hard disk management. The problems faced by an individual user are even more complex when it comes to networked hard disks. It's bad enough, for example, when you can't find a file in your own directory. Imagine what can happen when a dozen or more people start strewing work across as many hard disks.

From the beginning, your network should have a clearly defined storage strategy that each new user is thoroughly acquainted with. Moreover, the administrator should be willing to enforce the rules and regulations about accessing data on the network.

ELIMINATING AMBIGUITY

In effect, a network puts all your eggs in one basket. The potential for productivity is much greater but so is the potential for mishaps and mischief. To avoid confusion, keep things as clear-cut and aboveboard as possible.

Password strategy is discussed in Chapter 5.

Be scrupulous in the use of passwords—they're not only security devices but records of who was working at what time. Assign a unique password to each individual, not just to a department or work group. Make sure all passwords are confidential and purge the ones that aren't valid any longer.

MAKING BACKUPS

Making regular backups is very important when you're working with a LAN. This is because more people rely on a networked hard disk and because the higher volume of use means that backups are outdated faster. Make backups as frequently as you can. (You'll probably need to do it after regular working hours, since you have to shut down the network to make backups.)

IS IT WORKING?

One of the hardest parts of operating a LAN is evaluating its usefulness. Nonetheless, you should periodically take a hard look at the realities of your workplace. Find out if the workers are ignoring the electronic message system in favor of scribbled notes. Perhaps the software is inadequate or too difficult for them to use. If the network is so busy that performance has slowed to a crawl, it's time to consider adding another file server. On the other hand, if your department has been trimmed to a fraction of its former size, now might be the time to remove your Macs and hard disks from the network. Finally, be sure that laser printers and other shared resources are in a convenient location. It shouldn't take a long time to go to the printer and get your output.

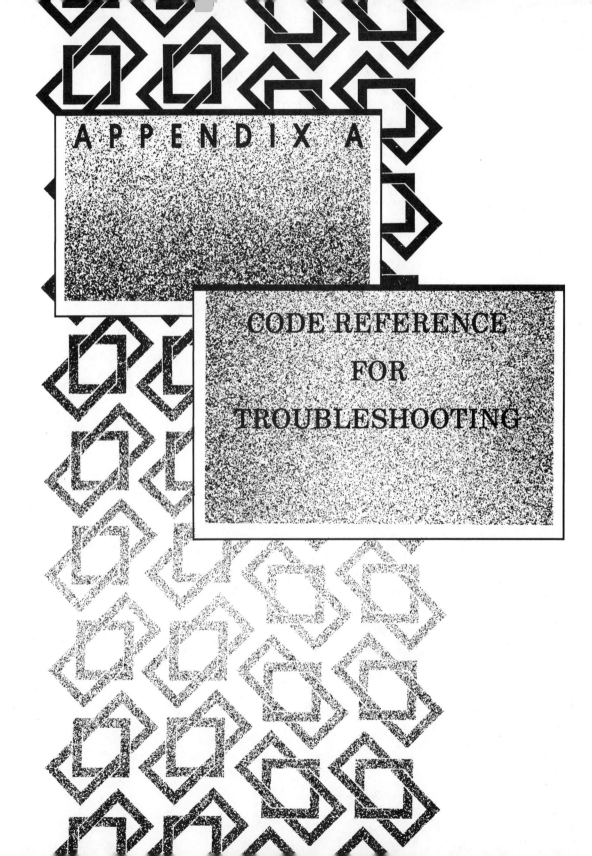

APPENDIX A

CODE REFERENCE
FOR
TROUBLESHOOTING

SYSTEM ERROR IDS

System error ID codes appear in the lower right-hand corner of bomb and other dialog boxes. Below are definitions and brief explanations of the codes.

ID NUMBER	*DEFINITION*	
ID 01	Bus error	The computer incorrectly accessed a portion of the RAM. This rare problem is limited to the Mac II and the obsolete XL (Lisa).
ID 02	Address error	The computer incorrectly accessed a portion of the RAM. One of the most common problems, especially on the Mac Plus, it is usually caused by a programmer's oversight.
ID 03	Illegal instruction	The currently running program used a command that the Mac didn't recognize.
ID 04	Zero divide	The Mac was told to divide a number by zero, an illogical instruction that can't be carried out.
ID 05	Check exception	The Mac has checked if a given value in some equation of the code is within a certain range of numbers, and it isn't.
ID 06	TrapV exception	A number that the program needs to continuously update, which is stored in a segment of RAM, has become too large for that segment before RAM can be reallocated.

ID 07	Privilege violation	An instruction for the user mode was given, but the Mac always runs in supervisor mode.
ID-08	Trace exception	A programming mistake—the trace bit in the status register is set.
ID 09	Line 1010 exception	A programming mistake—the 1010 trap dispatcher failed.
ID 10	Line 1111 exception	A programming mistake—there is an unimplemented instruction.
ID 11	Miscellaneous exception	An exception other than the ID 05, 06, 08, 09, or 010, often of hardware origin, has caused a crash.
ID 12	Unimplemented core routine	The programmer forgot to remove one of the temporary lines of code used to write an application.
ID 13	Spurious interrupt	Because it is running an application, the Mac's CPU can't access the routines it needs to carry out or give processing time to other, ongoing needs—noting the mouse cursor location, updating the screen display, etc.
ID 14	I/O system error	A function failure of the ROM Toolbox has occurred.
ID 15	Segment Loader error	A segment can't be found in memory or successfully loaded into memory.
ID 16	Floating point error	The halt bit of an important number-crunching function

		has mistakenly been set, disabling the function. Most likely the System software has been damaged.
ID 17–24	Can't load package	A PACK resource can't be loaded. PACKS, bits of code included in each System software release, update and augment the firmware resources in the ROM Toolbox.
ID 25	Can't allocate requested memory block	The Mac has run out of RAM. The memory size of the application is set too low (check its Get Info window) or the application was not intended to be run on the Mac model you are using.
ID 26	Segment Loader error	Either the application or the System file has been damaged severely and the launch process can't get underway.
ID 27	File map destroyed	There is a bad sector in the MFS volume's directory.
ID 28	Stack overflow error	Data assigned to one segment of RAM has overflowed its boundaries and crashed into other segments.

FILE TYPES AND CREATOR IDS

The table below lists the file types and creator IDs of some popular applications. The creator ID identifies which application created a file. The file type specifies which application the file can be read by. The Finder uses the file type to display the proper document icon and to launch applications. Damaged files can sometimes be repaired if their file type and creator ID are corrected with DiskTop, ResEdit, SUM, or a similar utility.

APPLICATION	FILE TYPE	CREATOR ID
ConcertWare + MIDI	CWMF	CWMP
FileMaker Plus	FMKL	FMKR
FreeHand	acf3	aca3
HyperCard	STAK	WILD
ImageStudio	RIFF	FSPE
MacDraw	DRWG	MDRW
MacPaint	PNTG	MPNT
MacProject	MPRD	MPRJ
MacWrite	WORD	MACA
Microsoft Word	WDBN	MSWD
PageMaker 2.0	ALDD	ALD2
PageMaker 3.0	ALT3	ALD3
PixelPaint	SCRN	PIXR
ReadySetGo!3	RSGJ	MRSN
SuperPaint	SPTG	SPNT
WriteNow	nX^d	nX^n
Xpress	XDOC	XPRS

FILE RESOURCES

Below is a list of all resources defined for System 4.1 or later. They are contained in the resource fork of files along with custom resources designed for the specific application.

RESOURCE NAME	
ADBS	Apple Desktop Bus service routine
ALRT	Alert template

BNDL	Bundle
CACH	RAM cache code
CDEF	Control definition function
CNTL	Control template
CODE	Application code segment
CURS	Cursor
DITl	Item list in a dialog or alert
DLOG	Dialog template
`DRVR	Desk accessory or other device driver
DSAT	System startup alert table
FKEY	Command-Shift-number routine
FMTR	$3\frac{1}{2}$-inch disk formatting code
FOND	Font family record
FREF	File reference
FRSV	IDs of fonts reserved for system use
FWID	Font widths
ICN#	Icon list
ICON	Icon
INIT	Initialization resource
INTL	International resource
INT#	List of integers owned by Find File
KCAP	Physical layout of keyboard (used by Key Caps desk accessory)
KCHR	ASCII mapping (software)
KMAP	Keyboard mapping (hardware)
KSWP	Keyboard script table
LDEF	List definition procedure
MBAR	Menu bar
MBDF	Default menu definition prodecure

MDEF	Menu definition procedure
MENU	Menu
MMAP	Mouse tracking code
NBPC	Appletalk bundle
NFNT	128K ROM font
PACK	Package
PAT	Pattern (The space is required.)
PAT#	Pattern list
PDEF	Printing code
PICT	Picture
PREC	Print record
PRER	Device type for Chooser
PRES	Device type for Chooser
PTCH	ROM patch code
RDEV	Device type for Chooser
ROvr	Code for overriding ROM resources
ROv#	List of ROM resources to override
SERD	RAM Serial Driver
SICN	Script symbol
STR	String (The space is required.)
STR#	String list
WDEF	Window definition function
WIND	Window template
actb	Alert color table
atpl	Internal AppleTalk resource
bmap	Bit maps used by the Control Panel
boot	Copy of boot blocks
cctb	Control color table

cicn	Color Macintosh icon
clst	Cached icon lists used by Chooser and Control Panel
clut	Color look-up table
crsr	Color cursor
ctab	Used by the Control Panel
dctb	Dialog color table
fctb	Font color table
finf	Font information
gama	Color correction table
ictb	Color table dialog item
insc	Installer script
itl0	Date and time formats
itl1	Names of days and months
itl2	International Utilities Package sort hooks
itlb	International Utilities Package script bundles
itlc	International configuration for Script Manager
lmem	Low memory globals
mcky	Mouse tracking
mctb	Menu color information table
mitq	Internal memory requirements for MakITable
mppc	AppleTalk configuration code
nrct	Rectangle positions
pltt	Color palette
ppat	Pixel pattern
snd	Sound (The space is required.)
snth	Synthesizer
wctb	Window color table

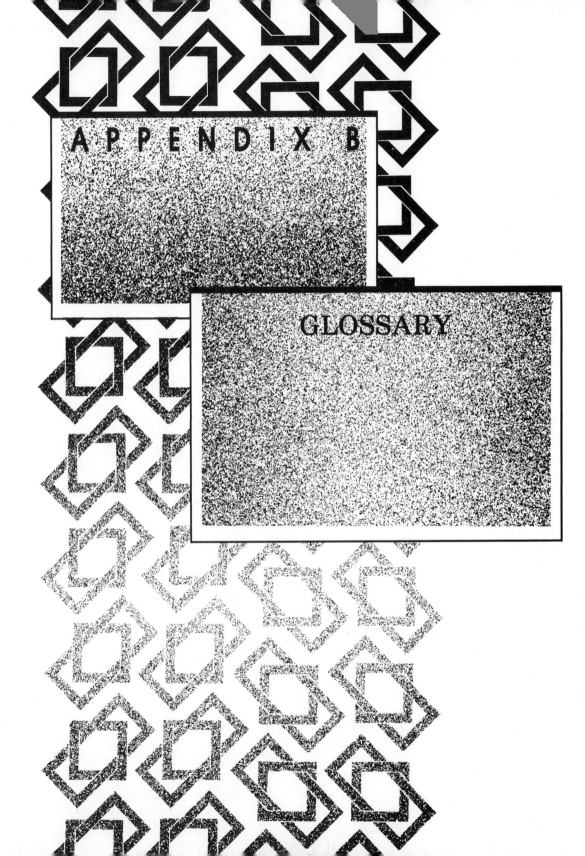

APPENDIX B

GLOSSARY

access time: The measurement of how quickly the read/write heads of a hard disk can retrieve data from storage.

address: The number that identifies a device on the SCSI bus or a location in the computer's memory.

Appletalk: See *LocalTalk*.

application: A user-initiated program, such as a word processor or spreadsheet, that saves work in document form and that assists in performing a task or series of tasks. Applications are launched by double-clicking on an icon.

archival data: Information that the user has preserved, but does not need to have readily available.

archive: A standby copy of the contents of a mass storage volume, usually comprising a collection of floppy disks.

backup: A duplicate copy of data, automatically compiled and updated with a utility program and stored for use in case the original becomes damaged or inaccessible. Backups may utilize floppy disks, hard disks, or other mass storage devices.

bit (binary digit): The smallest unit of information recognized by a computer; a single digit, either 0 or 1, that combines with others to represent numbers, characters, or instructions.

bit map: A set of dots or bits arranged by the computer to represent a graphic image.

bomb box: The dialog box displayed when a software problem has caused the operating system to lose control of the Macintosh. Distinguished by the round bomb icon in the upper-left corner.

bombing: The sudden cessation of all software functions, signaled by the appearance of the bomb box.

boot: To start or restart the computer by switching on the hardware and loading the system software. Also called a *cold boot.* (A *warm boot* refers to loading the system on an already-switched-on computer.)

boot blocks: The tracks on a startup disk read by the Macintosh as part of the booting-up process. These identify the disk and help the computer display the disk's contents; missing or damaged boot blocks usually render a disk unreadable.

buffer: An area of RAM memory used as interim storage for data being transferred from the computer to a peripheral. Since the Macintosh can export data faster than most printers and other devices can import it, holding data in a buffer allows the CPU to return to other tasks.

bus: A communication pathway. The Mac communicates with other SCSI devices by way of the SCSI bus; the mouse and keyboard by way of the Apple Desktop bus.

byte: A group of eight bits that the computer identifies as a number.

cartridge drive: A magnetic tape disk or optical disk that you can place on a disk drive without having to remove its container.

CDEV (Control Device): A resource file in the System Folder that contains device information and is used by the Control Panel desk accessory (found under the Apple menu).

CD-ROM (compact disk read-only memory): An optical device or medium capable of storing large amounts of permanent, unalterable data.

central processing unit (CPU):   The core of the computer, built around the CPU chip, that processes information and coordinates all functions.

client: A computer connected to a network that can access information from other computers or from file servers.

command key :   The ⌘ key, located in the lower left-hand corner of most Macintosh keyboards, used in conjunction with other keys for special functions.

commercial data: Any data that is purchased or otherwise provided by a secondary source. This can include applications.

compact disk (CD):   A storage technology, employing an optical rather than a magnetic media platter, on which data is created and accessed by a laser. CD drives for the Macintosh can store considerably more data than most hard disks. CD-ROM, WORM, and erasable optical disks are examples.

Control Device: See *CDEV*.

compact disk read-only memory: See *CD-ROM*.

controller: The circuitry that manages a hard disk's physical data access operations, such as moving read/write heads and erasing tracks and sectors. The term is sometimes used to mean the software that runs this circuitry (more correctly called the driver).

copy protection: Hardware and software methods of limiting data duplication in order to discourage illegal use and piracy of software. Some copy-protected software can be copied only a few times, some not at all; others require a password or special floppy in order to work.

CPU: See *central processing unit*.

crash: When the Mac stops functioning or functions incorrectly.

creator ID: The distinctive four-character code in each document's resource fork—MacWrite's is MACA, HyperCard's is WILD—that identifies the parent application. If a creator ID is changed or deleted, the Macintosh may be unable to open an otherwise intact document.

cursor: The symbol used to indicate position on the screen, usually manipulated with the mouse or keyboard. On the Mac, the cursor is a pointer arrow when items can be selected by pointing and clicking, an I-beam when text can be inserted, or a wait cursor when the computer is busy carrying out a command and can't acknowledge any new ones.

DA: See *desk accessory*.

daisychain: A configuration used by SCSI to connect multiple peripherals to a single Macintosh. Units are linked in a row, and each serves as an input/output relay for the others.

data encryption: A data protection method that makes use of codes. Data-encrypted files cannot be read except by users who know the code.

data fork: The part of a Macintosh file in which numbers, text, and graphics are stored.

dead key: A keystroke or keystroke combination that modifies the subsequent character rather than producing a character of its own. Option-U, for instance, will place an umlaut (¨) over the following letter.

desk accessory (DA):   A small program incorporated into the System file, such as Control Panel or Alarm Clock, that is run concurrently with applications. DAs are installed and removed with Font/DA Mover.

desktop: The icons and windows that the Finder displays. Also the area not occupied by any windows.

desktop file: The file in which the Finder stores the information it needs to accurately display and manage the contents of a volume. It records names, icons, directory structure, display formats, and instructions on loading and launching each file.

device: Any unit that can be controlled by the Macintosh to access, store, or display information. Hard disks and floppy drives are devices, and so is the internal speaker that emits warning beeps. In the Mac II, screen monitors also perform as devices.

dialog box: A box the Macintosh displays to request information or to issue warnings.

digitizer: A device that converts an image into a bit-mapped file that can be manipulated.

DIP switch: A small physical switch that can be in one of two positions, on or off. Often used to configure hardware.

directory: The organization of files on a disk or folder. In the Mac, files can be arranged by icon, small icon, name, date, size, kind, and color.

disk pack drive: The drive that accommodates a disk pack, one to eleven magnetic disk platters designed to be compatible with disk drives.

display font: Also known as the screen font, it is used to accurately display and manipulate a specific type style on the screen. The printer font is the one used to display type on a PostScript printer. The display font is installed and removed with Font/DA Mover.

document: Any file that stores the results of work done while using an application.

downloadable fonts: Fonts for a PostScript printer that reside on the Mac and can be downloaded to a printer for temporary use.

driver: Software used by the Macintosh to access and control devices. Hard disks, floppy drives, and printers have their own unique drivers.

dysfunction: Any or all of the conditions under which the Macintosh becomes entirely unusable. Bombs, crashes, freezes, and hangs are all dysfunctions.

Encapsulated PostScript (EPS) format: A graphic image format that combines two versions of an image, one in PostScript and one bit-mapped for the Mac screen. They can be printed in detail only on a PostScript printer.

erasable optical disk: A mass storage device that records and writes files to a photo-optical medium.

expansion card: A physical circuit card that plugs into a slot on the Mac SE or Mac II to add more functions.

expansion slot: The place on the bus for installing or connecting additional circuitry, or expansion cards, to a computer. The Macintosh SE has one; the Mac II has five.

external hard disk: A hard disk drive with its own enclosure and power supply, designed to be connected to a computer rather than installed inside one.

FAT (file allocation table):   A table showing which files are located on which sectors of a hard disk. To read a file to the disk, the Mac must first consult the FAT.

FKey: See *function key.*

file: A group of bytes in which data is stored. On the Macintosh, applications, documents, and specialized software (such as fonts and DAs) are considered files as long as they have a specific name, icon, and directory location.

file allocation table: See *FAT*.

file compressing utility: A program that compresses files, making them both easier to store and less expensive to send over a modem.

file dialog box: The screen display used to open or save a document. Often it is modified for other purposes as well. The contents and configuration of the box vary depending on the application being used and the task being performed.

file server: A hard disk or other storage device connected to other computers in a network. Usually used to designate a drive with files that can be accessed by several users.

file type: A four-character code that identifies the category to which a file belongs. For example, all Mac-compatible applications have the file type APPL.

Finder: The application launched automatically during startup, it displays and updates the desktop and directories of mounted volumes. It also performs basic functions such as opening, duplicating, relocating, and deleting files.

firmware: System software stored in read-only memory (ROM) and intended for continuous access by a computer. The Toolbox is an example.

floppy disk: A removable storage unit comprising a thin magnetic-medium platter in a protective enclosure. The Macintosh uses 3¹/₂-inch floppies, which can be single- or double-sided.

floppy disk drive: The internal or external mechanism that reads and writes data to and from a floppy disk.

folder: A subdirectory of a volume in which files and folders are grouped and stored.

font: An identifiable set of letters, numbers, and punctuation marks with a consistent design.

Font/DA Mover: A utility program provided with the System software, it is used for installing and removing fonts and desk accessories to and from the System file.

formatting: The process by which the driver of a storage device organizes and addresses tracks and sectors. Hard disk formatting varies according to model and manufacturer.

freeze: When everything on the screen, including the mouse cursor, cannot be altered. Faulty mouse and keyboard connections are usually what cause them.

function key: A keystroke combination that activates a small program incorporated in the system file. For example, Shift-⌘ 3 saves the current screen as a MacPaint file and Shift-⌘ 4 prints the screen on an ImageWriter. Not to be confused with the keys labeled F1 to F15 on the extended keyboard.

gigabyte: A unit for data technically totaling 1,073,741,824 bytes. Usually it is defined as either a million kilobytes or a thousand megabytes.

hang: When the Mac stalls and ignores commands from the mouse and keyboard.

hard disk: A storage device employing one or more permanently encased magnetic-media-coated platters. Capable of storing and quickly accessing a large quantity of data, it can be attached externally or installed internally.

hardware: The physical elements of a computer and its peripherals.

head crash: The condition that occurs when the read/write heads of a hard disk collide with the surface of a platter and damage the magnetic-media coating and the data contained in the area of contact.

head parking: Moving a hard disk's read/write heads from their operational position (hovering above a platter) to a safe "landing zone" when the drive is shut down. Unparked heads may touch the platter surface when the drive is moved, possibly causing a head crash.

HFS (Hierarchical File System):   A method of organizing applications, documents and folders, with folders nested inside other folders. HFS is the second and current volume directory standard used by the Macintosh; MFS (Macintosh File System) was the first.

Hierarchical File System: See *HFS*.

high-capacity floppy disk drive: A removable-media storage device, like a floppy disk, that can store more data than a floppy—as much as 10 megabytes.

I-Beam: The I-shaped cursor that indicates when text can be inserted.

incremental backup: A backup technique whereby only files altered since the previous backup are copied.

INIT: A program designed to be automatically launched whenever the Macintosh is booted up. To be activated, an INIT must first be placed in the System Folder of the startup volume.

initialization: The process of configuring a hard disk, floppy, or other storage volume for use by the Macintosh.

initiator: The SCSI device that initiates communication with another device on the daisychain.

installer: A utility included with the Macintosh's System software, it allows the user to replace a System file while retaining any custom features (fonts, DAs) that may have been installed.

interleave ratio: The ratio of hard disk platter rotations to the number of sectors to which the read/write heads read or write. For example, a drive with an interleave ratio of 1:1 will read or write to each sector as soon as it passes underneath. One with a 2:1 ratio will skip alternate sectors, waiting for them to rotate one more time before proceeding.

internal hard disk: A hard disk drive installed in the same casing as the computer it serves. The Mac SE and II have internal chassis and connectors for this purpose; earlier models do not.

invisible file: A file whose icon doesn't appear in the Finder or Standard File boxes.

kilobyte: A unit of memory totaling 1,024 bytes. Often abbreviated as KB or K (as in 800K floppy).

launching: The act of starting an application, it is done in a number of ways: automatically during startup, by double-clicking on an icon, or when a document created with a particular application is opened.

loading: The process in which the Macintosh conveys data from a storage volume to a location where it can be used or rapidly accessed (usually the RAM).

LocalTalk: Apple's connection standard, which allows multiple Macs to share laser printers and other AppleTalk devices. Formerly called AppleTalk.

logical volume: See *partition*.

Macintosh File System: See *MFS*.

macro: A sequence of commands distilled into a single, shorter command. Macro utilities save time by automating often-used functions. A complex series of commands can be activated with a single keystroke.

magnetic media: The types of media to which a computer can write magnetic patterns. These patterns are interpreted as data by the computer during the reading process. Magnetic tape, hard disks, floppy disks, and disk packs are examples.

megabyte: A quantity of data equal to 1,024 bytes (or 1,048,576 characters).

MFS (Macintosh File System):   A single-level organization standard for organizing files and folders on the Mac. Folders couldn't be nested under MFS, so it has been replaced by HFS (Hierarchical File System).

motherboard: The circuit board which contains the most important parts of the computer system—the CPU, memory, keyboard controller, etc.

mounted volume: An online volume.

mounting: The act of rendering a storage volume usable during the current work session. A hard disk, floppy, or other volume is mounted when its icon appears on the desktop.

non-copy-protected: Software that can be transferred and duplicated.

NuBus: The bus used in the Mac II.

offline: A device not currently accessible by the Macintosh. It may be nonoperational, turned off, or improperly connected, or it may be that the computer does not have the software necessary to control it. Volumes are considered offline when not mounted on the desktop.

online: A device currently accessible by the Macintosh, properly powered and connected, with the necessary controlling software provided. Synonymous with ''mounted'' in respect to storage volumes.

optical disk: A storage device on which data is written and read by means of a laser beam.

parameter RAM: See *PRAM*.

parent application: The application used to create a document, as opposed to any others that may be able to open, convert, or modify it. In order to know which application to launch when a document is opened, the Macintosh labels each document with the parent application's distinctive creator ID.

partition: A volume created by dividing the storage space on a hard disk into two or more separate entities. Also known as a logical volume.

path: The folder, parent folders (if any), and volume in which a file or folder is located. In other words, the location of a file or folder as specified by the volume and list of nested folders that lead to it. When written, the path (or *path name*) can include the name of the destination file or folder.

peripheral: A hardware device directly controlled by the Macintosh, but not an integral part of it. Hard disks, printers, and modems are peripherals.

platters: A flat, circular, rotating disk on which data is stored.

pointer arrow: The cursor in the shape of a left-slanting arrowhead used to select items and initiate commands.

PostScript: The page description language developed by Adobe Systems and used by many laser printers to produce high-resolution output of text and graphics.

PRAM (parameter RAM):   A part of the RAM, it is used to store Control Panel settings. It retains its contents when the power is turned off.

print spooler: A utility program that allows the user to operate the Mac and print at the same time. Print files are held by the spooler until the printer is ready to use them.

printer font: A file used by a printer or other output device to render text at a high degree of resolution.

progressive backup: Backing up all files that have changed since the last backup.

RAM (random access memory):   The area in which the Mac places data it is currently working with. The storage is temporary; the data disappears when the electrical current is discontinued.

read/write heads: The component of a hard disk that records and retrieves data to and from the sectors.

removable-media mass storage device: Similar to floppies, it can can be removed from the drive; however, unlike floppies, it can store 5 to 20 megabytes of data.

resource file: A file containing resources used by an application.

resource fork: The part of a Macintosh file in which specifications concerning the display and control of file contents are stored.

resource ID: A number that helps identify a resource in a resource file. Each resource must have an ID number.

resource type: A four-character code indicating the type of resource in a resource file.

ROM (read-only memory):   In the Mac, the unalterable memory used for storing the Toolbox, the Operating System, and programs that will never be modified, such as QuickDraw.

run-length limited coding: A method used to store data on a hard disk.

scanner: A device for converting printed images into a format that can be stored or reproduced by a computer.

SCSI (Small Computer Standard Interface):   An industry standard for electrical, functional, and mechanical interfaces for transferring data among hard disks, printers, and other peripherals.

SCSI bus: The bus which connects SCSI devices.

SCSI device: Any device that can be linked on the SCSI bus. Hard disks, printers, and optical disks are examples.

SCSI port: The communications port in a Macintosh or peripheral by which it is linked to the SCSI bus.

SE Bus: The bus used in the Mac SE.

sectors: A division of tracks on a disk. When accessing a disk, a disk drive must read or write complete sectors.

serial hard disk: A hard disk connected via a serial port.

serial port: The outlet used for connecting the Mac to serial peripherals.

shareware: Software that is not distributed commercially, but through user groups and bulletin boards. Owners of shareware are requested to pay a user fee to the software's manufacturer or author.

signature: A four-character code with which the Finder identifies an application.

SIMMs (Single Inline Memory Modules):   A package of memory chip that plugs into a Mac or other computer to increase memory size.

spliced application: An application too large for a single floppy disk, it is spread across several floppy disks for later installation on a hard disk. Usually one of the disks contains an installation program.

startup device: The device containing the active System file and the System Folder.

storage device: Any device that can store data. Examples are hard disks, floppies, and optical disks.

surge suppressor: A device that connects between a power source and the Macintosh and prevents surges of electricity from damaging the computer.

System file: The program the Mac uses to start itself. It launches automatically when the Mac is powered up.

System Folder: It contains the System file, the Finder, and other system software for basic Mac functions.

target device: The device on the SCSI daisychain that receives requests from the initiator to carry out an operation.

terminator: A device that prevents commands in a daisychain from echoing, or bouncing back, on the SCSI bus. The first and last devices in a daisychain must have terminators.

Toolbox: The software in the ROM whose purpose is to present the user interface of an application.

track: Composed of sectors, it is a ring around a hard disk.

transfer speed: The rate at which data can be carried between devices.

Trojan horse: A type of rogue software that pretends to be a useful application but actually carries a virus.

user interface: The way a computer communicates, with dialog boxes, icons, etc.

utility: A program that does not generate a document but instead performs service-oriented tasks, like spell-checking or screen color customization.

view format: The various ways of seeing files and folders on the desktop. The Mac offers seven view formats: by icon, small icon, name, date, size, kind, and color.

virus: A destructive program designed to be passed unknowingly from computer to computer.

volume: A storage medium for files. Each mounted volume appears as an icon on the desktop.

wait cursor: Usually a wristwatch but sometimes a spinning beach-ball, it tells the user to wait while the Macintosh completes a task.

Winchester drive: The standard hard disk drive, with read/write heads, platters, a fan, and a hermetically sealed case.

window: An enclosed area on the desktop which can be repositioned and resized. Disks and folder icons open into windows.

WORM (write-once read-many) drive: An optical mass storage device, it is used only for storing large amounts of data. Files are inscribed with a high-intensity laser and read with another, weaker laser beam.

write-protect tab: The small shutter in the upper left-hand corner of Macintosh floppy disks. When the tab is pushed up to reveal a square opening, the disk's contents can be read but not deleted or added to. Pushing the tab down will restore the floppy for normal writing functions.

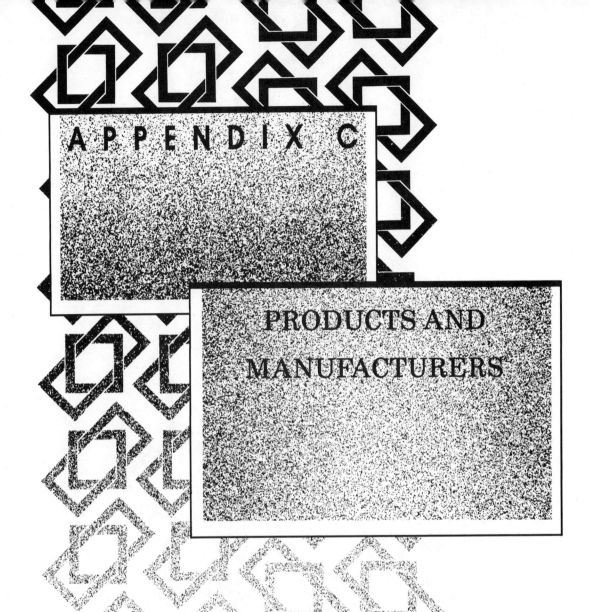

APPENDIX C

PRODUCTS AND MANUFACTURERS

Appleshare

Apple Computer, Inc.

20525 Mariani Avenue

Cupertino, CA 95014

(408) 996-1010

Bernoulli Box

Iomega Corp.

1821 W. 4000 South Street

Roy, UT 84067

(801) 778-1000

BlockCrypt

SuperMac Technologies

295 N. Bernardo Avenue

Mountain View, CA 94043

(415) 964-8884

Copy II

Central Point Software

15220 NW Greenbrier Parkway #200

Beaverton, OR 97005

(503) 690-8090

DES

SuperMac Technologies

295 N. Bernardo Avenue

Mountain View, CA 94043

(415) 964-8884

Disk First Aid
Apple Computer, Inc.
20525 Mariani Avenue
Cupertino, CA 95014
(408) 996-1010

DiskQuick
Ideaform, Inc.
P.O. Box 1540
612 West Kirkwood Street
Fairfield, IA 52556

DiskTop
CE Software
P.O. Box 65580
West Des Moines, IA 50265
(515) 224-1995

Excel
Microsoft Corporation
16011 NE 36th Way
Redmond, WA 98052
(800) 828-6293

Finder
Apple Computer, Inc.
20525 Mariani Avenue
Cupertino, CA 95014
(408) 996-1010

Find File

Apple Computer, Inc.

20525 Mariani Avenue

Cupertino, CA 95014

(408) 996-1010

Font/DA Mover

Apple Computer, Inc.

20525 Mariani Avenue

Cupertino, CA 95014

(408) 996-1010

GOfer

Microlytics

One Tobey Village Office Park

Pittsford, NY 14534

(716) 248-9150

HD Backup

Apple Computer, Inc.

20525 Mariani Avenue

Cupertino, CA 95014

(408) 996-1010

HD Tune Up

Symantec Corporation

Turner Hall Publishing Division

10201 Torre Avenue

Cupertino, CA 95014

(800) 888-0886

Hypercard

Apple Computer, Inc.

20525 Mariani Avenue

Cupertino, CA 95014

(408) 996-1010

ImageWriter

Apple Computer, Inc.

20525 Mariani Avenue

Cupertino, CA 95014

(408) 996-1010

Interferon

c/o Robert Woodhead

10 Spruce Lane

Ithaca, NY 14850

LaserWriter

Apple Computer, Inc.

20525 Mariani Avenue

Cupertino, CA 95014

(408) 996-1010

LocalTalk

Apple Computer, Inc.

20525 Mariani Avenue

Cupertino, CA 95014

(408) 996-1010

MacDraw

Claris, Inc.

440 Clyde Avenue

Mountain View, CA 94043

(415) 960-1500

MacPaint

Claris, Inc.

440 Clyde Avenue

Mountain View, CA 94043

(415) 960-1500

MacroMaker

Apple Computer, Inc.

20525 Mariani Avenue

Cupertino, CA 95014

(408) 996-1010

MacTools

Central Point Software

15220 NW Greenbrier Parkway #200

Beaverton, OR 97005

(503) 690-8090

MacWrite

Apple Computer, Inc.

20525 Mariani Avenue

Cupertino, CA 95014

(408) 996-1010

Microsoft Word
Microsoft Corporation
16011 NE 36th Way
Redmond, WA 98052
(800) 828-6293

MultiFinder
Apple Computer, Inc.
20525 Mariani Avenue
Cupertino, CA 95014
(408) 996-1010

The Muzzle
Ergotron, Inc.
P.O. Box 17013
Minneapolis, MN 55417
(800) 328-9829

NuBus
Texas Instruments, Inc.
P.O. Box 655012
Mail Stop 57
Dallas, TX 75265
(800) 527-3500

PackIt
Harry R. Chesley
1850 Union Street
San Francisco, CA 94123

PageMaker
Aldus Corporation
411 First Avenue South #200
Seattle, WA 98104
(206) 622-5500

PhoneNet
Farallon Computing
2150 Kittredge Street
Berkeley, CA 94704
(415) 849-2331

PrintMonitor
Apple Computer, Inc.
20525 Mariani Avenue
Cupertino, CA 95014
(408) 996-1010

QuicKeys
CE Software
P.O. Box 65580
West Des Moines, IA 50265
(515) 224-1995

ResEdit
Apple Computer, Inc.
20525 Mariani Avenue
Cupertino, CA 95014
(408) 996-1010

Sentinel

SuperMac Technologies

295 N. Bernardo Avenue

Mountain View, CA 94043

(415) 964-8884

StuffIt

Raymond Lau

100-04 70 Avenue

Forest Hills, NY 11375

Suitcase

Fifth Generation Systems, Inc.

2691 Richter Avenue #207

Irvine, CA 92714

(714) 553-0111

SUM (Symantec Utilities for the Macintosh)

Symantec Corporation

Turner Hall Publishing Division

10201 Torre Avenue

Cupertino, CA 95014

(800) 888-0886

SuperCrypt

SuperMac Technologies

295 N. Bernardo Avenue

Mountain View, CA 94043

(415) 964-8884

SuperPaint
Silicon Beach Software, Inc.
P.O. Box 261430
San Diego, CA 92126
(619) 695-6956

Switcher
Apple Computer, Inc.
20525 Mariani Avenue
Cupertino, CA 95014
(408) 996-1010

Teach Text
Apple Computer, Inc.
20525 Mariani Avenue
Cupertino, CA 95014
(408) 996-1010

TOPS
Sun Microsystems, TOPS division
950 Marina Village Parkway
Alameda, CA 94501
(800) 445-8677 (in California)
(800) 222-8677 (elsewhere in U.S.)

Virus Rx
Apple Computer, Inc.
20525 Mariani Avenue
Cupertino, CA 95014
(408) 996-1010

WriteNow

Airus, Inc.

10200 S.W. Nimbus Avenue #G-5

Portland, OR 97223

(503) 620-7000

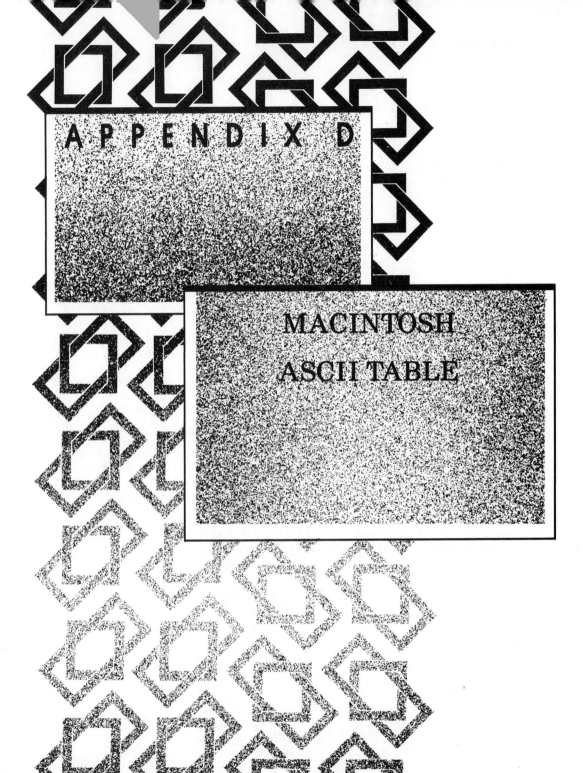

APPENDIX D

MACINTOSH
ASCII TABLE

The following table shows ASCII characters in the Chicago font. The box character (□) means that no symbol has been assigned to the specific character code. Equivalent symbols in fonts other than Chicago can be produced with these keystroke combinations. The codes Control-P through Control-S may not work with all applications, but you can insert the symbols they produce by cutting them from the Key Caps DA and pasting them into your document.

DEC	*HEX*	*KEYSTROKE*	*CHARACTER*
000	00	Control-@	
001	01	Control-A	□
002	02	Control-B	□
003	03	Control-C	□
004	04	Control-D	□
005	05	Control-E	□
006	06	Control-F	□
007	07	Control-G	□
008	08	Control-H	□
009	09	Control-I	
010	0A	Control-J	□
011	0B	Control-K	□
012	0C	Control-L	□
013	0D	Control-M	
014	0E	Control-N	□
015	0F	Control-O	□
016	10	Control-P	⌘
017	11	Control-Q	⌘
018	12	Control-R	✓
019	13	Control-S	◆
020	14	Control-T	
021	15	Control-U	□
022	16	Control-V	□
023	17	Control-W	□

DEC	*HEX*	*KEYSTROKE*	*CHARACTER*
024	18	Control-X	□
025	19	Control-Y	□
026	1A	Control-Z	□
027	1B	Control-[	□
028	1C		□
029	1D		□
030	1E		□
031	1F		□
032	20	space	
033	21		!
034	22		"
035	23		#
036	24		$
037	25		%
038	26		&
039	27		'
040	28		(
041	29		)
042	2A		*
043	2B		+
044	2C		,
045	2D		–
046	2E		.
047	2F		/
048	30		0
049	31		1
050	32		2
051	33		3
052	34		4
053	35		5
054	36		6

DEC	HEX	KEYSTROKE	CHARACTER
055	37		7
056	38		8
057	39		9
058	3A		:
059	3B		;
060	3C		<
061	3D		=
062	3E		>
063	3F		?
064	40		@
065	41		A
066	42		B
067	43		C
068	44		D
069	45		E
070	46		F
071	47		G
072	48		H
073	49		I
074	4A		J
075	4B		K
076	4C		L
077	4D		M
078	4E		N
079	4F		O
080	50		P
081	51		Q
082	52		R
083	53		S
084	54		T
085	55		U

DEC	HEX	KEYSTROKE	CHARACTER
086	56		V
087	57		W
088	58		X
089	59		Y
090	5A		Z
091	5B		[
092	5C		\
093	5D		]
094	5E		^
095	5F		_
096	60		`
097	61		a
098	62		b
099	63		c
100	64		d
101	65		e
102	66		f
103	67		g
104	68		h
105	69		i
106	6A		j
107	6B		k
108	6C		l
109	6D		m
110	6E		n
111	6F		o
112	70		p
113	71		q
114	72		r
115	73		s
116	74		t

DEC	HEX	KEYSTROKE	CHARACTER
117	75		u
118	76		v
119	77		w
120	78		x
121	79		y
122	7A		z
123	7B		{
124	7C		|
125	7D		}
126	7E		~
127	7F	space	
128	80	Option-u A	Ä
129	81	Shift-Option A	Å
130	82	Shift-Option C	Ç
131	83	Option-e E	É
132	84	Option-n N	Ñ
133	85	Option-u O	Ö
134	86	Option-u U	Ü
135	87	Option-e a	á
136	88	Option-' a	à
137	89	Option-i a	â
138	8A	Option-u a	ä
139	8B	Option-n a	ã
140	8C	Option-a	å
141	8D	Option-c	ç
142	8E	Option-e e	é
143	8F	Option-' e	è
144	90	Option-i e	ê
145	91	Option-u e	ë
146	92	Option-e i	í
147	93	Option-' i	ì

DEC	HEX	KEYSTROKE	CHARACTER
148	94	Option-i i	î
149	95	Option-u i	ï
150	96	Option-n n	ñ
151	97	Option-e o	ó
152	98	Option-' o	ò
153	99	Option-i o	ô
154	9A	Option-u o	ö
155	9B	Option-n o	õ
156	9C	Option-e u	ú
157	9D	Option-' u	ù
158	9E	Option-i u	û
159	9F	Option-u u	ü
160	A0	Option-t	†
161	A1	Shift Option-8	°
162	A2	Option-4	¢
163	A3	Option-3	£
164	A4	Option-6	§
165	A5	Option-8	•
166	A6	Option-7	¶
167	A7	Option-s	ß
168	A8	Option-r	®
169	A9	Option-g	©
170	AA	Option-2	™
171	AB	Option-e	´
172	AC	Option-u space	¨
173	AD	Option- =	≠
174	AE	Shift Option-'	Æ
175	AF	Shift Option-o	Ø
176	B0	Option-5	∞
177	B1	Shift Option- =	±
178	B2	Option-<	≤

DEC	HEX	KEYSTROKE	CHARACTER
179	B3	Option->	≥
180	B4	Option-y	¥
181	B5	Option-m	µ
182	B6	Option-d	∂
183	B7	Option-w	Σ
184	B8	Shift Option-p	∏
185	B9	Option-p	π
186	BA	Option-b	∫
187	BB	Option-9	ª
188	BC	Option-0	º
189	BD	Option-z	Ω
190	BE	Option-'	æ
191	BF	Option-o	ø
192	C0	Shift Option-/	¿
193	C1	Option-1	¡
194	C2	Option-l	¬
195	C3	Option-v	√
196	C4	Option-f	ƒ
197	C5	Option-x	≈
198	C6	Option-j	∆
199	C7	Option-\	«
200	C8	Shift Option-\	»
201	C9	Option-;	…
202	CA	space	
203	CB	Option-' A	À
204	CC	Option-n A	Ã
205	CD	Option-n O	Õ
206	CE	Shift Option-q	Œ
207	CF	Option-q	œ
208	D0	Option--	–
209	D1	Shift Option--	—

DEC	HEX	KEYSTROKE	CHARACTER
210	D2	Option-[	`` `` ``
211	D3	Shift Option-[	"
212	D4	Option-]	'
213	D5	Shift Option-]	'
214	D6	Option-/	÷
215	D7	Shift Option-v	◇
216	D8	Option-u y	ÿ
217	D9		□
218	DA		□
219	DB		□
220	DC		□
221	DD		□
222	DE		□
223	DF		□
224	E0		□
225	E1		□
226	E2		□
227	E3		□
228	E4		□
229	E5		□
230	E6		□
231	E7		□
232	E8		□
233	E9		□
234	EA		□
235	EB		□
236	EC		□
237	ED		□
238	EE		□
239	EF		
240	F0	Option-k	

DEC	HEX	KEYSTROKE	CHARACTER
241	F1		□
242	F2		□
243	F3		□
244	F4		□
245	F5		□
246	F6		□
247	F7		□
248	F8		□
249	F9		□
250	FA		□
251	FB		□
252	FC		□
253	FD		□
254	FE		□
255	FF		□

Most of the Control-key hex characters marked 00–1B can be generated on the Macintosh SE, II standard, and extended keyboards by holding down the Control key and typing the indicated character. For example, the hex character 07 is generated by typing Control-G. Hex characters generated with the Control key are used to make special symbols on the Macintosh and to control devices such as dot matrix printers. They are also used to access remote bulletin board systems. Some of the common Control-key hex characters used both on bulletin boards and the Macintosh are:

- Control-H (Backspace) makes the cursor move back one character space.

- Control-I (Tab) makes the next character print at the next tab stop to the right. Tab stops are typically placed every eight characters. Some applications let you set tab stops at any location.

- Control-M (Return) makes the cursor move to the beginning of the next line.

These functions are not usually used by the Macintosh, but are used by some bulletin board and telecommunication applications:

- Control-G sounds the speaker, beeper, or bell.
- Control-J (Line Feed) makes the cursor move down one line.
- Control-L (Form Feed) causes the device move to the top of the next page.
- Control-Q (XON) makes output suspended with Control-S resume.
- Control-S (XOFF) suspends output until Control-Q is typed.

Index

Selections from The SYBEX Library

APPLE/MACINTOSH

Encyclopedia Macintosh
Craig Danuloff/Deke McClelland
650pp. Ref. 628-6

Just what every Mac user needs—a complete reference to Macintosh concepts and tips on system software, hardware, applications, and troubleshooting. Instead of chapters, each section is presented in A-Z format with user-friendly icons leading the way.

Mastering Microsoft Word on the Macintosh
Michael J. Young
447pp. Ref. 541-7

This comprehensive, step-by-step guide shows the reader through WORD's extensive capabilities, from basic editing to custom formats and desktop publishing. Keyboard and mouse instructions and practice exercises are included. For Release 4.0.

Desktop Publishing with Microsoft Word on the Macintosh (Second Edition)
Tim Erickson/William Finzer
525pp. Ref. 601-4

The authors have woven a murder mystery through the text, using the sample publications as clues. Explanations of page layout, headings, fonts and styles, columnar text, and graphics are interwoven within the mystery theme of this exciting teaching method. For Version 4.0.

Mastering Adobe Illustrator
David A. Holzgang
330pp. Ref. 463-1

This text provides a complete introduction to Adobe Illustrator, bringing new sophisti-cation to artists using computer-aided graphics and page design technology. Includes a look at PostScript, the page composition language used by Illustrator.

HyperTalk Instant Reference SYBEX Prompter Series
Greg Harvey
316pp. Ref. 530-1, 4 ¾" × 8"

For serious HyperCard users, this finger-tip reference offers complete, cross-referenced summaries of HyperTalk commands, functions, properties, and constants. Examples of usage and an introduction to Scripting are provided.

Mastering AppleWorks (Second Edition)
Elna Tymes
479pp. Ref. 398-8

New chapters on business applications, data sharing DIF and Applesoft BASIC make this practical, in-depth tutorial even better. Full details on AppleWorks desktop, word processing, spreadsheet and database functions.

AppleWorks Tips and Techniques (Second Edition)
Robert Ericson
462pp. Ref. 480-1

An indispensible collection of timesaving techniques, practical solutions, and tips on undocumented problems for every AppleWorks user. This expanded new edition covers all versions through 2.0, and includes in-depth treatment of macros.

The ABC's of Excel on the Macintosh
Douglas Hergert
314pp. Ref. 562-X

This title is written for users who want a

quick way to get started with this highly-acclaimed spreadsheet program. The ABC's offers a rich collection of hands-on examples and step-by-step instructions for working with worksheets, charts, databases, and macros. Covers Excel through Version 1.5.

Mastering Excel on the Macintosh (Third Edition)
Carl Townsend
656pp. Ref. 622-7
This highly acclaimed tutorial has been updated for the latest version of Excel. Full of extensive examples, tips, application templates, and illustrations. This book makes a great reference for using worksheets, databases, graphics, charts, macros, and tables. For Version 2.2.

Understanding HyperCard (Second Edition)
Greg Harvey
654pp. Ref. 607-3
For Mac users who want clear-cut steps to quick mastery of HyperCard, this thorough tutorial introduces HyperCard from the Browsing/Typing and Authoring/Painting levels all the way to Scripting with HyperTalk, the HyperCard programming language. No prior programming experience needed. For Version 1.2.

Understanding Hard Disk Management on the Macintosh
J. Russell Roberts
334pp. Ref. 579-4
This is the most comprehensive and accessible guide to hard disk usage for all Macintosh users. Complete coverage includes SCSI and serial drives and ports, formatting, file fragmentation, backups, networks, and a helpful diagnostic appendix.

Using the Macintosh Toolbox with C (Second Edition)
Fred A. Huxham/David Burnard/Jim Takatsuka
525pp. Ref. 572-7
Learn to program with the latest versions of Macintosh Toolbox using this clear and succinct introduction. This popular title has been revised and expanded to include dozens of new programming examples for windows, menus, controls, alert boxes, and disk I/O. Includes hierarchical file system, Lightspeed C, Resource files, and R Maker.

DESKTOP PUBLISHING

The ABC's of Ventura
Robert Cowart/Steve Cummings
390pp. Ref. 537-9
Created especially for new desktop publishers, this is an easy introduction to a complex program. Cowart provides details on using the mouse, the Ventura side bar, and page layout, with careful explanations of publishing terminology. The new Ventura menus are all carefully explained. For Version 2.

Mastering Ventura (Second Edition)
Matthew Holtz
613pp. Ref. 581-6
A complete, step-by-step guide to IBM PC desktop publishing with Xerox Ventura Publisher. Practical examples show how to use style sheets, format pages, cut and paste, enhance layouts, import material from other programs, and more. For Version 2.

Ventura Tips and Techniques
Carl Townsend/Sandy Townsend
424pp. Ref. 559-X
Packed with an experienced Ventura user's tips and tricks, this volume is a time saver and design booster. From crop marks to file management to using special fonts, this book is for serious Ventura users. Covers Ventura 2.

Ventura Instant Reference SYBEX Prompter Series
Matthew Holtz
320pp. Ref. 544-1, 4 ¾" × 8"
This compact volume offers easy access to the complex details of Ventura modes and

options, commands, side-bars, file management, output device configuration, and control. Written for versions through Ventura 2, it also includes standard procedures for project and job control.

Ventura Power Tools
Rick Altman
318pp. Ref. 592-1
Renowned Ventura expert, Rick Altman, presents strategies and techniques for the most efficient use of Ventura Publisher 2. This includes a power disk with DOS utilities which is specially designed for optimizing Ventura use. Learn how to soup up Ventura, edit CHP files, avoid design tragedies, handle very large documents, and improve form.

Mastering PageMaker on the IBM PC (Second Edition)
Antonia Stacy Jolles
384pp. Ref. 521-2
A guide to every aspect of desktop publishing with PageMaker: the vocabulary and basics of page design, layout, graphics and typography, plus instructions for creating finished typeset publications of all kinds.

Understanding Professional Write
Gerry Litton
400pp. Ref. 656-1
A complete guide to Professional Write that takes you from creating your first simple document, into a detailed description of all major aspects of the software. Special features place an emphasis on the use of different typestyles to create attractive documents as well as potential problems and suggestions on how to get around them.

Understanding PFS: First Publisher
Gerry Litton
310pp. Ref. 616-2
This complete guide takes users from the basics all the way through the most complex features available. Discusses working with text and graphics, columns, clip art, and add-on software enhancements.

Many page layout suggestions are introduced. Includes Fast Track speed notes.

Mastering Ready, Set, Go!
David A. Kater
482pp. Ref. 536-0
This hands-on introduction to the popular desktop publishing package for the Macintosh allows readers to produce professional-looking reports, brochures, and flyers. Written for Version 4, this title has been endorsed by Letraset, the Ready, Set, Go! software publisher.

Understanding PostScript Programming (Second Edition)
David A. Holzgang
472pp. Ref. 566-2
In-depth treatment of PostScript for programmers and advanced users working on custom desktop publishing tasks. Hands-on development of programs for font creation, integrating graphics, printer implementations and more.

Your HP LaserJet Handbook
Alan R. Neibauer
564pp. Ref. 618-9
Get the most from your printer with this step-by-step instruction book for using LaserJet text and graphics features such as cartridge and soft fonts, type selection, memory and processor enhancements, PCL programming, and PostScript solutions. This hands-on guide provides specific instructions for working with a variety of software.

DESKTOP PRESENTATION

Mastering Harvard Graphics
Glenn H. Larsen
318pp. Ref. 585-9
Here is a solid course in computer graphing and chart building with the popular software package. Readers can create the perfect presentation using text, pie, line, bar, map, and pert charts. Customizing and automating graphics is easy with

these step-by-step instructions. For Version 2.1.

NETWORKS

The ABC's of Novell Netware
Jeff Woodward
282pp. Ref. 614-6

For users who are new to PC's or networks, this entry-level tutorial outlines each basic element and operation of Novell. The ABC's introduces computer hardware and software, DOS, network organization and security, and printing and communicating over the netware system.

Mastering Novell Netware
Cheryl C. Currid/Craig A. Gillett
500pp. Ref. 630-8

Easy and comprehensive, this book is a thorough guide for System Administrators to installing and operating a microcomputer network using Novell Netware. Mastering covers actually setting up a network from start to finish, design, administration, maintenance, and troubleshooting.

Networking with TOPS
Steven William Rimmer
350pp. Ref. 565-4

A hands on guide to the most popular user friendly network available. This book will walk a user through setting up the hardware and software of a variety of TOPS configurations, from simple two station networks through whole offices. It explains the realities of sharing files between PC compatibles and Macintoshes, of sharing printers and other peripherals and, most important, of the real world performance one can expect when the network is running.

UTILITIES

Mastering the Norton Utilities
Peter Dyson
373pp. Ref. 575-1

In-depth descriptions of each Norton utility make this book invaluable for begin-

ning and experienced users alike. Each utility is described clearly with examples and the text is organized so that readers can put Norton to work right away. Version 4.5.

Mastering SideKick Plus
Gene Weisskopf
394pp. Ref. 558-1

Employ all of Sidekick's powerful and expanded features with this hands-on guide to the popular utility. Features include comprehensive and detailed coverage of time management, note taking, outlining, auto dialing, DOS file management, math, and copy-and-paste functions.

COMMUNICATIONS

Mastering Crosstalk XVI
(Second Edition)
Peter W. Gofton
225pp. Ref. 642-1

Introducing the communications program Crosstalk XVI for the IBM PC. As well as providing extensive examples of command and script files for programming Crosstalk, this book includes a detailed description of how to use the program's more advanced features, such as windows, talking to mini or mainframe, customizing the keyboard and answering calls and background mode.

HARDWARE

The RS-232 Solution
(Second Edition)
Joe Campbell
193pp. Ref. 488-7

For anyone wanting to use their computer's serial port, this complete how-to guide is updated and expanded for trouble-free RS-232-C interfacing from scratch. Solution shows you how to connect a variety of computers, printers, and modems, and it includes details for IBM PC AT, PS/2, and Macintosh.

Mastering Serial Communications
Peter W. Gofton
289pp. Ref. 180-2
The software side of communications, with details on the IBM PC's serial programming, the XMODEM and Kermit protocols, non-ASCII data transfer, interrupt-level programming and more. Sample programs in C, assembly language and BASIC.

Microprocessor Interfacing Techniques (Third Edition)
Austin Lesea/Rodnay Zaks
456pp. Ref. 029-6
This handbook is for engineers and hobbyists alike, covering every aspect of interfacing microprocessors with peripheral devices. Topics include assembling a CPU, basic I/O, analog circuitry, and bus standards.

From Chips to Systems: An Introduction to Microcomputers (Second Edition)
Rodnay Zaks/Alexander Wolfe
580pp. Ref. 377-5
The best-selling introduction to microcomputer hardware—now fully updated, revised, and illustrated. Such recent advances as 32-bit processors and RISC architecture are introduced and explained for the first time in a beginning text.

HOME COMPUTERS

Amiga Programmer's Handbook, Volume I (Second Edition)
Eugene P. Mortimore
624pp. Ref. 367-8
The complete reference for Amiga graphics programming. System commands and function calls are presented in detail, organized by funcitonal class: Exec, Graphics, Animation, Layers, Intuition and the Workbench. Includes AmigaDOS version 1.2.

Amiga Programmer's Handbook, Volume II
Eugene P. Mortimore
365pp. Ref. 384-8
In-depth discussion of Amiga device I/O programming—including programming with sound and speech—with complete details on the twelve Amiga devices and their associated commands and function calls. Inclues AmigaDOS version 1.2.

Programmer's Guide to the Amiga
Robert A. Peck
352pp. Ref. 310-4
A programmer's hands-on tour through the Amiga system—AmigaDOS, Exec, Graphics, Intuition, Devices, Sound, Animation, and more—packed with in-depth information and sample programs (in Amiga C) showing proper use of system routines.

SPREADSHEETS AND INTEGRATED SOFTWARE

Visual Guide to Lotus 1-2-3
Jeff Woodward
250pp. Ref. 641-3
Readers match what they see on the screen with the book's screen-by-screen action sequences. For new Lotus users, topics include computer fundamentals, opening and editing a worksheet, using graphs, macros, and printing typeset-quality reports. For Release 2.2.

The ABC's of 1-2-3 Release 2.2
Chris Gilbert/Laurie Williams
340pp. Ref. 623-5
New Lotus 1-2-3 users delight in this book's step-by-step approach to building trouble-free spreadsheets, displaying graphs, and efficiently building databases. The authors cover the ins and outs of the latest version including easier calculations, file linking, and better graphic presentation.

The ABC's of 1-2-3 Release 3
Judd Robbins

290pp. Ref. 519-0

The ideal book for beginners who are new to Lotus or new to Release 3. This step-by-step approach to the 1-2-3 spreadsheet software gets the reader up and running with spreadsheet, database, graphics, and macro functions.

The ABC's of 1-2-3 (Second Edition)
Chris Gilbert/Laurie Williams

245pp. Ref. 355-4

Online Today recommends it as "an easy and comfortable way to get started with the program." An essential tutorial for novices, it will remain on your desk as a valuable source of ongoing reference and support. For Release 2.

Mastering 1-2-3 Release 3
Carolyn Jorgensen

682pp. Ref. 517-4

For new Release 3 and experienced Release 2 users, "Mastering" starts with a basic spreadsheet, then introduces spreadsheet and database commands, functions, and macros, and then tells how to analyze 3D spreadsheets and make high-impact reports and graphs. Lotus add-ons are discussed and Fast Tracks are included.

Mastering 1-2-3 (Second Edition)
Carolyn Jorgensen

702pp. Ref. 528-X

Get the most from 1-2-3 Release 2 with this step-by-step guide emphasizing advanced features and practical uses. Topics include data sharing, macros, spreadsheet security, expanded memory, and graphics enhancements.

The Complete Lotus 1-2-3 Release 2.2 Handbook
Greg Harvey

750pp. Ref. 625-1

This comprehensive handbook discusses every 1-2-3 operating with clear instructions and practical tips. This volume especially emphasizes the new improved graphics, high-speed recalculation tech-niques, and spreadsheet linking available with Release 2.2.

The Complete Lotus 1-2-3 Release 3 Handbook
Greg Harvey

700pp. Ref. 600-6

Everything you ever wanted to know about 1-2-3 is in this definitive handbook. As a Release 3 guide, it features the design and use of 3D worksheets, and improved graphics, along with using Lotus under DOS or OS/2. Problems, exercises, and helpful insights are included.

Lotus 1-2-3 Desktop Companion SYBEX Ready Reference Series
Greg Harvey

976pp. Ref. 501-8

A full-time consultant, right on your desk. Hundreds of self-contained entries cover every 1-2-3 feature, organized by topic, indexed and cross-referenced, and supplemented by tips, macros and working examples. For Release 2.

Advanced Techniques in Lotus 1-2-3
Peter Antoniak/E. Michael Lunsford

367pp. Ref. 556-5

This guide for experienced users focuses on advanced functions, and techniques for designing menu-driven applications using macros and the Release 2 command language. Interfacing techniques and add-on products are also considered.

Lotus 1-2-3 Tips and Tricks
Gene Weisskopf

396pp. Ref. 454-2

A rare collection of timesavers and tricks for longtime Lotus users. Topics include macros, range names, spreadsheet design, hardware considerations, DOS operations, efficient data analysis, printing, data interchange, applications development, and more.

Lotus 1-2-3 Instant Reference Release 2.2 SYBEX Prompter Series
Greg Harvey/Kay Yarborough Nelson

254pp. Ref. 635-9, 4 ¾" × 8"

The reader gets quick and easy access to any operation in 1-2-3 Version 2.2 in this handy pocket-sized encyclopedia. Organized by menu function, each command and function has a summary description, the exact key sequence, and a discussion of the options.

Lotus 1-2-3 Instant Reference
SYBEX Prompter Series
Greg Harvey/Kay Yarborough Nelson
296pp. Ref. 475-5; 4 ¾" × 8"
Organized information at a glance. When you don't have time to hunt through hundreds of pages of manuals, turn here for a quick reminder: the right key sequence, a brief explanation of a command, or the correct syntax for a specialized function.

Mastering Symphony
(Fourth Edition)
Douglas Cobb
857pp. Ref. 494-1
Thoroughly revised to cover all aspects of the major upgrade of Symphony Version 2, this Fourth Edition of Doug Cobb's classic is still "the Symphony bible" to this complex but even more powerful package. All the new features are discussed and placed in context with prior versions so that both new and previous users will benefit from Cobb's insights.

The ABC's of Quattro
Alan Simpson/Douglas J. Wolf
286pp. Ref. 560-3
Especially for users new to spreadsheets, this is an introduction to the basic concepts and a guide to instant productivity through editing and using spreadsheet formulas and functions. Includes how to print out graphs and data for presentation. For Quattro 1.1.

Mastering Quattro
Alan Simpson
576pp. Ref. 514-X
This tutorial covers not only all of Quattro's classic spreadsheet features, but also its added capabilities including extended graphing, modifiable menus, and the macro debugging environment. Simpson brings out how to use all of Quat-

tro's new-generation-spreadsheet capabilities.

Mastering Framework III
Douglas Hergert/Jonathan Kamin
613pp. Ref. 513-1
Thorough, hands-on treatment of the latest Framework release. An outstanding introduction to integrated software applications, with examples for outlining, spreadsheets, word processing, databases, and more; plus an introduction to FRED programming.

The ABC's of Excel
on the IBM PC
Douglas Hergert
326pp. Ref. 567-0
This book is a brisk and friendly introduction to the most important features of Microsoft Excel for PC's. This beginner's book discusses worksheets, charts, database operations, and macros, all with hands-on examples. Written for all versions through Version 2.

Mastering Excel on the IBM PC
Carl Townsend
628pp. Ref. 403-8
A complete Excel handbook with step-by-step tutorials, sample applications and an extensive reference section. Topics include worksheet fundamentals, formulas and windows, graphics, database techniques, special features, macros and more.

Excel Instant Reference
SYBEX Prompter Series
William J. Orvis
368pp. Ref.577-8, 4 ¾" × 8"
This pocket-sized reference book contains all of Excel's menu commands, math operations, and macro functions. Quick and easy access to command syntax, usage, arguments, and examples make this Instant Reference a must. Through Version 1.5.

Understanding PFS:
First Choice
Gerry Litton
489pp. Ref. 568-9

From basic commands to complex features, this complete guide to the popular integrated package is loaded with step-by-step instructions. Lessons cover creating attractive documents, setting up easy-to-use databases, working with spreadsheets and graphics, and smoothly integrating tasks from different First Choice modules. For Version 3.0.

Mastering Enable
Keith D. Bishop
517pp. Ref. 440-2
A comprehensive, practical, hands-on guide to Enable 2.0—integrated word processing, spreadsheet, database management, graphics, and communications—from basic concepts to custom menus, macros and the Enable Procedural Language.

Mastering Q & A (Second Edition)
Greg Harvey
540pp. Ref. 452-6
This hands-on tutorial explores the Q & A Write, File, and Report modules, and the Intelligent Assistant. English-language command processor, macro creation, interfacing with other software, and more, using practical business examples.

Mastering SuperCalc5
Greg Harvey/Mary Beth Andrasak
500pp. Ref. 624-3
This book offers a complete and unintimidating guided tour through each feature. With step-by-step lessons, readers learn about the full capabilities of spreadsheet, graphics, and data management functions. Multiple spreadsheets, linked spreadsheets, 3D graphics, and macros are also discussed.

ACCOUNTING

Mastering DacEasy Accounting
Darleen Hartley Yourzek
476pp. Ref 442-9
Applied accounting principles are at your fingertips in this exciting new guide to using DacEasy Accounting versions 2.0

and 3.0. Installing, converting data, processing work, and printing reports are covered with a variety of practical business examples. Through Version 3.0

DATABASE MANAGEMENT

The ABC's of Paradox
Charles Siegel
300pp. Ref.573-5
Easy to understand and use, this introduction is written so that the computer novice can create, edit, and manage complex Paradox databases. This primer is filled with examples of the Paradox 3.0 menu structure.

Mastering Paradox (Fourth Edition)
Alan Simpson
636pp. Ref. 612-X
Best selling author Alan Simpson simplifies all aspects of Paradox for the beginning to intermediate user. The book starts with database basics, covers multiple tables, graphics, custom applications with PAL, and the Personal Programmer. For Version 3.0.

Quick Guide to dBASE: The Visual Approach
David Kolodney
382pp. Ref. 596-4
This illustrated tutorial provides the beginner with a working knowledge of all the basic functions of dBASE IV. Images of each successive dBASE screen tell how to create and modify a database, add, edit, sort and select records, and print custom labels and reports.

The ABC's of dBASE IV
Robert Cowart
338pp. Ref. 531-X
This superb tutorial introduces beginners to the concept of databases and practical dBASE IV applications featuring the new menu-driven interface, the new report writer, and Query by Example.

SYBEX®

TO JOIN THE SYBEX MAILING LIST OR ORDER BOOKS
PLEASE COMPLETE THIS FORM

NAME _____ COMPANY _____

STREET _____ CITY _____

STATE _____ ZIP _____

☐ PLEASE MAIL ME MORE INFORMATION ABOUT **SYBEX** TITLES

ORDER FORM (There is no obligation to order)

PLEASE SEND ME THE FOLLOWING:

TITLE	QTY	PRICE
_____	_____	_____
_____	_____	_____
_____	_____	_____
_____	_____	_____

TOTAL BOOK ORDER   _____ $_____

CUSTOMER SIGNATURE _____

SHIPPING AND HANDLING PLEASE ADD $2.00 PER BOOK VIA UPS   _____

FOR OVERSEAS SURFACE ADD $5.25 PER BOOK PLUS $4.40 REGISTRATION FEE   _____

FOR OVERSEAS AIRMAIL ADD $18.25 PER BOOK PLUS $4.40 REGISTRATION FEE   _____

CALIFORNIA RESIDENTS PLEASE ADD APPLICABLE SALES TAX   _____

TOTAL AMOUNT PAYABLE   _____

☐ CHECK ENCLOSED   ☐ VISA
☐ MASTERCARD   ☐ AMERICAN EXPRESS

ACCOUNT NUMBER _____

EXPIR. DATE _____ DAYTIME PHONE _____

CHECK AREA OF COMPUTER INTEREST:

☐ BUSINESS SOFTWARE

☐ TECHNICAL PROGRAMMING

☐ OTHER: _____

THE FACTOR THAT WAS MOST IMPORTANT IN YOUR SELECTION:

☐ THE SYBEX NAME

☐ QUALITY

☐ PRICE

☐ EXTRA FEATURES

☐ COMPREHENSIVENESS

☐ CLEAR WRITING

☐ OTHER _____

OTHER COMPUTER TITLES YOU WOULD LIKE TO SEE IN PRINT:

_____

_____

OCCUPATION

☐ PROGRAMMER   ☐ TEACHER

☐ SENIOR EXECUTIVE   ☐ HOMEMAKER

☐ COMPUTER CONSULTANT   ☐ RETIRED

☐ SUPERVISOR   ☐ STUDENT

☐ MIDDLE MANAGEMENT   ☐ OTHER:

☐ ENGINEER/TECHNICAL   _____

☐ CLERICAL/SERVICE

☐ BUSINESS OWNER/SELF EMPLOYED

CHECK YOUR LEVEL OF COMPUTER USE

☐ NEW TO COMPUTERS

☐ INFREQUENT COMPUTER USER

☐ FREQUENT USER OF ONE SOFTWARE

   PACKAGE:

   NAME _____

☐ FREQUENT USER OF MANY SOFTWARE

   PACKAGES

☐ PROFESSIONAL PROGRAMMER

OTHER COMMENTS:

_____

_____

_____

_____

_____

_____

_____

PLEASE FOLD, SEAL, AND MAIL TO SYBEX

SYBEX, INC.
2021 CHALLENGER DR. #100
ALAMEDA, CALIFORNIA USA
           94501

SEAL

SYBEX Computer Books are different.

Here is why . . .

At SYBEX, each book is designed with you in mind. Every manuscript is carefully selected and supervised by our editors, who are themselves computer experts. We publish the best authors, whose technical expertise is matched by an ability to write clearly and to communicate effectively. Programs are thoroughly tested for accuracy by our technical staff. Our computerized production department goes to great lengths to make sure that each book is well-designed.

In the pursuit of timeliness, SYBEX has achieved many publishing firsts. SYBEX was among the first to integrate personal computers used by authors and staff into the publishing process. SYBEX was the first to publish books on the CP/M operating system, microprocessor interfacing techniques, word processing, and many more topics.

Expertise in computers and dedication to the highest quality product have made SYBEX a world leader in computer book publishing. Translated into fourteen languages, SYBEX books have helped millions of people around the world to get the most from their computers. We hope we have helped you, too.

For a complete catalog of our publications:

SYBEX, Inc. 2021 Challenger Drive, #100, Alameda, CA 94501
Tel: (415) 523-8233/(800) 227-2346   Telex: 336311
Fax: (415) 523-2373

Special Function Keystroke/Mouse Combinations

Special keystroke/mouse functions are not supported by all software. The keystroke/mouse combinations below may not be used with some applications and fonts.

⌘-A	Selects all items in the currently active Finder window.
⌘-C	Copies the selection to the Clipboard.
⌘-D	Creates a duplicate of the selected file or folder.
⌘-E	Ejects the selected floppy disk without removing it from the desktop.
⌘-I	Summons the Get Info box of the selected file, folder, or volume.
⌘-N	Creates a new folder from the Finder.
⌘-O	Opens a preexisting document.
⌘-P	Summons the Print dialog box.
⌘-Q	Closes the currently active application.
⌘-S	Saves all changes made to the document.
⌘-V	Inserts the Clipboard's contents into the document.
⌘-W	Closes the currently active window or document.
⌘-X	Removes the selected text or graphic, saving it to the Clipboard.
⌘-Z	Undoes the previous document entry.
⌘-Shift-1	Ejects the floppy disk in the first internal disk drive (the right one in the Mac II, the top one in the SE).
⌘-Shift-2	Ejects the floppy disk in the external disk drive (or the second internal disk drive on the Mac II and SE).
⌘-Shift-3	Takes a snapshot of the current screen, saving the image as a MacPaint file.
Option-`	Places a grave accent (`) over the following character.
Option-e	Places an acute accent (´) over the following character.
Option-i	Places a circumflex (^) over the following character.
Option-n	Places a tilde (˜) over the following character.
Option-u	Places an umlaut (¨) over the following character.
Option-Clean Up	Orders the items in the active window into a grid pattern (used with View by Icon only).
Option-Close	Closes all opened windows in the Finder.
Option-Shift	Allows multiple item selection in the Finder.